Complete Chess Strategy
2: Principles of Pawn-Play and the Center

Also by Ludek Pachman

Complete Chess Strategy
1: First Principles of the Middle Game

COMPLETE CHESS STRATEGY

Volume 2
Principles of Pawn Play
and the Center

Ludek Pachman
International Grandmaster

Translated by John Littlewood

CORNERSTONE LIBRARY   *NEW YORK*

Reprinted 1978

© Ludek Pachman 1976

This new Cornerstone Library edition is published by
arrangement with Doubleday & Co., and is a complete and
unabridged reprint of the original hardcover edition designed and
produced by Chancellor Hall.

The trademark of Cornerstone Library, Inc. consists of the words
"Cornerstone Library" and the portrayal of a cube and is registered
in the United States Patent Office.

ISBN: 346 • 12343 • 7

Manufactured in the United States of America
under the supervision of
Rolls Offset Printing Co., Inc., N.Y.

Contents

Preface

Is it possible to learn how to play the middle game correctly, or must we rely on our own imagination, combinative powers and experience when tackling this complex phase of the game?

There is no doubt that the theory of the middle game is vastly different from that of the opening. The latter has been studied in detail, with theoreticians attempting to supply us with the 'best' moves. We must of course try to grasp the strategic and tactical ideas behind each opening, but there is no escaping the need for a wide knowledge of many concrete variations.

When studying the middle game we cannot learn specific variations off by heart, but are concerned with basic principles and typical positions or manoeuvres. It becomes vitally important to recognize the characteristic features of a position and plan our play accordingly, but how can this be done? My purpose in the present volume is to give the ordinary club player an answer to this question. I am not seeking a new approach to chess strategy, but offering practical guide-lines for the study of the middle game.

It is well-known that the evaluation of many positions and many strategic problems depends on individual style. For this reason no author of a work on chess strategy can escape the criticism that he is bringing in his personal opinion and approach to the game. The objectivity of such a book can only be guaranteed if it is based upon material from master and grandmaster games, and if the advice given represents the views of various outstanding players.

This book is based on games from practical play. Only in a few cases have I restricted myself to quoting a position. Usually the whole game is presented, for the reader must learn above all to view a game as an entity and to recognize the transition stages between one part of the game and another. This has naturally compelled me to limit the number of examples used to illustrate the various strategic ideas.

The material is a mixture of old and new, with examples from modern tournament practice alongside games from the past which have permanent value and are often easier to understand than the complicated struggles from the present chess scene. The reader will also find a relatively large number of my own games. These have not been included because I am so immodest as to think they represent the best examples of correct play, but because every chess player knows his own games best and can therefore explain his thought processes more effectively.

The present volume is the second of three which aim to give the reader an insight into the whole field of chess strategy. The structure of the book remains the same as in previous (German-language) editions, but the contents have in part been revised and brought up to date.

Ludek Pachman
West Berlin, 1975

PART ONE
THE PAWNS

Already in our chapter 'The fundamentals of chess strategy' (Vol. 1) we demonstrated the extraordinary importance of handling pawns correctly. Though they are the weakest element in the game, they often determine the character of the position and the strategic plan to be followed. They are usually better suited for guarding important squares and pieces than are the pieces themselves, as the latter are less expendable. They are the best means of blockading enemy pawns, or, (by their advance) opening vital files and diagonals, creating weaknesses in the opposite camp and taking important squares away from the enemy pieces. For this reason it is hardly surprising that we devote more space to the pawn than to any other piece. In the present volume the pawn occupies pride of place, with over two thirds of the text allocated to it, divided into seven chapters as follows:

1 The passed pawn: its creation and exploitation.
2 Blockading the passed pawn.
3 Special kinds of passed pawn.
4 The isolated pawn.
5 The backward pawn.
6 The isolated pawn couple and hanging pawns.
7 Doubled pawns.

1 The Passed Pawn: Its Creation and Exploitation

Despite its limited power, the pawn has one special advantage over the other pieces in that it can be promoted once it reaches the eighth rank. A successful pawn advance can completely change the balance of power and decide the game. However, it is not easy to advance our pawns. The greatest obstacle is the enemy pawns which will sooner or later bring our own to a standstill unless they can be removed. We are referring not only to those enemy pawns immediately in front of ours but also to those on the adjacent files which cannot even be by-passed when our pawn is allowed to cover two squares on its first move (the 'en passant' rule sees to that!). In certain positions, however, there are pawns facing no such obstacle, and we call these 'passed' pawns. They represent an important strategic factor, for often the whole game can revolve around a single passed pawn. Such a pawn can be created in the following ways:

UTILIZATION OF A PAWN MAJORITY

(*1*) White has a Q-side and Black a K-side majority, from both of which a passed pawn can be created by correctly advancing the pawns. We term this a mobile pawn majority. However, it is not always so easy to exploit a pawn majority, as we see in the next diagram.

Although both sides have a pawn majority (*2*), a passed pawn cannot be created merely by advancing the pawns without any help from the pieces. In such situations we talk of a compromised pawn majority. It is clear that any method of advancing Black's pawns only results in a blocked position. Black must first try to weaken the white pawns in the hope of exchanging his pawn on QB3 e.g. if White is forced to play P–N3, then Black can proceed . . . P–B4–B5×NP. Of course, this is only possible in certain circumstances.

White, too, requires the help of a piece so that he can recapture after 1 P-KB4 P×P, as otherwise Black has a passed pawn to compensate for the one White creates by 2 P-KR4 followed by P-N5, P-R5, P-N6 etc. In such cases Black can thwart White's aim by controlling the 'hole' on . . . KB5.

Let us turn to diagram 1 and see how both sides should proceed. Clearly 1 P-N4? would be a grave positional mistake, for 1 . . . P-QN4! prevents any further effective advance of White's Q-side pawns. The same applies to 1 . . . P-KR4? 2 P-KR4! After 1 P-QR4 P-QR4 White still has to play 2 P-B3 and 3 P-N4 before he can create a passed pawn, whereas 2 P-B4? once again cripples his own majority.

The logical. (and usually the only correct) pawn advance is 1 P-B4 so as to play 2 P-B5, 3 P-N4, 4 P-N5 and 5 P-B6 creating a passed pawn without any difficulty. If Black replies 1 . . . P-QR4 then White must not play 2 P-QR3? P-R5 but 2 P-N3 followed by 3 P-QR3 and 4 P-N4 etc. In the same way, Black creates a passed pawn on the K-side by 1 . . . P-KN4 followed by 2 . . . P-KR4, 3 . . . P-N5 (not 3 . . . P-R5), 4 . . . P-R5 and 5 . . . P-N6.

Two principles emerge from the above:
1. To create a passed pawn from a pawn majority it is best to begin by advancing the pawn which has no enemy pawn in front of it.
2. The fewer pawns there are in the majority, the quicker a passed pawn can be created. In diagram 1, Black's majority of two against one produces a passed pawn before White's majority of three against two, even if White is first to move e.g. 1 P-B4 P-QR4! 2 P-N3 P-KN4 3 P-QR3 P-N5 4 P-N4 P×P 5 P×P P-R4 6 P-B5 P-R5 7 P-N5 P-N6. It is clear that we are only

considering basic pawn structure here, without reference to the number and placing of the pieces. However, these general principles should be taken as the rule, exceptions arising purely in unusual circumstances.

Although we intend to show in more detail in the third section how to exploit a pawn majority, we give here an example of the successful creation of a passed pawn from such a majority.

1 Furman-Holmov

Sverdlovsk 1963, Nimzo-Indian Defence

1 P-Q4 N-KB3 2 P-QB4 P-K3 3 N-QB3 B-N5 4 P-K3 0-0 5 B-Q3 P-Q4 6 N-B3 N-B3 7 0-0 P-QR3 8 P-KR3 P-R3 9 P-R3 P×P 10 B×P B-Q3 11 P-K4 P-K4 12 B-K3 R-K1 13 R-K1 P×P 14 N×P N×N
    15 B×N   P-B4

Black's Q-side pawn majority is already a force to be reckoned with. White ought to have played 14 B×QP! when P-K5 would be a serious threat, whereas in this position it only gives White equality e.g. 16 P-K5 P×B 17 Q×P B×P 18 Q×Q R×Q 19 R×B P-QN4 20 B-N3 R-R2 etc.

    16 B-K3   P-QN4
    17 B-Q5?

Only now is White at a serious disadvantage. He should play 17 B-N3 B-N2 18 P-B3 P-B5 19 B-B2, or even 17 B-KB1.

    17 . . .   N×B
    18 Q×N   B-K3
    19 Q-R5   B-QN6!

The exchange of White's KB has led to a glaring weakness on the white squares, with the result that White cannot even use the important Q-file. Nor can he play 20 B×BP? P-N3 when his bishop is lost.
    20 Q-N4 *(3)*

3
B

Black has achieved two important strategic advantages: a Q-side pawn majority and the two bishops. White's last move leads at least to the elimination of the second advantage.

20 ...   Q-B1!

Less experienced players usually avoid the exchange of queens when playng for a win, reserving it for when they stand worse. However, such an exchange often increases winning chances, as in this case. After 21 Q×Q R×Q White would no longer be able to exchange the black-squared bishops, and Black's Q-side majority would be relatively easy to set into motion, backed by the two bishops which are ideal in such situations (see Volume 1).

21 Q-B3!   Q-K3
22 B-B4   B×B
23 Q×B   QR-Q1

Black has lost the power of the two bishops working together, but White's manoeuvre has given him time to post his queen effectively on K3 and occupy the Q-file, thus completing the development of his forces.

24 P-B3   R-Q5
25 N-K2   R-Q2
26 Q-K3   P-B5!
27 N-B3

Exchange of knight for bishop would not help White, for after 27 N-Q4 Q-KB3 28 N×B (or *28 P-K5 Q-KN3*) 28 ... R-Q6! and 29 ... R×N, the

pressure of Black's major pieces would quickly decide the issue.

27 ...   R-Q6
28 Q-B2   Q-K4
29 R-K2

White settles for passive defence which is equivalent to certain defeat. Now, or on the next move he must play N-Q5. On the other hand if he tried to use his own majority, he would have a very poor endgame, after 29 P-B4 Q-Q5! 30 P-K5 Q×Q+ 31 K×Q R-Q7+ 32 R-K2 R×R+ 33 N×R (*33 K×R P-B3*) 33 ... R-Q1. Or here 30 Q×Q R×Q 31 R-K2 R1-Q1 32 N-Q5 K-B1 when Black's pieces are so active that he has no trouble preparing the advance of his Q-side pawns.

29 ...   R1-Q1
30 R1-K1(?)   R1-Q5!

This nullifies the effect of an eventual N-Q5, as the black rook will be no longer cut off.

31 Q-R4   P-QR4
32 Q-B2   P-N5
33 P×P   P×P
34 N-Q5   P-B6
35 P×P   P×P(4)

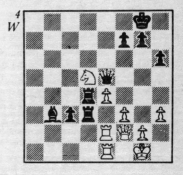

4
W

Within the space of a few moves, Black has completed his strategic plan. He has created a strong passed pawn, whereas White's pawns are static. If now 36 P-B4 Q-Q3, the white knight has no good retreat (37 N–K3 R×P 38 N–B5 R×R).

36 N–K3   R–Q7!

A typical use of the passed pawn. If now 37 R×R P×R and Black wins.

37 R–QB1   R5–Q6
38 N–B1

Black was threatening 38 ... R×R 39 Q×R Q–Q5

38 ...   R–Q8!
39 R–K1   R×R.K8
40 Q×R   Q–Q5+
41 Q–B2   P–B7
0–1

The passed pawn costs White at least a piece after 42 Q×Q R×Q 43 N–K3 R–Q8+ etc.

FORCED EXCHANGE OF PIECES ON A SQUARE
GUARDED BY A PAWN

(5) White plays 1 R–Q5 R×R (forced, or he loses a pawn) 2 P×R obtaining a passed QP.

Our next game is a good example of this method of creating a passed pawn.

2 Alekhine–Fine

Kemeri 1937, Queen's Gambit Accepted

1 P–Q4 P–Q4 2 P–QB4 P×P 3 N–KB3 N–KB3 4 Q–R4+ Q–Q2 5 Q×BP Q–B3 6 N–R3 Q×Q 7 N×Q P–K3 8 P–QR3! P–B4 9 B–B4 N–B3

10 P×P B×P 11 P–QN4 B–K2 12 P–N5! N–QN1 13 N–Q6+ B×N 14 B×B N–K5 15 B–B7 N–Q2 16 N–Q4 N–N3 17 P–B3 N–Q4 18 B–R5 N.K5–B3 19 N–B2 B–Q2 20 P–K4 R–QB1 21 K–Q2 N–N3 22 N–K3 0–0 23 P–QR4! KR–Q1 24 B–Q3 P–K4 25 KR–QB1 B–K3 26 R×R R×R 27 B–N4 N–K1 28 P–R5 N–Q2 (6)

Alekhine has succeeded in posting his pieces effectively and now obtains a passed pawn by playing his knight to Q5. It is interesting to note that he obtains his second passed pawn in exactly the opposite way, by capturing Black's knight on ... QB4 (see move 34).

29 N–Q5!   B×N
30 P×B   N–B4
31 B–B5!   R–Q1
32 K–B3   P–QN3
33 P×P   P×P
34 B×N!

The two bishops have completed their task, and now the two advanced passed pawns bring about a quick decision.

34 ...   P×B
35 P–N6   N–Q3
36 B–Q7!   R×B?
37 R–R8+   N–K1
38 R×N mate

The next example, from Korchnoi–Karpov, Moscow 1971, is interesting in that Black twice forces an exchange of pieces on squares controlled by his pawn. The first exchange gives him a passed pawn and the second forces his pawn to the seventh rank. (We have already seen this second factor at work in game No. 1, the note to Black's 36th move, and the final comment: 43 . . . R–Q8+ 44 N×R P×N= Q+).

7
B

Play, from the diagram (7), went: **12 . . . N–Q5! 13 N×N** After 13 Q–Q1 then 13 . . . N–N5 is very strong. **13 . . . P×N 14 N–B3 Q–N3 15 N–K5 B×N 16 B×B P–B3 17 B–B4 QR–B1 18 Q–R4** 18 Q–Q2? P–KN4 wins a piece. **18 . . . P–KN4 19 B–B1** 19 B–Q2? Q×P **19 . . . B–K7 20 R–K1 P–Q6 21 B–B1! B×B 22 R×B R–B7 23 B–K3 N–B4 24 Q–Q4 ?** So far White has defended very well and should now play 24 Q–R3! R–B1 25 B×N Q×B 26 Q×QP R×NP with a slight edge to Black. **24 . . . P–K4! 25 P×Pep Q×KP 26 QR–B1 R–B1 27 P–QN4 N×P! 28 R×R** After 28 Q×QP, the beautiful diversionary move 28 . . . N×BP! wins. **28 P×R 29 R–B1 P–N3 30 P–B3 N–Q3 31 Q–Q3 R–B3 32 P–QR4 Q–B5 33 Q–Q2 N–B2 34 P–B4 P–N5 35 P–N5 R–B1 36 Q–Q7 P–KR4 37 K–B2** 37 Q×RP Q–K7 38 Q×P R–Q1 and 39 . . . R–Q8+ **37 . . . Q–B6 38 Q–B5 R–K1 0–1**

TACTICAL MEANS

In many games a passed pawn is obtained as a result of various tactical strokes. These really belong to the sphere of chess tactics, so we will restrict ourselves here to quoting the three basic 'themes'.

A

(*A*) Material is equal but White has a break-through combination with 1 P–N6 RP×P 2 P–B6! P×BP 3 P–R6, or here 1 . . . BP×P 2 P–R6! P×RP 3 P–B6. Similar break-throughs occur in various forms, usually associated with loss of material and therefore only succeeding when the resulting passed pawn is sufficient compensation.

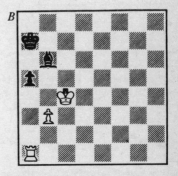

B

(*B*) White exploits the pin of Black's RP in order to create a passed pawn by 1 P–N4 K–R3 2 P–N5+ etc.

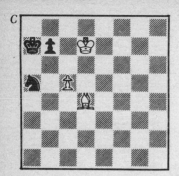

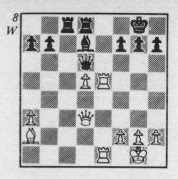

In this position (*C*) the passed pawn is created by means of a discovered check: **1 P–B6+** and **2 P–B7** winning.

Now we turn to the problem of exploiting the passed pawn. It seems obvious and logical that our main strategic aim should be to push the pawn on to promotion. Nevertheless, this method of utilizing a passed pawn is found only infrequently in the middle-game. It is usually extremely difficult to prevent enemy pieces from blocking the pawn somewhere in its path.

The following games illustrate the simplest as well as the most complex ways of exploiting a passed pawn.

3 Filip–Urbanec

Czechoslovak Championship 1954, Nimzo–Indian Defence

1 P–Q4 N–KB3 2 P–QB4 P–K3 3 N–QB3 B–N5 4 P–K3 P–B4 5 B–Q3 0–0 6 N–B3 P–Q4 7 0–0 N–B3 8 P–QR3 BP×P 9 KP×P P×P 10 B×BP B–K2 11 B–KN5 11 Q–Q3! P–QN3 12 B–KN5 **11 ... N–Q4 12 B×B N3×B 13 Q–Q3 N×N** 13 ... P–QN3! **14 P×N N–N3 15 KR–K1 B–Q2 16 N–K5 R–B1 17 B–R2 N×N 18 R×N B–B3** Both 18 ... P–QN4 and 18 ... Q–K2 are better. **19 QR–K1 Q–Q3** 19 ... P–QN4! **20 P–QB4 KR–Q1 21 P–Q5 P×P 22 P×P B–Q2** (*8*)

By failing to take appropriate counter-measures Black has allowed White to create a passed QP. However, a cursory glance at the diagram tells us that it will be very difficult to advance this pawn, for no fewer than three enemy pieces are standing in the path to its queening square.

23 P–KR4!

A dual-purpose move, firstly cutting out back-rank possibilities against his king, such as 23 ... Q×R and 24 ... R–B8+, and secondly planning to fix Black's K-side by advancing the pawn further.

23 ...　　　R–B8?

A typical case of faulty exchanging. This move only helps White to achieve his strategic goal of advancing the QP. After 23 ... R–K1 Black could still hold the game.

**24 R×R　　　Q×R
25 Q–B4**

25 P–Q6 B–B4! would be premature. The text-move is thematic in such positions i.e. preparing the advance of the pawn by first manoeuvring the pieces. In this case by controlling the QB-file and threatening to penetrate to the seventh rank. White intends 26 Q–B7, and 25 ... R–QB1?? obviously fails to 26 Q×R+

25 ...　　　Q–K1

The only defence! Now 26 Q–B7 is answered by 26 ... R–B1, so White regroups his pieces to occupy the seventh rank via the K-file.

26 Q–QN4   P–QN3
27 R–K1!

Once again 27 P–Q6 would be premature in view of 27 ... B–K3 28 B×B Q×B, and 27 R–B7 R–B1! 28 R×P? fails to 28 ... R–B8+ 29 K–R2 Q–N1+ .

27 ...   Q–B1
28 R–K7!   P–QR4
29 Q–K4   B–B4
30 Q–K5   B–K3
31 R–B7   B–B1
32 P–Q6!

Now this advance is decisive, for it is coupled with an attack on KB7, and after 32 ... B–Q2 33 Q–K7! there is no defence to the double threat of 34 R×B and 34 B×P+ .

32 ...   R–K1
33 Q×R!   1–0

The pawn triumphs after 33 ... Q×Q 34 B×P+ Q×B 35 R×B+ Q–B1 36 P–Q7.

4 Unzicker–Donner

Goteborg Interzonal 1955, French Defence

1 P–K4 P–K3 2 P–Q4 P–Q4 3 N–QB3 P×P 4 N×P N–Q2 5 N–KB3 B–K2 6 B–Q3 KN–B3 7 Q–K2 N×N 8 B×N P–QB4 Better is 8 ... 0–0 and 9 ... N–B3. **9 P–Q5! P–K4** (9)

Already White has obtained a passed pawn, . which is not necessarily advantageous in such positions, especially if Black manages to mobilize his K-side pawns. For this reason, White's next move prevents ... P–B4 which would be threatened after 10 0–0 0–0.

10 B–B5   0–0
11 0–0   B–B3

Black must accept this further hindrance to the advance of his K-side pawns, as 11 ... B–Q3 12 N–N5 is very unpleasant for him.

12 N–Q2!

Otherwise Black would have no difficulties after 12 ... P–KN3 followed by ... B–N2 and ... P–B4. The knight is now brought to the tactically favourable K4 square before Black's KBP can control it.

12 ...   P–KN3
13 B×N   Q×B!

Not 13 ... B×B? 14 N–K4 with a clear advantage to White. Note that the opposite-coloured bishops which result from 14 ... P–N3 15 N×B+ place Black at a grave disadvantage, as he has no effective counterplay against White's pressure on the long black diagonal (P–QB4, B–Q2–B3, and P–KB4.

14 N–K4   B–N2
15 R–Q1   P–N3?

A natural but wrong move, allowing White to eliminate the only advantage of Black's position, his two bishops. He should play 15 ... Q–B2! 16 B–K3 P–N3 wih an even game.

16 B–R6!   P–B4
17 B×B   Q×B

Black's main problem is that he cannot blockade the passed pawn by occupying ... Q3. e.g. if 17 ... K×B 18 N–B3 Q–Q3 White plays 19 N–N5 when 19 ... B–R3 allows 20 N×Q B×Q 21 R–K1 etc.

18 N–B3   B–N2?

Even if it is not possible to prevent P–Q6, Black should at least do all in his power to blockade on his Q2 square. So 18 ... B–Q2! is essential! Probably Black did not relish the prospect of N–Q5 after P–Q6, but the advance of White's pawn to Q7 is a greater evil.

19 P–QR4!

An excellent move! To gain the full value from his advanced pawn, White must create additional points of attack. He now aims to weaken Black's QNP after 19 ... QR–Q1 20 P–R5 followed by 21 P×P. After Black's next move this weakness is even more glaring.

19 ...	**P–QR4!**
20 Q–N5	**Q–QB2**
21 P–Q6	**Q–Q1**

Or 21 ... Q–B3 22 Q×Q B×Q 23 P–Q7! KR–Q1 24 R–Q6! B×QP 25 QR–Q1 R–R2 26 N–Q5 etc. Again the passed pawn decides the game, but this time by sacrificing itself. Such a sacrifice is by no means an exception, as the remaining games in this chapter will demonstrate.

22 N–Q5 (*10*)

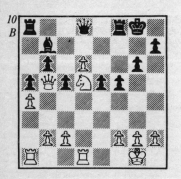

This move forces the exchange of Black's last minor piece (22 ... R–R3? 23 N–B7 and 24 N–K6), leading to an easy win because Black's major pieces will be tied to the blockade of the white pawn on Q7.

22 ...	**B×N**

23 R×B	**P–K5**
24 R1–Q1	**K–N2**
25 P–Q7	**R–B3**
26 P–R3	**R–K3**
27 Q–B4	**R–K2**
28 R–Q6	**R–R2**
29 Q–B3+	**K–N1**
30 Q–B6	**R–R1**
31 Q×R!	**1–0**

The final obstacle is removed, and after 31 ... Q×Q 32 P–Q8=Q+ R×Q 33 R×R+ K–B2 34 R–Q7 White comes out a whole rook ahead.

The above two games have one thing in common: the relatively rapid advance of the pawn to the queening square made possible not only by inexact defence but also by subsidiary threats, such as the atack on KB7 in Game 3, or the attack on the weak QNP in Game 4. We can take it as a basic principle that tactical threats like this are essential in order to divert the enemy pieces from the blockade of our pawn which can then advance.

As we have already mentioned, we seldom find the pawn actually achieving promotion in the middle game, whereas in the endgame with it reduced material, the passed pawn has a veritable field-day. It would be quite wrong to assume from this that a passed pawn is of no use in the middle game, apart from on those exceptional occasions when it can be promoted! Here are two further games which teach us a little more about the rôle of the passed pawn.

By threatening to advance, the passed pawn can tie down enemy pieces which cannot play their part in defending another section of the board. In the following game Capablanca used his passed pawn both to create a strong-point and to limit the action of the enemy pieces, then finally brought about a decision by an attack on the king, again involving the pawn.

5 Capablanca–Zubarev

Moscow 1925, Queen's Gambit

**1 P–Q4 P–Q4 2 P–QB4 P–K3 3
N–KB3 P×P 4 P–K4 P–QB4 5
P–Q5?!** 5 B×P is better. **5...P×P 6
P×P N–KB3** Black has a good game
after 6 ... B–Q3 and 7 ... N–K2. **7
B×P B–Q3 8 0–0 0–0 9 B–KN5 B–N5
10 N–B3 QN–Q2** 10 ... P–KR3! **11
N–K4 Q–B2 12 B×N N N×B 13 N×N+
P×N** *(11)*

11
W

It is clear that White's passed QP is
well and truly blockaded. However, he
has an additional trump-card: Black's
weakened K-side. In the further course
of the game he manoeuvres his pieces in
such a way that they are well-placed for
a possible advance of the QP as well as
for an attack on the king.

**14 P–KR3 B–R4
15 R–K1 KR–K1
16 Q–N3 P–QR3
17 P–QR4 B–N3**

If the reader is surprised that Black
does not go in for bishops of opposite
colour by 17 ... B×N, he must realize
that after 18 Q×B Black's K-side is
without defence.

**18 B–Q3 Q–Q2
19 N–Q2 R–K2
20 B×B**

If White does not exchange Black's
strong defensive bishop, he has no real
attacking chances. However, Black

should now play 20 ... RP×B!
followed by 21 ... K–N2 with near
equality. The move he chooses gives
him a serious weakness on ... K3 which
White uses as an important strong-
point for his pieces.

**20 ... BP×B?
21 N–K4 K–N2**

After 21 ... K–B2 White has the
unpleasant 22 Q–KB3

**22 Q–QB3 B–K4
23 Q×P B×P
24 N–N5!**

We now see why Black should have
played 20 ... RP×B. White's knight
obtains a splendid post on K6.

**24 ... R1–K1
25 N–K6+ K–B2
26 QR–N1 B–K4
27 Q–B4 R–QB1
28 Q–N3 B–N1?**

After this move Black soon has a
hopeless position. Admittedly, it is
doubtful if his game can be held, even
with other moves. If 28 ... Q–Q3 29
R.K1–QB1! and White seizes the vital
open file. Some annotators recommend
28 ... R–B6 when White must not
continue 29 Q×P? Q×Q 30 R×Q
R×R 31 N–Q8+ K–B1 32 N×R
R–Q6 with a drawn ending. However,
he can simply play 29 Q–R2 or 29
Q–Q1 threatening 30 R×P!

**29 P–N3 Q–Q3
30 N–B4 R1–K1
31 R–K6! Q–Q2
32 R×R+ K×R**

Not of course 32 ... R×R? 33
P–Q6+. Black now hopes for 33 Q×P
B×N 34 P×B Q×Q 35 R×Q+
K–Q3 with drawing chances.

33 Q×P B×N *(12)*

Capablanca now concludes the game
with a pretty combination in which the
passed pawn plays a vital rôle.

**34 R–K1+! B–K4
35 P–Q6+! K–K3**

He is mated or loses his queen after 35

... K–Q1 36 Q–N6+ or 35 ... K×P 36 R–Q1+

36	Q–N3+	K–B4
37	Q–Q3+	K–N4
38	Q–K3+	K–B4
39	Q–K4+	K–K3
40	Q–QB4+	K×P
41	R–Q1+	K–K2
42	R×Q+	K×R
43	Q×P	R–QN1
44	Q–R7+	K–B3
45	Q×P	R–N7
46	Q×P	1–0

As we have already seen, the pawn sacrifice on move 35 is a common feature of such positions. When the passed pawn cannot advance without being lost, it is sacrificed at an opportune moment in order to open attacking lines. In the above game the sacrifice was a simple one, as the capture of the pawn loses the queen. The pawn sacrifice in our next game is much more complicated.

6 Szabo–Wade

Trencianske Teplice 1949, Grünfeld Defence

1 P–Q4 N–KB3 2 P–QB4 P–KN3 3 N–QB3 P–Q4 4 N–B3 B–N2 5 Q–N3 P×P 6 Q×BP 0–0 7 P–K4 N–R3 8 B–K2 P–B4 9 P–Q5 P–K3 10 0–0 P×P

11 P×P

We have reached a position in which the passed pawn has no particular dynamic strength. White's pieces are not well placed for supporting a speedy advance of the pawn, whereas Black has counterplay down the long black diagonal. Theory now recommends 11 ... Q–N3 followed by ... R–K1 and ... B–B4 with the constant threat of ... N–K5

11 ...   N–K1(?)

In the next section we shall show that it is strategically correct · policy to blockade the QP by placing a knight on Q3, but in this position the immediate attempt to do so is tactically faulty. Black must now relinquish his main advantage of pressure down the long black diagonal, and his pieces become unco-ordinated.

12 B–N5!   P–B3

Of course 12 ... Q–N3 13 B–K7 loses the exchange.

13 B–B4   R–B2

It would be more logical to play 13 ... N–Q3. After 14 Q–N3! (*14 B×N Q×B 15 N–QN5 Q–N3* or *15 N–K4 Q–N3* gives White nothing) 14 ... R–K1 15 QR–Q1, although White has a more active position, it is by no means easy to exploit this advantage.

14 QR–Q1   B–B1? (*13*)

Black intends to play this bishop to Q3 with a view to exchanging White's active bishop or forcing it to retreat. However, 14 ... N–Q3 is essential to

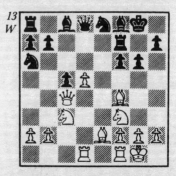

prevent the next move which allows White to obtain a decisive positional advantage by sacrificing his QP.

15 P-Q6!　　　N-N2!

The pawn cannot be captured by the knight or bishop because of a subsequent Q-Q5 winning a piece. With the text-move Black hopes to regroup his pieces by . . . B-K3 and . . . R-Q2, but White's next energetic move puts an end to this idea.

16 P-Q7!

On Q6 the pawn is a clear weakness, whereas this sacrifice destroys the co-ordination of Black's pieces. Nimzow-itsch once wrote that the most dangerous pawns are those that have 'the death wish'.

16 . . .	**B× P**
17 Q-K4	**Q-B1**

Forced, as White was threatening both 18 Q× QNP and 18 B-B4

18　B-B4	**B-K3**
19　KR-K1!	**B× B**
20　Q× B	**N-N5**
21　N-QN5	**N-K1**
22　P-QR3	**N-R3**

The knight cannot go to QB3, as White then plays 23 B-Q6 B× B 24 N× B N× N 25 R× N Q-B4 26 N-R4

Q-N4 27 R-Q7 R1-KB1 28 R-K8! etc.

23　P-KR4	**N1-B2**
24　B× N	**N× B**
25　N-Q6	**B× N**
26　R× B	**K-N2**

Black loses after 26 . . . N-K1 27 R6-K6 followed by 28 R-K7

27　P-R5!

Threatening 28 P-R6+ against which there is no defence, as 27 . . . P× P 28 N-R4! would only help White's attack.

27　. . .	**N-K1**
28　P-R6+ !	**K-B1**
29　R6-K6	**Q-B2**
30　P-QN4	**N-Q3**

Not of course 30 . . . P× P?? 31 Q× P+ . Black's QBP cannot be defended by 30 . . . P-N3 when 31 Q-K4 follows e.g. 31 . . . Q-B1 32 R-K7 or 31 . . . Q-Q1 32 Q-B6 N-B2 33 R-Q6 etc.

31　Q-B3	**N-B4**
32　N-N5!	**N-Q5**
33　N× R	**N× R**
34　R× N	**R-K1**

Black, in time-trouble, was still hoping to trap the knight, but it simply returns the same way it came in.

35　N-N5!　　　1-0

2 Blockading the Passed Pawn

14

The black knight on Q3 (*14*) effectively prevents the passed pawn from advancing. We term such a piece a *blockader*, the simplest, most effective and therefore most common means of blocking a passed pawn. In the diagrammed position, White has no chance at all of exploiting the passed pawn. Prospects are even. Black has a mobile K-side majority which he can push forward after due preparation (. . . P–B4, . . . P–K5, . . . P–B5) when he threatens either . . . P–K6 creating a passed pawn, or . . . P–B6 with an attack on the white king. An interesting position arises after 1 . . . P–B4 2 P–B4 P–K5 3 N–Q1! and 4 N–K3. Although Black has a protected passed pawn, he has no advantage, because White's knight is a very strong blockader on K3 and the black KP can later be undermined by P–R3 and P–KN4.

Even this simple example tells us that the blockader fills two rôles:

1. A defensive one, holding up the enemy pawn.
2. An active one, as it often draws strength from its post in front of the pawn (especially when this is a centre pawn), being protected from a frontal attack.

Let us consider two games which illustrate these points.

7 Vesely–Pachman

Prague 1951, Ruy Lopez

1 P–K4 P–K4 2 N–KB3 N–QB3 3 B–N5 P–QR3 4 B–R4 N–B3 5 P–Q4 P×P 6 0–0 B–K2 7 P–K5 N–K5 8 N×P 0–0 9 R–K1 N–B4 10 B×N QP×B 11 N–QB3 (*15*)

15
B

A well-known theoretical position which occurred in the game Alekhine–Keres, Kemeri 1937, with the continuation 11 . . . R–K1 12 B–K3 B–B1 13 P–B4 P–B3 14 P×P Q×P 15 Q–B3 and a better game for White. As a result, many theoreticians were of the opinion that 8 ... N-K3 was better, instead of 8 ... 0-0. I obtained the diagrammed position in an earlier game, as Black against Foltys in the 1946 Championship of Czechoslovakia. After long thought, it became clear to me that Black's bishop pair would give him an advantage if he could stem the advance of White's K-side pawns. There is only one way to do this, by a move which at first sight appears to do the very opposite.

11 ...   P-B4!

Black gives White a protected passed pawn which he will then permanently restrain by placing a blockader on ... K3, giving him active play on both wings.

12 N3-K2

The best move! In the above-mentioned game Foltys played 12 P-B4 N-K3 13 B-K3 N×N 14 Q×N Q×Q 15 B×Q B-K3, after which White is strategically lost, as he has no effective counter to the advance of Black's Q-side pawns. Nor can White improve in this line by 13 N-B3 B-N5 14 B-K3 B×N 15 P×B P-B4 16 Q-Q3 Q-K2 17 QR-Q1 P-R3 18 P-KR3 P-QN3 19 K-B2 B-N2 20 Q-Q7 Q×Q 21 R×Q B-K5 22 R-K2 QR-Q1 23 R2-Q2 R×R 24 R×R R-Q1 25 R-K7? K-B1 and Black won, Darga-Ivkov, Hastings 1955-6. The blockading knight on K3 did an excellent job here too. If 12 P×P ep P×B, Black's pieces come into action more quickly than White's.

12 ...   N-K3
13 N×N   Q×Q
14 R×Q   B×N
15 N-B4?

White obviously wishes to remove Black's strong blockading bishop, but a better way of doing thas is 15 N-Q4 when 15 ... QR-Q1? fails to 16 B-N5! etc. However, Black can play 15 ... K-B2 16 N×B K×N when the game is

clearly drawn, as the king is such a good blockader here that White has not the slightest chance of exploiting his pawn majority. Even better, however, is 15 N-Q4 B-B1! when the White knight will soon be driven from the centre e.g. 16 P-QN3 (*16 B-K3 P-B5*) 16 ... P-KN4! followed by ... P-B4 and ... B-K3

15 ...   QR-Q1!
16 B-K3   B-B1
17 N-Q3

After 17 N-K2 Black plays ... P-B4 and ... P-KN4 (in any order) followed by ... B-K3. This bishop would then be secure on K3 and White would have to defend on both wings.

17 ...   P-QN3
18 P-QN4

It is already clear that White is not content to defend passively but is striving for active counterplay. The text-move prepares P-QR4-5 but White is given no time for this, because Black immediately begins operations.

18 ...   P-B5!
19 N×P

Not of course 19 B×BP? R×N! and if instead 19 B-Q2 P-B6 20 P-N3 B-KB4, White's position is equally unattractive.

19 ...   B×P
20 N-K2

Or 20 N-Q3 B-B6 21 QR-N1 B-B4 22 P-B4 P-B4.

20 ...   B-KB4!

A little surprise, as the seemingly strong 21 N-Q4 fails to 21 ... B-B6 e.g.

a. 22 N×B B×R 23 N-K7+ K-B2 24 R×B K×N 25 B-N5+ K-K3 26 B×R R×B 27 P-KB4 R-Q7 winning.

b. 22 QR-B1 B-N7 23 R-N1 B×N and 24 ... B×P wins.

21 P-QB3   B-R4
22 QR-B1   P-B4
23 P-B3   B-K3

White would have no prospects now

after 24 P–QR3 B–B5, so he tries to conjure up a few complications.

24 K–B2   B–B5

Cutting out any slight counter-chance that White may have after 24 ... R×R 25 R×R B×RP 26 R–Q7 or 24 ... B×RP 25 R×R R×R 26 P–QB4.

25 N–B4	KR–K1
26 R×R	R×R
27 P–QR3	R–K1
28 P–K6	B×KP
29 N×B	R×N
30 P–QB4	K–B2
31 B–B4	P–QN4!
32 B–K3	B–N3
33 P×P	P×P
34 R–QN1	

Not 34 B×P? R–QB3

34 ...	P–B5!
35 B×B	R×B
36 K–K3	P–B4
37 K–K4	K–K3
0–1	

8 Euwe–Pilnik

Amsterdam 1950, Grünfeld Defence

1 P–Q4 N–KB3 2 P–QB4 P–KN3 3 P–KN3 B–N2 4 B–N2 P–Q4 5 P×P N×P 6 P–K4 N–N3 7 N–K2 P–QB4 8 P–Q5 0–0 9 0–0 P–K3 10 N1–B3? *10 P–QR4!* 10 ... N–R3 11 N–B4 P–K4 12 N4–K2 *(16)*

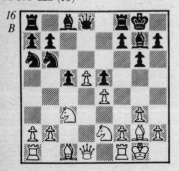

This is a position that often arises in play. White has a protected passed pawn on Q5 (see Chapter 3), whilst Black has a Q-side pawn majority. Black's most immediate task is to place a blockading knight on Q3.

12 ...   N–B5!

13 P–N3?

To hand over the blockading square without a fight is equivalent to strategic capitulation. The correct plan is 13 N–N5! e.g. 13 ... B–Q2 *(13 ... N–B2 14 Q–B2)* 14 N2–B3 Q–N3 15 P–QR4 and White has more chance of active play than after the text-move.

13 ...	N–Q3
14 B–K3	P–N3
15 Q–Q2	R–K1

Black is not afraid of a possible exchange of his bishop after 16 B–R6, as he would then be left with his 'good' bishop, but the text-move is a good prophylactic measure against White's next move.

16 P–B4?

This only helps Black. It was essential to set up a passive defence with 16 P–B3 followed by 17 KR–Q1 (or B2) and 18 B–B1, aiming to restrain Black's Q-side pawns. This would indeed be a thankless task, but the game continuation gives White even more difficulties.

16 ...   N–B2

17 R–B2?

Apparently under-estimating the importance of the blockading square on ... K4 which Black now obtains. However, other moves would be answered by 17 ... B–QR3 and 18 ... N2–N4 with good prospects for Black.

17 ...   P×P!

18 B×KBP

Forced, as 18 P×P loses a pawn without compensation after 18 ... N×KP! 19 B×N R×B, whereas now 18 ... N×KP? 19 B2×N R×B 20 N×R B×R 21 N2–B3! gives White an irresistible attack.

18 ...	B–QR3!
19 R–K1	Q–K2
20 P–KN4	B–K4 (17)

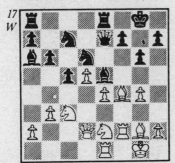

A strategically important position. Black's knight on Q3 blockades the QP, but equally important is the blockade of the KP by the bishop on K4, as the advance of this pawn would activate his colleague on Q5.

21 B× B	Q× B
22 N–N3?	

It is not clear what White has in mind with this move. He could instead fight for the blockading square in front of his KP by 22 K–R1! threatening N–KN1–B3. Black would still have the advantage after 22 ... B× N, but it would not be as great as in the game.

22 ...	R–K2
23 B–B1	B–B1
24 B–K2	B–Q2
25 R1–KB1	R–KB1
26 Q–B1	N2–K1
27 K–R1	P–B3
28 R–N1	N–KN2?

The knight does nothing here. The correct plan was to transfer his knight on Q3 to K4 via KB2. However, Black's position is so strong that he can afford an inexactitude. It even goads White into making another mistake!

29 B–B3?	Q–N4!!

A splendid positional move! Black is willing to give White two connected passed pawns and double his own

pawns, in order to set up a complete blockade on the Black squares. It is only eight moves later that Black's plan comes to fruition.

30 Q× Q	P× Q
31 R1–KB1	N2–K1
32 B–K2	R× R
33 R× R	K–N2
34 P–KR3	N–B3
35 B–B3	B–K1!
36 R–K2	N–Q2
37 R–Q2	N–K4 (18)

Everything is now clear. The blockading knights dominate the position, fixing White's pawns on white squares and helping the black Q-side pawns to advance. The rest of the game is pure logic:

38 B–K2 P–N4! 39 R–B2 R–QB2 40 N–Q1 P–B5 41 P× P P× P 42 N–B3 or 42 N–N2 K–B3 42 ... K–B3 43 N–N1 R–QN2 44 N–Q2 B–R5! 45 R–B1 R–N7! 46 N× P N.K4× N 47 B× N B–B7! 48 B–N3 R–N8! 49 R× R B× R 50 N–K2 B× KP+ 51 K–R2 K–K4 52 N–B3 B–Q6 53 K–N3 N–K5+ 54 N× N B× N 55 P–Q6 K× P 56 B–N8 P– KR3 57 B–B7 B–Q4 58 B× P B× P 59 P–R4 P–QR4 60 P× P P× P 61 K–B3 P–R5 62 K–K3 B–K3 63 K–Q4 B× P 64 K–B3 B–Q8 65 B–B5 K–K4 66 B–Q7 K–B5 67 K–N4 B–B7 68 K–B3 B–N6 69 K–N4 B–B2 70 K× P B–N3

71 K–N4 B–B4 72 B–B6 P–N5 73 K–B5 B–K5 74 B—Q7 P–N6 75 B–R3 K–K6 76 K–Q6 B–B4! 77 B–N2 K–B7 0–1.

Both these games are good illustrations of the importance of blockading. In the first game Black deliberately gave White a protected passed pawn after 11 . . . P–B4! and we saw that a blockaded passed pawn is often less dangerous than a mobile pawn majority. During the game and the variations arising, the K5 pawn was blockaded by various pieces, and it is worthwhile considering which piece is the most effective blockader. It is usually the knight, and we saw such a knight remaining on K3 until the game was decided (Darga–Ivkov, quoted in the annotation to White's 12th move in game 7), fulfilling both a defensive and attacking rôle (attack on the KBP). However, in the games against Vesely and Foltys the bishop on K3 proved an effective blockader, with the important support of the 'reserve blockader' on K2. Nimzowitsch gave this name to a piece which can still blockade the pawn when his colleague moves away. Such a set-up is particularly useful, as it gives the bishop on K3 more scope for tactical operations on several diagonals. In the note to move 15 of game 7, we also showed the king as a blockader. With few exceptions such a rôle is only possible in the endgame, for obvious reasons. The rook and queen are basically unsuitable as blockaders, mainly because they are powerful attacking pieces which do not like to be tied down in this way. Such a blockade by the major pieces is therefore usually a matter of necessity (see game 3). Here is a good example of the contrasting effectiveness of the blockade by a minor and major piece.

9 Korchnoi–Pachman

Bucharest 1954, Nimzo–Indian Defence

1 P–Q4 N–KB3 2 P–QB4 P–K3 3 N–QB3 B–N5 4 P–B3 P–Q4 5 P–QR3 B–K2!? 6 P–K4 P×KP 7 P×P P–K4! 8 P–Q5 0–0 9 N–B3 N–N5! 10 B–Q3 B–QB4 11 Q–K2 B–B7+ 12 K–Q1 B–Q5!

13 K–B2

If 13 N×B P×N 14 N–N5 N–K4! 15 N×QP B–N5 16 N–B3 P–KB4, Black has a very strong attack for the pawn.

13 ...   P–QB4!

Allowing White a protected passed QP which Black intends to blockade by placing a knight on Q3.

14	**R–B1**	**B×N**
15	**K×B**	**Ň–Q2**
16	**K–B2**	**P–QR3**
17	**B–Q2**	**N5–B3**
18	**B–B3**	**Q–B2**
19	**N–R4**	**N–K1**
20	**Q–R5**	**P–QN4!**

A correctly timed counter-attack, as now 21 N–B5 P×P 22 B×BP N–Q3 would give Black a good game.

21 N–B3

Returning to the defence of QB4 square.

21	**...**	**P–B3**
22	**N–Q2**	**N–N3**
23	**P–QN3** *(19)*	

19 B

So far the game has gone well for Black who has contained White's attack and could now consolidate his advantage by 23 ... N–Q3. If White then continued in attacking style with 24 P–KN4, Black would obtain a winning position after 24 ... P×P 25 N×P N.Q3×N 26 B×N (otherwise *26 ...N–R5* follows) 26 ... N×B 27 P×N Q–Q2! 28 P–N5 Q–R5+ 29 K–Q3 P–B4 etc.

23 ...   P×P??

The correct idea but in the wrong sequence. Black overlooks a tactical possibility at White's disposal.

24 N×P   N×N
25 B×N   Q–Q3

Only now does Black realize that his intended 25 ... N–Q3 fails to 26 B×KP! P×B 27 R×R+ K×R 28 Q×RP winning for White. This means that he must blockade the QP with his queen rather than his knight, and a strategically won position is suddenly transformed into a clear positional disadvantage.

26 P–KN4   B–Q2
27 P–N5   P–B4?

The game could probably still be saved by the stronger 27 ... B–N4! 28 P×P P×P.

28 P×P   B×P+
29 K–N2   N–B2

It is difficult to find a good square for the knight, and the KP is weak. White won in simple and convincing fashion as follows: **30 QR–K1 P–K5 31 Q–R4! N–N4 32 Q–B4! Q×Q 33 R×Q N×B 34 K×N P–N3 35 B–B1! P–QR4 36 B–N5! QR–N1 37 P–QR4 K–N2 38 K–B4 R.N1–B1 39 R–K3 P–R3 40 P–R4 P×P 41 P×P 1–0.** The Q-side pawns cannot be held.

And now one or two comments on game 8, whose closing stages clearly show the strength of the blockade. Although Black's pawns are weakened and he gives White two connected

passed pawns, the splendidly posted blockading knights win the game for him. This game reveals another interesting point, however. Black was blockading the QP with his knight, but as soon as he captured the KBP with his KP he was obliged to set up a blockade of White's KP, even though the latter was not passed. On the basis of this observation, we can now extend the concept of the blockade as follows: it is important to restrain not only passed pawns but any pawn whose advance can improve the enemy position. For this reason, we must also blockade weak pawns whose immobility then often becomes a vital strategic factor. Sometimes a few pieces and pawns can blockade a whole wing, or, in specially favourable circumstances, the entire enemy position!

We shall later be examining this extended form of the blockade, but let us linger on the blockade of a passed pawn. The examples we have quoted so far may give the reader the impression that the blockade of a passed pawn always restricts its mobility to such an extent that it practically loses all its value. The blockade is no such panacea and there are effective means of countering it. The simplest method is to exchange the blockader, but sometimes a sacrifice will lure it away from the blockading square. We saw this kind of sacrifice in the famous Botvinnik–Capablanca encounter at the A.V.R.O. tournament (see volume 1) where 30 B–R3! drew away the black queen, which is a poor blockader as it is so vulnerable to attacks. Here is another way of dealing with the blockader:

Nimzowitsch quotes this position (*20*) as an example of 'changing the blockader'. White wins by **1 R–N8+ R–B1 2 R×B! R×R 3 K–N7 R–KB1 4 P–R8=Q R×Q 5 K×R K–B2 6**

K–N7 K–N3 7 K–B7 K–N4 8 K–Q7!
K–B4 9 K–Q6 etc. By sacrificing the

exchange White replaces a blockading bishop with a rook so that his king can approach the queening square. In our next game White sacrifices the exchange in order to prevent the blockade of his passed pawn.

10 Grünfeld–Steiner

Ostrava 1933, Queen's Gambit

1 P–Q4 P–Q4 2 P–QB4 P–K3 3 N–QB3 P–QB3 4 N–B3 N–B3 5 P–K3 QN–Q2 6 B–Q3 B–K2 7 0–0 0–0 8 P–QN3 P–QN3 9 B–N2 B–N2 10 Q–K2 P×P 11 P×P P–B4 12 QR–Q1 Q–B2 13 N–K5 P–QR3 13 . . . N×N 14 P×N N–Q2 15 P–B4 gives White a strong attack. 14 P–B4 KR–Q1 15 P–Q5! N–B1 if 15 . . . P×P 16 N×P N×N 17 B×P+! K×B 18 Q–R5+ etc. 16 P–K4 P–QN4 17 N–N4 P–N5 18 N–N1 N–K1

19 P–B5!

By removing Black's KP White strengthens his QP and forces through P–K5. However, he has to foresee the following sacrifice, as otherwise Black can set up an effective blockade of the centre pawns.

    19 . . .   P×BP

    20 R×P

This is stronger than 20 P×P P–B3 21 R.Q1–K1 R–Q2 and 22 . . . N–Q3

    20 . . .   B–B1 *(21)*

It now seems that Black will be able to blockade the pawns after exchanging White's knight on KN4 e.g. 21 R–R5 B×N 22 Q×B N–B3 23 B×N B×B etc. Or 21 R5–B1 B×N 22 Q×B B–Q3. However, the following sacrifice gives White mobile centre pawns supported by his pieces, leading to a decisive attack.

    21 P–K5!   B×R

    22 B×B   Q–R4

    23 N–Q2   Q×P

Other moves also give White an irresistible attack by N–K4 or N–B3.

    24 N–B3

This is not only threatening to win a piece by P–Q6 but also sets up a winning attack on Black's queen, as the game continuation shows. Black has no defence, as his minor pieces are completely hemmed in by the White pawns.

	24 . . .	P–B3 ?
	25 R–R1!	Q–N6
	26 B–B2!	Q×B.N7
	27 B×P+	N×B
	28 Q×Q	P×P
	29 Q×KP	B–Q3
	30 Q–K6+	K–R1
	31 N3–K5	B×N
	32 N×B	N–B1
	33 Q–K7	N–Q3
	34 R–KB1	K–N1
	35 R–B3	1–0

As we have already stated, the side with the passed pawn(s) usually tries to exchange or drive away the blockader. We see both ideas in the following game.

11 Nimzowitsch–Gottschall

Breslau 1925, Queen's Pawn Game

1 N–KB3 P–K3 2 P–Q4 P–Q4 3 P–K3 N–KB3 4 P–QN3 QN–Q2(?) 5 B–Q3 P–B3(?) 6 0–0 B–Q3 7 B–N2 Q–B2 8 P–B4 P–QN3 9 N–B3 B–N2 10 R–B1 R–QB1 11 P×P(?) KP×P 12 P–K4 P×P 13 N×P N×N 14 B×N 0–0
15 P–Q5   P–QB4? (22)

As Black's opening errors have not been exploited, he could now equalize by 15 ... N–B4! when 16 B×RP+ K×B 17 N–N5+ K–N3 is bad for White, and 16 P×P N×B 17 Q–Q4 P–B4 likewise gives him nothing e.g. 18 Q–Q5+ Q–B2! 19 Q×Q+ R×Q.20 P×B R×R 21 R×R R×P 22 R–B8+ K–B2.

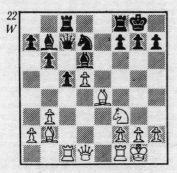

Gottschall now appears to have set up an effective blockade of the QP, with a reserve blockader on Q2. However, we shall see that this blockade cannot be maintained. By threats against the enemy king, White succeeds in enticing away the blockading knight and exchanging the bishop, after which the QP shows its power.

16 R–K1   Q–Q1
17 B–N1!   R–K1
18 Q–Q3(?)

A slight inexactitude. He should first exchange rooks, as Black could now improve his defensive chances by 18 ... R×R+.

18 ...   N–B1(?)
19 R×R!   Q×R
20 N–R4!

One of the blockaders is tied to the defence of the KRP, and the other will be exchanged.

20 ...   P–B3

After 20 ... B–K4 21 B×B Q×B 22 P–Q6 (or 22 N–B5) White would also stand far better, but he now increases his advantage by a simple tactical point.

21 N–B5   R–Q1
22 B×P!

Black had hoped for 22 N×B? R×N with pressure on the QP. Now, after 22 ... P×B 23 N×B R×N, 24 Q–N3+ wins the rook, so Black's reply is forced.

22 ...   B×RP+
23 K×B   P×B
24 Q–N3+   N–N3
25 P–B4 (23)

The real point of White's 22nd move. Black was threatening not only to capture the QP but also to exchange queens by 25 ... Q–K4.

After the text move, 25 ... R×P or 25 ... B×P fails to 26 R–K1 followed by

27 N–K7+ Black's position has become much worse over the last few moves. His blockading KB has gone and the knight is far away from . . . Q2. In addition Black's king position is weak, so White can combine the advance of his pawn with an attack on the king. This quickly leads to the win of material.

25 . . .	K–R1
26 R–K1	Q–B1

It is interesting to see how the QP is used after 26 . . . Q–N1 27 N–K7! N×N 28 R×N Q×Q+ 29 K×Q R–KN1+ 30 K–B2 R–N2 31 P–Q6 R×R 32 P×R B–B3 33 B–K4 B–K1 34 P–B5 K–N2 35 B–Q5 K–R3 36 K–B3 K–N4 37 K–K4 followed by B–N7, K–Q5 and B–B6.

27 P–Q6! **R–Q2**

He is forced to blockade in this way, as 27 . . . B–B1 loses to 28 N–K7 Q–R3+ 29 K–N1 N×P 30 N×B R×N 31 P–Q7.

28 Q–QB3! **R×P**

The threat was 29 R–K8! and if 28 . . . R–KB2 29 P–Q7! R×P 30 R–K8! again wins. The rest of the game is a matter of technique: **29 N×R Q×N 30 B×N P×B 31 R–K8+ K–N2 32 Q–N3 B–B3 33 R–K3 B–Q2 34 P–B5! Q×Q+ 35 K×Q B×P 36 R–K7+ K–R3 37 R×P B–N8 38 R–R6 P–QN4 39 P–R4 P×P 40 P×P K–N4 41 R–N6 B–K5 42 P–R5 P–B4 43 P–R6 P–QB5 44 P–R7 P–B6 45 R–N3 P–B5+ 46 K–B2 P–B7 47 R–QB3 1–0.**

Let us now consider examples of the blockade other than that of a passed pawn, when a particular pawn or group of pawns is immobilized.

12 Nimzowitsch–Salve

Karlsbad 1911, French Defence

1 P–K4 P–K3 2 P–Q4 P–Q4 3 P–K5 P–QB4 4 P–QB3 N–QB3 5 N–B3 Q–N3 6 B–Q3 B–Q2? 6 . . . P×P! 7 P×P! B×P 8 0–0 P–B3 *(24)*

White's KP is an important strategic factor as it exerts a severe restraining effect on Black's K-side. With his last move Black aims to exchange this pawn, even if this means weakening his own KP, and of course White cannot avoid this exchange. It is clear that 9 P×P would only help Black's development, so it seems more advantageous to guard the pawn and force Black to make the exchange. At first sight 9 Q–K2 seems best, giving us 9 . . . P×P 10 N×P N×N 11 Q×N N–B3. The queen would then be blockading the KP, preventing the freeing . . . P–K4. However, as we have already seen, the queen is not a good blockader, apart from the fact that it cannot remain on K5 for long (e.g. the possibility of B–Q3). With a deep understanding of the strategic character of the position, Nimzowitsch selects a manoeuvre which uses the bishop as a blockader.

9 P–QN4!	B–K2
10 B–KB4	P×P
11 N×P	N×N
12 B×N	N–B3

If Black tries to contest the blockading square at once by 12 . . . B–B3 he loses after 13 Q–R5+ P–N3 14 B×P+! P×B 15 Q×P+ K–K2 16 B×B+ N×B 17 Q–N7+ etc.

13 N–Q2!

It would be a strategic mistake to

play to win a pawn by 13 Q–B2? when Black replies 13 . . . 0–0! 14 B×N B×B 15 B×P+ K–R1 followed by 16 . . . P–K4 with a clear advantage in view of his two bishops and strong centre. Thus the win of a pawn would divert White from his correct strategic plan which lies in blockading on his Q4 and K5 squares.

13 ...	0–0
14 N–B3	B–Q3 (25)

25
W

Black aims to play . . . Q–B2 and . . . N–N5 to contest his K4 square. White's correct plan is to replace the blockading bishop with the knight, then support it with Q–K2 and R–K1. Note that it would be wrong to play immediately 15 B–Q4? Q–B2 16 Q–K2 N–N5! 17 P–KR3 P–K4! with an excellent game for Black.

15 Q–K2!	QR–B1

Or 15 . . . B×B 16 N×B QR–B1 17 P–QB4!

16 B–Q4	Q–B2
17 N–K5	

White's spatial superiority and the weakness of the Black KP give him a clear advantage. The remainder of the game is extremely instructive for the way in which White speedily and accurately converts this advantage into a win.

17...	B–K1
18 QR–K1	B×N
19 B×B	Q–B3

20 B–Q4	B–Q2
21 Q–B2!	

Compare the note to move 13. White's attack against KR7 is successful, only because the black centre is now blockaded.

21 ...	R–KB2
22 R–K3	P–QN3
23 R–N3	K–R1
24 B×RP!	P–K4

He cannot play 24 . . . N×B 25 Q–N6. The game now concluded: **25 B–N6 R–K2 26 R–K1 Q–Q3 27 B–K3 P–Q5 28 B–N5 R×P 29 R×R P×R 30 Q×P K–N1 31 P–QR3 K–B1 32 B–R4 B–K1 33 B–B5 Q–Q5 34 Q×Q P×Q 35 R×R K×R 36 B–Q3 K–Q3 37 B×N P×B 38 P–KR4 1–0.**

26
W

In this position (26), which comes from Ciocaltea–Darga, 1972 Skopje Olympiad, White's main task is to blockade Black's QBP and QP. The simplest way to achieve this is by 15 B×B Q×B 16 P–QB3 and 17 Q–Q4, but White chose a more complex manoeuvre: **15 B–Q4 B×B 16 Q×B Q–N3!** Now Black threatens both 17 . . . Q×BP and 17 . . . B–R6 which would force a serious weakening of White's K-side by P–N3. White cannot play 17 R–K2 B–R6 18 P–KB3 QR–K1 19 R1–K1? B×P! when Black wins. **17 R–K3! Q×BP 18 N–B5** Black's extra pawn is meaningless, as White's pieces dominate the whole board. He now threatens 19 R1–K1 and 20 R–N3. **18 ... B–B4 19 R1–K1! P–QR4??** surprisingly, Black overlooks the main threat, but his position is difficult anyway. After 19 ... Q×RP 20 P–KN4 B–N3 21 P–R4 P–R3 22 P–R5 B–R2 23 P–N5! P×P 24 P–R6 P×P 25 N–Q7 wins; or here 21 ... P–B3 22 P–R5 B–B2 23 P–R6! P×P 24 N–Q7 and White's attack breaks through. **20 R3–K2 1–0.**

13 Schlechter–Janowski

Paris 1900, Ruy Lopez

1 P–K4 P–K4 2 N–KB3 N–QB3 3 B–N5 N–B3 4 0–0 N×P 5 P–Q4 B–K2 6 Q–K2 N–Q3 7 B×N NP×B 8 P×P N–N2 9 N–B3 0–0 10 R–K1 R–K1? A serious error which gives Black a clear disadvantage; 10 ... N–B4! was the correct move. **11 Q–B4! N–B4**
   12 N–KN5!
White already begins his blockading plan. If now 12 ... N–K3 13 N×N BP×N 14 B–B4 followed by 15 QR–Q1 makes it difficult for Black to develop his QB. After Black's next move, involving the exchange of two minor pieces, his important black-squared bishop disappears and this piece was needed to support the freeing advance of the QP.

12 ...	B×N
13 B×B	Q×B
14 Q×N	R–K3
15 Q–Q4!	

An important move which counters Black's attempt to free his game. In the game Janowski–Chigorin, London 1899, the weak 15 QR–Q1? was played and 15 ... P–B3! was in Black's favour whereas now this move is answered by either 16 P–B4 or 16 P×P with advantage to White.

| 15 ... | B–N2 |

Hoping for 16 Q×QP P–QB4 with a strong counter-attack, but White is not to be denied his blockade.

| **16 Q–QN4!** | **B–B1** |

Not of course 16 ... R–N1 17 N–K4 Q×KP 18 N–B5 Q–Q3 19 R.K1–Q1 winning.

| **17 N–K4** | **Q–K2** |

Again 17 ... Q×KP is bad, as 18 N–B5 Q–Q3 19 Q–R5 R×R+ 20 R×R gives White a decisive positional superiority.

18 N–B5	**R–N3**
19 R–K3	**P–QR4**
20 Q–Q4 (27)	

The black position is now blockaded to such an extent by White's pawn on K5 and his advantageously posted pieces, that there is no adequate way of developing Black's Q-side pieces. White's task now is to open up the position on the K-side so that he can attack the enemy king with his more active pieces.

| **20 ...** | **R–N1** |

Threatening 21 ... R–QN4, but White soon puts an end to the QR's attempt to free itself.

21 P–QB4	**P–R3**
22 P–QN3	**K–R2**
23 R–Q1	**Q–N4**
24 R–KN3	**Q–B4**
25 R×R	**P×R**
26 P–KR3	**R–R1**
27 P–QR4	**R–N1**
28 R–Q3	**Q–N4**

29	K-R2	Q-K2
30	P-B4	Q-B2
31	P-K6!	

A very fine positional sacrifice which increased operational points for his pieces and begins the final attack on the king.

31	...	P×P
32	Q-K5	Q-K2
33	P-KN4	R-N5
34	K-N3	R-N3

35	P-R4	Q-B1
36	P-R5	P×P
37	Q×RP	R-N1
38	Q-K5	R-N3
39	P-N5	P-R4
40	P-N6+	K×P
41	Q-N5+	K-R2
42	Q×RP+	K-N1
43	Q-N5	K-B2
44	R-Q8	Q-K2
45	Q-R5+	1-0

3 Special Kinds of Passed Pawn

Among passed pawns there are three special kinds which have a particular importance: the outside, protected and connected passed pawns.

The outside passed pawn usually comes into its own in the end-game.

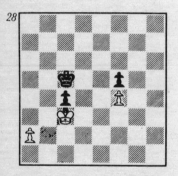

28

White's QRP in diagram 28 is classed as an outside passed pawn, as it is further than Black's QBP from the pair of blocked pawns on the K-side. White wins easily by **1 P–R4 K–Q4 2 P–R5 K–B4 3 P–R6 K–N3 4 K×P** etc.

The advantage of an outside passed pawn resides in the fact that it lures the enemy king away from our future object of attack. Of course, such a pawn is more difficult to utilize in an ending with many pieces on the board. All the same, it can tie down enemy pieces on one wing while the decisive break-through occurs on the other. This means that simplification and transition to the endgame are the most

important prerequisites for utilizing an outside passed pawn.

14 Flohr–Romanovsky

Moscow 1935, Nimzo–Indian Defence

1 P–Q4 N–KB3 2 P–QB4 P–K3 3 N–QB3 B–N5 4 Q–B2 N–B3 5 P–K3 P–Q4 6 N–B3 0–0 7 P–QR3 B×N+ 8 Q×B B–Q2 9 P–QN4! 9 . . . P×P?9 . . . P–QR4! 10 P–N5 N–R2 10 B×P P–QN4?! 11 B×NP N×NP 12 B×B N5–Q4 13 Q–B2 N×B 14 P–K4 N–K2·15 0–0 R–B1 16 B–K3 P–QB3 17 KR–B1 K–R1 18 Q–K2 P–KR3 19 N–K5 P–B3 20 N–Q3 Q–K1 21 B–B4 Q–B2 22 QR–N1 N–QN3 23 P–QR4! KR–Q1 23 . . . N×P 24 R–R1 N–QN3 25 R×RP would have been better. **24 P–R5 N–R1**

25 R–N7!

White could also play 25 B–K3 with pressure against Black's pawns on QR2, QB3 and K3. He prefers instead the slight but lasting advantage afforded him by an outside passed pawn which he now obtains after the forced exchange of his QP for Black's QRP.

25 . . .	**R×P**
26 N–B5	**P–K4**
27 B–K3	**R5–Q1**
28 R×P *(29)*	

The strategic picture is now clear. The further course of the game shows that it is not easy to force this pawn through. However, to prevent its advance, Black must maintain at least

46 R–Q2!	R–R2
47 R–Q7+	R×R
48 N×R	K–K3
49 N–B5+	K–Q3
50 B–B2	N–B2?

This makes White's task much easier. 50 . . . N–B5 was stronger; White would first have to dislodge this powerfully placed knight by 51 K–B1 followed by B–K3, K–B2 and K–B3.

51 P–N3	N–QR1 (*30*)

The final phase really belongs to a book on endgame theory, but is an excellent illustration of our theme. By threatening to advance his QRP, White diverts his opponent's pieces away from the centre and the K-side, even though this entails the loss of his outside passed pawn.

52 K–N2	N–K2
53 K–B3	P–N3
54 N–Q3	N–B1
55 B–B5+	

White's bishop takes over as a blockader, while the knight attacks the KP and KNP.

55 . . .	K–K3
56 N–N2	

White now threatens 57 N–B4 and 58 N–R5, then, after the forced . . . K–Q2, 59 B–B8 P–R4 60 P–N4 would allow the decisive entry of his king to attack the weak pawns. This plan is only possible because Black's pieces are tied to holding up the QRP.

---

one of his minor pieces on an unfavourable square where it has little scope. In contrast, White's blockading knight on QB5 is extremely well posted.

28 . . .	N–B2

Black must quickly drive White's rook from the seventh rank.

29 P–R3	N–N4
30 R–N7	N–Q3
31 R–N2	N–N4
32 R–Q2	P–B4
33 P–B3	P×P

It would have been better to keep the K-side position blocked by playing 33 . . . P–B5, as White himself will later need to open up this wing.

34 P×P	N–N3
35 Q–N4	K–R2

Now White's aim is to bring about a minor piece ending.

36 R–KB2	Q–K2
37 R1–KB1	R–B1
38 Q–K6	Q×Q
39 N×Q	R×R
40 R×R	R–K1
41 N–B5	R–QR1
42 P–R6	K–N1
43 R–R2	N–B1

Even now White cannot force his QRP through, so he must exchange the last pair of rooks. To do this, he must first drive Black's knight away from . . . KB1, in order to penetrate to Q7 with his rook.

44 B–B2!	K–B2
45 B–N3	N–N3

56 ...   **N–Q3**

Allowing further simplification.

57 B×N!   **K×B**

58 N–B4+   **K–B4**

After 58 ... K–K3 White's QRP would win the game for him. His king would cross to the Q-side, then play to QN7 after P–R7. So Black prefers to remove this thorn in his side, but at the expense of his K-side pawns.

59 N×P   **K–N3**

60 N×NP   **K×P**

Black's QBP has now become the outside passed pawn, but this means little compared to White's material and positional superiority.

61 P–K5   **K–N2**

62 K–K4   **K–B2**

63 K–B5   **K–Q2**

64 P–K6+   **K–K1**

65 N–K5!   **P–B4**

66 N–Q7!   **P–B5**

67 N–B6+   **K–B1**

68 N–Q5   **K–N2**

69 K–K4   **1–0**

It is much more difficult to utilize an outside passed pawn in the middle game, but even here in many positions it may force the opponent to direct some of his pieces away from the main scene of action, which makes it easier to begin an attack.

31
B

In this game (*31*), Czerniak–Unzicker, from the 1956 Moscow Olympiad, Black carried out a well-

planned manoeuvre to exchange his QBP for White's QRP, then to advance his outside passed pawn in instructive fashion, despite the fact that White activated his pieces and penetrated to the seventh rank with his rook: **25 ... B–N5! 26 N–Q5 K–N2 27 R–Q4 B×P 28 R×P B–N4 29 R–B7 B–Q3 30 R–R7 P–R5 31 P–N5** An interesting but unsuccessful counter-attack, but 31 P–B4 would not have saved the game because after 31 ... B–K1 32 N–B7 B×N 33 R×B R–N5! the black QRP is much more dangerous than the white QBP e.g. 34 R–B8 P–R6! 35 R×B P–R7 36 R–QR8 R–N8+ wins. Or 34 B–Q5 P–R6 35 R–R7 R–R5! 36 R×R B×R 37 P–B5 B–B3! wins. White loses a piece after 31 N–B3 B–K1 32 N×P R–N5 33 N–B3 B–K4. **31 P×P 32 P–B6+ K–B1 33 N–B3 B–K1 34 B–Q5 B–B4! 35 R–R6 R–Q1! 36 B–B4 B–Q5 37 N–K4** if 37 N×P R–B! 38 B–Q5 R×P **37 ... R–B1 38 B–Q5 R×P 39 R–R8** not 39 N×P? R–B8+ 40 K–N2 R–KN8+ **39 ... P–N5 40 P–R3 P–N6 41 N×P B×P 42 N–B5 R–Q7! 43 B–K4 R–Q1 44 R–K6 B–N7 45 N–Q6 B–Q2 46 B×P B–K3! 47 N×P! R–Q8+ 48 K–N2 B–N6!** Now the one remaining black pawn wins! **49 N–Q6 P–R6 50 N–B5 B–Q4+ 51 K–N3 B–K4+ 52 K–B2 P–R7 53 N–K3 R–Q7+ 54 K–K1 B–QB6! 55 N–Q1 R–K7+! 0–1.**

The protected passed pawn has already been seen at work in games 8 and 9, but once again its power is best demonstrated in simple endgames (*32*).

White wins by first capturing Black's QRP then returning to the K-side to force through his protected passed pawn on KN5. The advantage of such a pawn is two-fold: not only is it free to advance to the queening square at a favourable moment, like any other passed pawn, it is also protected from capture by the enemy king without requiring the support of its own king. As

32

a result, the latter can head for more profitable fields without any risk. A protected passed pawn is also a vital factor in a middle game situation, always threatening to advance and free from attacks by enemy pieces. The following two games illustrate this point.

15 Gligoric–Sanchez

Stockholm–Saltsjobaden Interzonal 1952, Queen's Gambit

1 P–Q4 N–KB3 2 P–QB4 P–K3 3 N–QB3 P–Q4 4 P×P N×P 5 N–B3 B–K2 5 ... P–QB4! 6 P–K4 N×N 7 P×N P–QB4 8 B–QB4 0–0 9 0–0 N–Q2 10 Q–K2 Q–B2 10 ... P×P 11 P×P N–B3 followed by ... P–QN3 and ... B–N2 is better. 11 R–Q1 P–QR3 12 P–QR4 P–QN3

    13 P–Q5   P–K4 *(33)*

After 13 ... P×P White might try 14 B×QP B–N2 15 P–B4. After the text

33
W

move we reach a typically advantageous position for the side with the protected passed pawn.

14 N–K1!

A very important move, making it impossible for Black to blockade the QP with his knight. If now 14 ... N–B3 (intending ... *N–K1–Q3*) 15 P–B4 follows, with these possibilities:

a. 15 ... P×P? 16 P–K5 winning.
b. 15 ... N–K1 16 P×P Q×P 17 N–B3 Q×BP 18 B–N2 etc.
c. 15 ... B–Q3 16 N–B3 B–N5 17 P–B5 with advantage.

    14 ...   **B–Q3**
    15 N–B2   **R–K1**
    16 B–Q3   **N–B1**
    17 N–K3   **N–N3**
    18 P–N3

Not only a defence against ... N–B5 but also a preparation for the important strategic advance P–KB4. Black's pieces are now posted most unfavourably. He cannot play the natural ... B–Q2 because his QRP needs protection, and a preliminary ... P–QR4 would cut out his own chances on the Q-side.

    18 ...   **B–N2**
    19 N–B4!

A well-known strategic motif. White threatens to eliminate the blockader whilst gaining a tempo with his secondary threat of 20 R–N1 winning a pawn.

    19 ...   **KR–N1**
    20 B–K3?

An inexactitude giving Black the chance to play 20 ... B–KB1! threatening 21 ... P–N4. White should instead take the bishop immediately, but Black also does not appreciate the value of this piece and neglects the opportunity of retaining it.

    20 ...   **B–QB1?**
    21 N×B   **Q×N**
    22 P–B3   **P–KR4**
    23 Q–KB2!

An excellent move, preparing P–KB4 and at the same time forcing Black to block the Q-side in view of the powerful threat 24 P–R5! winning the QBP.

23 ...	P–R4
24 P–KB4!	

This begins the second part of White's plan, operations on the K-side. He now threatens 25 P–B5 N–B1 26 B–K2 P–N3 27 P×P P×P 28 R–KB1 R–R2 29 Q–B6, so Black is compelled to exchange pawns in order to have ... K4 for his knight after P–B5. However, this merely strengthens White's centre, and P–K5 is now always in the air.

24 ...	P×P
25 P×P	B–N5
26 R–Q2	Q–Q2
27 B–B1	

He could also play 27 P–K5, but he does not even want to give his opponent the slight counter-chance of ... N–K2–B4.

27 ...	B–R6
28 B×B	Q×B
29 Q–N3!	Q–R5

After 29 ... Q×Q+ 30 P×Q followed by 31 P–B4 and 32 R–N1 White wins easily. Even now he would have the superior ending after 30 Q×Q N×Q 31 K–B2 R–K1 32 P–K5.

30 B–B2	Q–B3

But not 30 ... Q×BP 31 Q×Q N×Q 32 B–N3 P–KN4 33 B×N P×B 34 P–B4 with a won rook ending for White.

31 P–B5	

Gligorić selects this move rather than P–K5. He has the slow but sure plan in mind of exchanging the minor pieces on K5, then exploiting his protected passed QP in the major piece ending by building up an attack against Black's QNP.

31 ...	N–K4
32 K–R1	R–K1
33 R–K2	N–N5
34 B–N1	Q–K4

35 Q–B3	Q–B3
36 R–KB1	QR–Q1
37 P–R3	Q–R5
38 B–R2!	N×B

38 ... N–B3 would be weaker because of 39 R1–K1 threatening both B–B7 and Q–N3.

39 K×N	R–K4
40 R–KN1	R–Q2

Black could have made it a little harder for White with 40 ... K–B1 41 P–B4.

41 R2–KN2!	P–B3
42 R–K2	

The rook manoeuvre has forced Black to block in his queen which can now be exchanged after due preparation.

42 ...	K–R1
43 P–B4	K–N1
44 R1–K1	K–B1
45 Q–KN3	Q×Q+
46 K×Q	K–K1
47 R–QN1	R–N2
48 K–B4	K–Q1 (*34*)

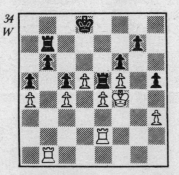

34
W

Now comes a characteristic manoeuvre in such positions. White sacrifices his QP in order to win the QNP and penetrate with his rooks into the enemy camp.

49 P–Q6!	K–Q2
50 R2–QN2	K–B3
51 P–Q7	K×P
52 R×P	R–B2

53 R–Q1+	**K–K1**
54 R–Q5	**1–0**

After 54 . . . R4–K2 55 R–N8+ K–B2 56 R5–Q8 Black must lose material.

16 Unzicker–Neikirch

Leipzig Olympiad 1960, Ruy Lopez

1 P–K4 P–K4 2 N–KB3 N–QB3 3 B–N5 P–QR3 4 B–R4 P–Q3 5 P–B3 B–Q2 6 P–Q4 N–B3 7 QN–Q2 B–K2 8 0–0 0–0 9 R–K1 P×P 10 P×P N–QN5 11 B×B Q×B 12 N–B1 P–B4 13 P–QR3 N–B3 14 P–Q5 N–K4 15 N×N P×N

16 N–N3

White has obtained a protected passed pawn from this opening variation, but it is unclear whether this constitutes an advantage. Black can blockade on Q3 with a minor piece, then utilize his Q-side pawn majority. An alternative to the text move is Bronstein's idea of 16 N–K3, after which Black must play accurately to keep the balance: 16 . . . N×KP (after *16 . . . N–K1 17 N–B4 Q–B2 18 P–QR4* Black's position would be uncomfortable) 17 N–B4 Q–B4 18 Q–B2 N–Q3 19 Q×Q N×Q 20 R×P N–Q3! 21 R×B N×N 22 R×NP KR–Q1 and Black wins the QP with equality.

16 . . .   B–Q3(?)

This unobtrusive move is a serious error. Black should postpone as long as possible the decision whether to blockade the QP with his bishop or his knight. He has two stronger alternatives which keep his options open:

a. 16 . . . N–K1 17 P–B4 B–Q3, or here 17 N–B5 N–Q3!

b. 16 . . . P–B5! and the bishop takes up an active position on . . . QB4 while the knight heads for . . . Q3.

17 N–B5	**N–K1**
18 B–K3	**R–B1**
19 R–QB1	**P–B5** (35)

We can now see that 16 . . . B–Q3 has cost Black a valuable tempo. If the white rook were on QR1, Black would have nothing to fear, whereas now White can clear up the situation on the Q-side in an interesting way.

20 P–QN3!   B×P

20 . . . P–B6 would be bad in view of 21 P–QN4! when Black's QBP is lost, a good example of the danger in advancing a passed pawn without preparation. Also bad is 20 . . . P–QN4 21 P–QR4! when Black remains with a weak pawn after 21 . . . BP×P 22 R×R Q×R 23 P×P P×P 24 Q×P etc. If 20 . . . P×P 21 R×R Q×R 22 Q×P, White can render Black's Q-side majority harmless by R–QB1, and P–QR4–R5 because 22 . . . P–QN4 allows 23 R–QB1 and 24 R–B6!

21 R×P   N–Q3

21 . . . R×R 22 P×R is positionally bad, for although Black has an outside passed pawn, White can exert decisive pressure down the QN-file by Q–N3, R–N1 and P–B5

22 N×N	**B×N**
23 Q–B2	**R.QB1–K1**

As 23 . . . R×R is still bad for Black, he must give up the QB-file now or after 24 R–QB1.

24 B–B5!

The keen reader who remembers what we said about the 'good' and 'bad' bishops will wonder why White decides to exchange this active bishop for Black's inactive one. The reason is that the latter is a very useful blockader, whereas after its exchange the pawn must be blockaded uneconomically by the queen or rook.

24 ...   P-B4

The only way to obtain counterplay, weakening his KP but the resulting open file will make White's task more difficult.

25 P-B3

After the hasty 25 P×P B×B 26 R×B Black could equalize in two ways, by 26 ... Q×BP 27 Q×Q R×Q 28 R-B7 R-Q1 29 R-Q1 P-K5 30 P-Q6 R-QN4, or by 26 ... P-QN3 and 27 ... Q×QP.

25 ...   P×P
26 P×P   R-B2
27 B×B   Q×B
28 R-B8!

Once again a purposeful exchange, as White needs a point of entry on the file he controls. In general, when one has a permanent advantage such as a protected passed pawn, there is no need to fear simplification. With this particular pawn structure, Q+ R versus Q+ R is the most favourable material balance. With minor pieces it is much more difficult and usually even

impossible to exploit such an advantage.

28 ...   R1-B1
29 R×R+   R×R
30 Q-B3   Q-QN3+
31 K-R1 *(36)*
31 ...   Q-B7?

The threat of mate is tempting but completely wrong from a strategic point of view. Black must patiently maintain the blockade of the QP, as active play only hastens his defeat. After 31 ... Q-Q3 White would probably continue 32 P-R3 P-R3 33 R-QB1 K-R2 (if *33 ... R-B5 34 Q-B8+*) 34 Q-Q3! followed by 35 R-B4. He would then have a clear positional plus, but it would be far from easy to convert this into a win.

32 P-R3   P-KN4
33 R-QB1   Q-B5

The QP would still advance after 33 ... Q-B3 34 Q-B7 R-B2 35 P-Q6!, whereas the text move prevents this variation, as White's rook would then be attacked, and in addition Black is threatening 34 ... P-N5. However, the QP can now play its part.

34 P-Q6!   P-N5

Not 34 ... Q×P 35 P-Q7! and there is no answer to the various threats e.g. 35 ... Q-K7 36 Q-B4+ wins, or 35 ... K-N2 36 Q-B7 wins, or 35 ... Q-B4 Q-B8! wins, or 35 ... Q-Q4 36 Q-B4 Q-B2 37 R-B1! wins.

35 R-Q1   P-N6

Again threatening mate. He still cannot capture the KP because of (35 ... Q×P.) 36 P-Q7 R-Q1 37 Q-B8, and 35 ... P×P fails to 36 Q×RP Q×P 37 P-Q7 R-Q1 38 Q-K6+ etc.

36 Q-Q3   R-Q1
37 P-Q7

Black's rook now blockades the pawn, but in a typically bad way, as it stands completely passive. White's queen only needs to reach K8 or QB8 and the game is over.

37 ...   Q–N4
38 Q–Q5+   K–R1

Or 38 ... K–B1 39 R–KB1+ K–N2
40 Q–B7+ K–R1 41 Q–K8+ K–N2 42
R–B7+ K–R3 43 Q–K6+ etc.

39 Q–B7   Q–N3

Covering K1 but he cannot also
cover QB1.

40 Q–K7   Q–N3
41 R–QB1!   1–0

Of course, a protected passed pawn
does not always constitute an advantage, as we saw in games 8 and 9.
The strength of such a pawn can be
sapped if it is blockaded, if possible by a
knight, and an attack is mounted
against the pawn guarding it.

In this set-up (*37*), Black will aim for
pressure on White's QBP by ...
P–QR3 and ... P–QN4. But above all
he will try to attack the KP by ... P–N3
and ... P–B4, as the latter has no
neighbouring pawn to support it.

Our next game illustrates some
problems arising from protected passed
pawns. We see how White's QP is first
blockaded and then converted into a
weak isolated pawn, whereas Black's
QBP brings about the decision by
advancing at the right moment.

17 Christoffel–Boleslavsky

Groningen 1946, King's Indian
Defence

1 P–Q4 N–KB3 2 P–QB4 P–KN3 3
N–QB3 B–N2 4 P–K4 0–0 5 B–K2
P–Q3 6 N–B3 QN–Q2 7 0–0 P–K4 8
R–K1 R–K1 9 B–B1 P–B3 10 P–Q5
P–B4 11 P–QR3 R–B1 12 P–QN4
N–K1 13 P–N3 P–KR3

14 N–KR4

It was precisely the plan chosen here
by White which drove Black's opening
system out of fashion. White prevents
the freeing ... P–B4 and prepares to
exploit his active position on the Q-side.

14 ...   N2–B3

Preventing the immediate 15 B–K3
because of 15 ... N–N5. White should
prepare this by 15 P–B3.

15 P×P(?)

It is not easy to resist such a tempting
opportunity of creating a passed pawn.
Nevertheless, this move is unfavourable
here, as Black is ready to blockade the
pawn immediately with a knight and
thereby improve immensely the co-
ordination of his pieces.

15 ...   P×P
16 P–QR4!?   P–QR4

Otherwise, after 17 P–R5 followed
by B–K3 Black's QBP would be
constantly difficult to protect. White
has thus achieved a certain success, as
he has cut out Black's possibility of
counterplay on the Q-side. However,
White's QRP turns out to be tactically
weak, so it is not possible to pass a
definitive judgement on 16 P–QR4.

17 R–N1   N–Q3 (*38*)

A typical position in which the protected passed pawn offers no real advantage. It is well blockaded by the knight and Black can eventually carry out the counter-thrust . . . P–B4.

18 B–QR3?

A developing move of doubtful value. White is tempted by tactical threats down the QN-file, but these in no way compensate for the strategically poor posting of his QB. With 18 P–B3 he could have obtained an approximately even game.

18 . . .   **P–N3**
19 Q–N3   **R–R3**

Nor 19 . . . R–N1? 20 B×P. White now thought that the passively placed rook justified his previous manoeuvre, but as Euwe rightly pointed out in the tournament book, Black's QR stands no worse than White's queen!

20 Q–B2   **N–R2**
21 N–N5!

An idea which is well-known to us from the previous section on the blockade of passed pawns. White intends to eliminate the blockader. The move also has an interesting tactical point, for 21 . . . N×N is answered by 22 BP×N! (not *22 R×N? B–Q2 23 R5–N1 Q–K1* winning a pawn) 22 . . . R–R2 23 N–B3, when it is White who will blockade Black's QBP by playing his knight to the splendid QB4 square. From there it would guard the important blockading square of the QP whilst attacking Black's QNP and KP.

21 . . .   **N–N4!**
22 K–R1?

Black's last move has so changed the tactical situation, that he can now profitably exchange knights on QN4. 22 N×N was essential.

22 . . .   **N×N!**
23 BP×N   **R–R2**

Now White's knight can no longer reach QB4 in time, as KB3 is guarded and 24 N–N2 (aiming for *N–K3–B4*)

allows 24 . . . N–B6 and 25 . . . N–Q5 when Black obtains an overwhelming positional superiority by . . . P–B4.

24 B–QN2   **Q–Q3**

As we have already mentioned, the queen is usually a poor blockader, but every rule has its exception. The queen is well placed here, as it not only blockades the QP, but also protects Black's KP and KNP and thus helps to prepare the vital . . . P–B4.

25 Q–Q2   **R–K2**
26 B–N2   **B–R6!**

This exchange of bishops favours Black, as it increases the power of the coming . . . P–B4 by removing one of White's controls of K4 and Q5.

27 B×B   **N×B**
28 N–N2   **N–N4**

White was threatening both 29 P–B4 and also 29 N–K3 followed by N–B4.

29 Q–Q1

Preventing the threatened win of the exchange and finally hoping to play his knight to QB4 by 30 N–K3! (*30 . . . N×P? 31 N–B4*). However, Black has meanwhile prepared the decisive break-through.

29 . . .   **P–B4!**
30 P×P   **P×P** (*39*)

39 W

The diagram shows how surprisingly the situation has changed since move 17. Both supports of White's QP have disappeared and this pawn has suddenly become weak. In contrast,

Black's QBP is very strong and its advance will bring about the final decision. It is important to note that White cannot carry out his intention of playing his knight to the strategically important QB4 square. After 31 N–K3 P–KB5! 32 N–B4 Q–Q2, Black would have a winning attack on the K-side:

a. 33 B×P Q–R6 34 B×P R×R+ 35 Q×R R×B! 36 P×R Q–B6+ 37 K–N1 N–R6+ 38 K–B1 Q–Q6+ etc; or here 34 B×B P–B6 35 R–N1 R–K7! 36 R–QN2 (or *36 Q–KB1*) 36 . . . N–K5! etc.

b. 33 N×KP Q–Q3! (*33 . . . Q–R6? 34 N–B6*) 34 N–B3 R×R+ 35 N×R B–Q5! 36 B×B Q×P+ etc.

c. 33 N×NP Q–R6 34 P–Q6 P×P 35 Q–Q5+ R–K3! etc.

d. 33 P–Q6 Q–N2+ etc.

31 P–B4

This prevents . . . P–KB5 but gives Black's knight an excellent post on . . . K5

| 31 . . . | N–K5 |
| **32 K–N1 ?** | |

Hastening his defeat. White could have put up a longer fight after 32 R–KB1.

| 32 . . . | P–B5! |

Perfectly timed, as both 33 . . . P–B6 and 33 . . . Q–B4+ are threatened.

| **33 P×P** | **B×P** |
| **34 B×B** | **R×B** |

And now both 35 . . . R×P and 35 . . . N–B6 are threatened. White could resign, but plays on a little longer: **35 N–K3 N–B6 36 Q–Q4 N×R 37 R×N R–K5 38 N×KBP R×Q 39 N×Q P–B6 40 R–QB1 R×QP 41 N–K4 R–Q5 42 N×P R–B1 0–1.**

Connected passed pawns are usually so strong that sacrifices are often made in order to create them. It is not easy to blockade them, as they can often support each other as they move forward together. It is interesting to note that we frequently see a fight

between a minor piece and three connected pawns. In an ending the pawns are a little stronger than the knight or bishop, but the situation in the middle-game is much more complex, as the extra piece can be used in the attack before the pawns become dangerous. However, after the exchange of queens the value of the pawns increases, as the following game shows.

18 Bronstein–Najdorf

Argentine–USSR 1954, Sicilian Defence

1 P–K4 P–QB4 2 N–KB3 P–Q3 3 P–Q4 P×P 4 N×P N–KB3 5 N–QB3 P–QR3 6 B–KN5 P–K3 7 Q–B3 QN–Q2 8 0–0–0 Q–B2 9 Q–N3 P–QN4 10 B×P!? P×B 11 N4×NP Q–N1 ? He cannot play 11 . . . Q–B4? 12 B–K3, but 11 . . . Q–R4! would have avoided the coming exchange of queens which makes White's task easier. **12 N×P+ B×N 13 Q×B Q×Q 14 R×Q** (*40*)

40
B

Let us consider Bronstein's assessment of this position: 'White has won three pawns for his piece, an approximate material equivalent, but it would be wrong to judge this position merely from a material point of view. Whilst it is relatively easy for White to restrict the activity of the black knight, it is much more difficult for Black to battle against White's passed pawns. In this game Black by no means exploited the possibilities at his disposal.'

14 ...   P-R3!

15 B-Q2(?)

Both 15 B-K3 N-N5 and 15 B-R4 P-N4 favour Black, but 15 B×N! is possible. Bronstein wrote about this move: 'In the given position the black-squared bishop is extremely strong. It would be a pity to give it up for a rook, never mind a knight.' He was probably over-estimating the importance of this bishop, and a game Fichtl–Dolezal (1954 Czechoslovak Championship) continued: 15 B×N! N×B 16 KR–Q1 B-N2 17 P-B3 when White successfully utilized his passed pawns in the ending, as follows: 17 ... K-K2 18 R-N6! KR–QN1 19 P-QN3 B-R3? 20 R×R R×R 21 R-Q2 R-Q1 22 N-Q1! R×R? 23 K×R P-N4 24 P-KR3 K-Q3 25 P-QB4 N-R4 26 N-K3 N-B5 27 P-QN4 P-R4 28 P-QR4 B-B1 29 K-B3 N-K7+ 30 K-N3 N-Q5+ 31 K-N2 P-B4 32 P-B5+! K-B2 33 P-N5 P×P 34 P×P B-N2 35 K-B3 N-K7+ 36 K-Q3 N-B5+ 37 K-Q4 N-K7+ 38 K-K5 N-B6 39 P-B6 B-B1 40 N-B4! N×RP 41 N-Q6 and White won.

However, after Bronstein's move, Black could have equalized.

15 ...   B-N2

16 P-B3   0-0?

The decisive mistake. He had to castle on the Q-side when his king can play a vital part in the fight against the passed pawns whilst he can carry out a sharp counter-attack on the K-side by ... P-N4-N5. Prospects are probably about even in the complex position that arises, but it is clear that White's 15th move has cost him an important tempo allowing Black to complete his development by castling long.

17 P-QN3   KR-B1

18 K-N2   N-B4

19 B-K3   P-K4

20 KR-Q1   N-K3

21 R-N6   B-B3

22 N-Q5!   B×N

23 P×B

White now has four connected passed pawns and the outcome is already clear.

23 ...   N-B4

24 R-N5   N3-Q2

25 P-QB4   P-K5

26 B×N

White finally exchanges his bishop, as the two knights would otherwise make it difficult to advance the pawns. As it is, White plans to sacrifice a pawn to give him time to advance the others.

26 ...   N×B

27 P×P   N×KP

28 P-Q6!   R×RP+

29 K×R   N-B6+

30 K-R3   N×R.Q8

31 P-B5   N-B6

32 R-R5   N-Q4

33 P-B6   N-B3

34 R-R6   K-B1

35 P-QN4   K-K1

36 P-N5   N-Q2

The last part of the game was played in severe time-trouble, so Najdorf tries to complicate matters. The game ended: **37 R-R7 R-N1 38 R×N R×P 39 R-R7 R-N1 40 P-Q7+ K-K2 41 P-Q8=Q+ K×Q 42 P-B7+ K-B1 43 P×R=Q+ K×Q 1-0.**

Two connected passed pawns are seen far more frequently than three, but great care must be taken to stop them being blockaded. As a rule they should be advanced together when possible. For example, with pawns on QN4 and QB4, one should only play P-N5 or P-B5 when the other pawn is ready to advance. The following game clearly illustrates the extraordinary importance of blockading such a pair of pawns.

19 Gligoric–Szabo

Helsinki Olympiad 1952, Nimzo-Indian Defence

1 P–Q4 N–KB3 2 P–QB4 P–K3 3 N–QB3 B–N5 4 P–K3 P–B4 5 KN–K2 P–Q4 6 P–QR3 BP×P 7 KP×P B–K2 8 P–B5 0–0 9 P–QN4 P–QN3! 10 P–N3 P×P

11 QP×P

To capture with the NP would be weaker, as after 11 . . . N–B3 and 12 . . . B–R3 White's passed pawn is blockaded and Black's pieces are well co-ordinated.

11 . . .   P–QR4!

A seemingly illogical move, as it allows White to obtain two fairly advanced connected passed pawns. However, it is soon clear that these pawns are not as dangerous as they look, for it is precisely their advanced position which makes a blockade easier to achieve.

12 R–QN1

Not, however, 12 B–QN2? N–B3 13 P–N5 N–K4 etc.

12 . . .   P×P
13 P×P *(41)*

At first sight the situation looks dangerous for Black, as White's two passed pawns are already on the 4th and 5th ranks, whereas Black has only one passed pawn which will take some time to push forward. However, we have already mentioned in our note to move 11 that pawns can sometimes be blockaded more easily if their advance has to some extent outstripped the development of the pieces behind them, which means that they momentarily lack support. Black now has two strategic aims:

1. To blockade the white pawns, especially the QNP, by playing a knight to QN4 (moves 13–27).
2. To force his centre pawns through (moves 18–56).

As regards the first aim, it is worth noting that it is always best to blockade the rear of the two pawns to prevent them moving forward together, and thus depriving them of their strongest asset.

13 . . .   N–B3!

The first blockading move does not fulfil the above condition but is based on a tactical point: if 14 P–N5 N–K4 15 P–B4 N–B6+! 16 K–B2 B×P+ 17 K×N P–Q5! wins.

14 B–KN2   R–N1!
15 B–QR3

15 P–N5 now allows 15 . . . B×P! 16 P×N R×R 17 N×R Q–N3 with a strong attack, and Black can answer 15 Q–R4 with 15 . . . B–Q2! 16 P–N5 N–K4 17 P–B6 N–Q6+ 18 K–B1 B×P! 19 P×B R×R 20 N×R Q–N3 etc.

15 . . .   B–Q2!
16 0–0

For the third time 16 P–N5 cannot be played, as 16 . . . N–QR4 17 0–0 N–B5 wins a pawn.

16 . . .   N–R2!
17 R–K1   N–K1!

It is important not to blockade too early. After 17 . . . N–N4? 18 N×N B×N 19 N–Q4, the blockader is removed, as White also has B–KB1 to follow. With the text-move Black brings up another knight to control QN4.

18 B–QB1   B–KB3

The first move of Szabo's attacking

plan. White should now play 19 P–B4 N–B2 20 B–K3 (*20 N–Q4? B×N+ 21 Q×B N–B3*); after 20 ... N.B2–N4 Black stands better. Instead White chooses the dubious plan of enticing the black pawns forward so as to attack them and increase the scope of his KB.

19 B–B4?	P–K4
20 B–Q2	P–Q5
21 N–Q5	B–B3
22 N×B+	

The knight cannot be maintained on Q5, as 22 Q–N3 is answered by 22 ... N–B2. Nevertheless, it was best to play this and capture the knight rather than the bishop, for as we have seen a knight is a better blockader.

22 ...	Q×N
23 B×B	Q×B
24 P–B4	P–B3

It would, of course, be a grave error to give up his connected pawns by 24 ... P×P?

25 Q–N3+	K–R1
26 R–KB1	N–B2
27 Q–B4	N.R2–N4
28 R.N1–K1	

The end of all White's hopes of advancing his Q-side pawns. He now regroups his pieces for defence against Black's centre pawns, but it is already too late.

28 ...	P–R3
29 P–N4	

Intending to blockade by N–N3–K4.

29 ...	R.N1–K1?

A tactical error which could have made Black's task much more difficult. The correct move was 29 ... KR–K1! 30 N–N3 P–K5 winning quickly. After the text-move White should play 30 P×P P×P 31 N–N3 when 31 ... R×R+ 32 Q×R P–K5? fails to 33 N×P! R×N 34 Q–B8+ K–R2 35 Q–B5+ . White misses this chance and goes in for a desperate K-side attack.

30 P–B5?	Q–Q4
31 Q–B1	

Or 31 Q×Q N×Q 32 N–N3 R–R1 and his better placed pieces guarantee Black a won ending.

31 ...	K–R2
32 N–N3	P–K5
33 B–B4	P–K6
34 Q–Q1	Q–B5

Preventing a possible blockade by 35 Q–Q3.

35 P–R4	N–Q4
36 P–N5	P–Q6
37 Q–N4	R–KN1!
38 N–R5	R–K5 (*42*)

42 W

It is instructive to compare this diagram with the previous one. White's Q-side pawns have not advanced a single square, whereas Black's centre pawns now bring about the decision.

39 P–N6+	K–R1
40 Q–N3	0–1

When both sides have connected passed pawns or a pawn majority on different sides of the board, the most important factor is the mobility of the pawns.

This position (*43*) occurred in Gligoric–Matulovic, Palma de Mallorca 1967. The continuation was: **30 R×N! P×R** Black is now the exchange up, but this is irrelevant here. The main point is that White's pawns are far more mobile than Black's. **31 P–Q6 Q–N3 32 B–B4 R–R2 33 P–K5 P–QR4 34 Q–Q5 P–R5 35 P–Q7 R–KB1 36 R–Q1 R2–R1 37 P–K6!** P×P 37 ... Q×P? 38 Q×R! **38 Q–K5! K–B2 39**

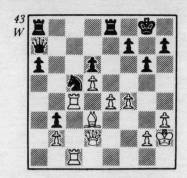

R–Q6 Q–B2 40 B×KP+ K–K2 41
P–Q8= Q+ ! KR×Q 42 B–B4+ 1–0.

The following opening is interesting
as regards mobile passed pawns: 1
P–Q4 N–KB3 2 P–QB4 P–KN3 3
N–QB3 B–N2 4 P–K4 P–Q3 5 P–B3
0–0 6 B–K3 P–N3 7 B–Q3 B–N2 8
KN–K2 P–B4 9 P–Q5 P–K3 10 0–0
P×P 11 BP×P QN–Q2 12 R–N1!
N–K4 13 P–QN4 N×B 14 Q×N N–Q2
15 P×P N×P 16 B×N! QP×B 17
P–B4 (*44*)

What is the point of this variation
which I have recommended for White
although he has conceded the two
bishops? The fact is that his mobile
centre pawns give him a clear
superiority. They can easily advance,
with P–Q6 and P–K5 played in either
order, and at the same time vacate
squares which will prove excellent posts
for the knights. On the other hand,
Black's Q-side pawn majority is
immobile (17 . . . P–QR3 18 P–QR4).

4 The Isolated Pawn

Every player has often found how troublesome a pawn can be when it is separated from other pawns and so cannot be supported by any of them. Such a pawn is termed an isolated pawn. As it has lost the simplest and most economical protection of another pawn, it is clearly vulnerable. Even if it is not captured, the defending pieces can be passively tied down to guarding it, while the more active attacking pieces obtain an advantage elsewhere. The following game illustrates this indirect exploitation of the weakness of an isolated pawn.

20 Zita–Pachman

Czechoslovak . Championship 1954, Bird's Opening

1 P–K3 P–KN3 2 P–KB4 B–N2 3 N–KB3 P–Q4 4 B–K2 N–KB3 5 0–0 0–0 6 P–Q3 P–N3 7 Q–K1 P–B4 8 QN–Q2 B–N2 9 B–Q1 Q–B2 10 N–K5? he should play 10 P–KN3 followed by P–K4, although his K-side is then weakened a little. **10 . . . N–K1!** so that after 11 P–K4 B×N 12 P×B Q×P this knight can replace the bishop on KN2 **11 N2–B3 P–B3 12 N–N4 N–Q3 13 N–B2 P–K4!** So Black is the first to advance in the centre, but this important gain of space is only possible because the ensuing tactics have been carefully assessed. **14 P×P P×P 15 P–K4 P×P 16 N2×P** the point is that he cannot play 16 N–N5? P×P! 17

N–K6 Q–B3 18 B–B3 R×B and Black wins. But for this combination White would have a clear advantage after 16 . . . Q–K2? 17 N×KP, for Black would be left with an unpleasant isolated K P. **18 . . . N×N 19 P×N** (45)

45
B

Both sides have an isolated KP but close study reveals that White's pawn is much the weaker of the two. The reason for this is that Black's pieces are placed most favourably both for defending his own KP (queen and KB) and also for attacking his opponent's KP (his QB and . . . N–Q2–B3). White's pieces in contrast are far less effective. For example, if he tries to develop his QB aggressively by P–QN3 and B–N2, his KB4 becomes an ideal post for Black's KR attacking the KP. Black's plan now is to prevent the regrouping of the enemy pieces and tie his opponent down to the defence of the KP.

17 . . .   P–KR3!

Otherwise after 17 . . . N–Q2 White obtains counter-play with 18 N–N5!

18 N–Q2?

Attempts to attack the king fail because of the weakness of the KP e.g. 18 N–R4 R×R+ 19 Q×R Q–B2! with a clear advantage to Black. However, White should try to activate his pieces by 18 B–K2! e.g. 18 . . . P–B5 19 Q–N4 when Black can create a passed pawn after 19 . . . B×P 20 Q×BP+ Q×Q 21 B×Q+ K–R2 or else play 19 . . . B–R3 followed by . . . N–Q2–B3, but in both cases his task would be more difficult than in the game.

18 . . .   **N–Q2**
19 R×R+   **R×R**
20 B–B3   **N–B3**
21 N–B1   **Q–B2!**

Threatening 22 . . . N×P which is of course still possible after 22 B–Q2.

22 N–N3   **Q–B5**
23 Q–B3

With his last moves Black has succeeded in positioning all his pieces effectively and after the passive 23 P–B3 R–Q1 White would soon be embarrassed for good moves. So Zita decides to exchange queens, hoping that piece play will compensate for the weakness of his pawns.

23 . . .   **Q×Q**
24 P×Q (46)

Although White's Q-side pawns are now seriously weakened, I decided after

lengthy deliberation that at the moment this weakness is not easy to exploit, and White's KP must still be the main object of attack. However, a successful attack is only possible if Black can exchange his 'bad' bishop on KN2.

24 . . .   **P–KR4!**
25 B–N5   **N–R2**
26 B–K3   **B–KB3**
27 R–Q1   **B–N4**

The first stage of the plan is over. Pressure against the KP now forces White to exchange into an extremely disadvantageous minor piece ending.

28 B×B   **N×B**
29 R–Q7   **R–B2**
30 R×R   **K×R**

If Black tries instead to attack the weak Q-side pawns, White defends after 30 . . . N×R? 31 N–B1! N–Q3 32 N–Q2 N–N4 33 N–N1. The text move threatens . . . P–R5 winning the KP.

31 P–KR4   **N×B+ !**

This move is only possible because White has played P–KR4 which will later allow Black to create an outside passed pawn by . . . P–KN4. This is a typical case of pressure against one weakness (the white KP) leading to another weakening move (P–KR4) forced by the consequential unfavourable placing of his pieces.

32 P×N   **B–B1!**

Not at once 32 . . . P–KN4? 33 N–B5. The rest of the game belongs to the end game proper, but contains a number of interesting points which are worth our consideration: **33 K–B2 P–KN4! 34 P×P K–N3 35 N–B1 B–K3!** It would be a bad mistake to play 35 . . . K×P? 36 P–QB4! drawing. **36 P–R3 K×P 37 N–K3 B–R7!** This deliberate enclosure of his own bishop is the only way to win, as 37 . . . P–R5 allows White to draw by 38 P–QB4 followed by 39 N–Q5. **38 P–QB4**. This makes Black's task easier, although his strong passed pawn still guarantees the win against other defences e.g. 38 N–Q5? B×N 39 P×B P–N4 40 K–N3 K–B3 41 K–R4 K–K2 42 K×P K–Q3 43 K–N5 K×P 44 K–B5 P–R4 etc. Or 38 K–N3 P–R5+ 39 K–B2 P–R6 40 K–N3 P–R7 41 K×P K–B5 42 N–N4 B–K3 wins. Or 38 N–B5 P–R5 39 N–K7 B–B5! 40 N–B6 K–B5 41 N×RP P–R6 42 N–B8 B–K7 43 N×P B×P 44 N–Q5+ K×P 45 N–B6+ K–B5 wins. **38 ... P–R5 39 N–N4 K–B5 40 N–K3 P–R6 41 P–R4** if 41 N–Q5+ K–N4 White loses after both 42 N–K3 P–R7 43 K–N2 P–R8= Q+ 44 K×Q K–B5, or 42 K–N3 B×P 43 K×P B×N 44 P×B P–N4! It is this last variation which the text-move is designed to prevent. **41 ... K–N4** The sealed move; Black obviously plays a waiting move before committing himself to the final winning manoeuvre. **42 N–N4 K–B5 43 N–K3 B–N8!** It would be premature to play 43 ... P–R7 44 N–Q5+ K–N4 45 K–N2 B×P 46 K×P B×N 47 P×B when the pawn ending has become a veritable study: 47 ... P–B5 48 N–N2!! (not *48 K–N3 K–B3 49 P–B4 K–B4!* winning) 48 ... K–B3 49 K–N3! (zugzwang) 49... K–K2 50 P–B4 draws. **0–1.** If 44 N–Q5+ K–N4 45 N–K3 P–R7 etc. Or 44 P–B3 K–N4! 45 N–N4 B×P 46 N×P K–B5 wins.

The isolated pawn in the above example was not on an open file, so it was not possible to attack it from the front with the major pieces. We deliberately chose this untypical example for our first illustration of the isolated pawn, because many books only deal with isolated pawns on an open file. Clearly an isolated pawn is just as much of a weakness, even if it cannot be attacked from the front, as the previous game showed. Of course, as our next example illustrates, an open line greatly helps us to exploit the weakness of an isolated pawn.

21 Sokolsky–Simagin

1st USSR Correspondence Championship, Grünfeld Defence

1 P–Q4 N–KB3 2 P–QB4 P–KN3 3 N–QB3 P–Q4 4 P×P N×P 5 P–KN3 B–N2 6 B–N2 N–N3 7 N–B3 0–0 8 0–0 N–B3 9 P–Q5 N–N5 10 P–K4 P–QB3 11 P–QR3 N–R3 12 P×P P×P (47)

47
W

Black has an unpleasant isolated pawn on QB3, but his open QN-file might give him chances of counterplay if White does not play exactly. White's first task, therefore, is to develop his pieces in such a way that they attack the QBP whilst preventing Black from exerting pressure on the QNP.

    13 Q–B2   Q–B2
    14 P–N3!   P–K4?

Black voluntarily blocks the important long diagonal of his KB. 14 ... B–K3 15 B–K3 KR–Q1 was better.

    15 B–K3   P–B3
    16 KR–B1   B–K3
    17 B–B1   Q–N2
    18 N–QR4!

The decisive move after which Black has no reasonable way of defending his QBP. It is interesting to note that a similar situation arose in the game Pachman–Dolezal (Czech Championship 1954). The first six opening moves were the same, then the game continued: 7 N–B3 N–B3(?) 8 P–K3 0–0 9 0–0 P–QR4 10 P–Q5 N–N5 11

P–K4 P–QB3 12 P–QR3 N–R3 13 P×P
P×P 14 Q–B2 Q–B2 15 R–Q1 (*15
P–N3? P–R5!*) 15 ... P–K4 (the threat
was *16 N–Q4*) 16 P–N3 B–K3 17 B–K3
KR–Q1 18 B–KB1 Q–N2 19 R×R+
R×R 20 N–Q2 B–KB1 21 N–R4! N×N
22 P×N N–N1 23 R–N1 Q–K2 24
Q–B3 P–B3 25 N–B4 R–B1 26 Q×RP
and White won quickly.

18 ...   N×N

In comparison with the above-
quoted game, the situation here is even
more favourable for White, as he can
immediately win a pawn if he wishes by
19 Q×P Q×Q 20 R×Q B×P 21 R×N
N–N3 22 B×N etc. However, Black's
bishop pair would enable him to put up
stiff resistance, so White selects another
plan. He leaves Black's weak pawn on
the board, compelling his opponent to
post his pieces unfavourably in order to
defend it. He then uses the superior
activity of his own pieces to begin a
quick attack. The variation with 19
Q×P and the game continuation are
good examples of direct and indirect
exploitation of the weakness of an
isolated pawn.

19 P×N!   N–N1

White also wins easily after 19 ...
P–QB4 20 QR–N1 Q–B3 21 Q–Q3!
B–B1 (*21 ... P–B5 22 R×P!* etc.) 22
Q–N3+ K–R1 23 B–QN5 Q–B2 24
Q–B4 etc.

20 QR–N1   Q–QB2
21 N–Q2   R–B1
22 P–R5   N–Q2

White was threatening 23 P–R6 and
24 R–N7. If 22 ... Q×P 23 B–QB4
B×B 24 Q×B+ K–R1 25 R–N7 Q–Q1
26 N–N3 R–B2 27 R×R Q×R 28
R–Q1 and Black is stuck for a good
move, as 28 ... N–Q2 fails to 29 Q–B7.

23 B–QR6   Q×P

As 23 ... R.B1–N1 24 Q×P is
hopeless for Black, he offers the
exchange, but this is equally
unsatisfactory.

24 B×R   R×B
25 R–N7   P–QB4
26 Q–Q3   Q–R5
27 Q–Q6   R–B3
28 Q–K7   B–B1

After 28 ... R–R3 Sokolsky gives the
following interesting variation: 29
Q–K8+ N–B1 (*29 ... B–B1 30 B–R6*)
30 R×B+ ! K×R 31 Q–K7+ B–B2 32
B–R6+ ! winning.

29 Q–K8   1–0

If 29 ... R–Q3 30 B–R6 followed by
31 R×N, and if 29 ... R–N3 30 R×R
B–B2 31 R–R6! wins.

The reader may well have the
impression from all this that the isolated
pawn must constitute a weakness in all
circumstances, but matters are not so
simple. Of course, the isolated pawn is
almost always a serious disadvantage in
the endgame, but in the middle game it
can even become a vital attacking
factor. For convenience, we will deal
only with the isolated QP, which is a
good example of the contrast between
static weakness and dynamic strength.

We meet the isolated QP in many
openings, especially in countless
variations of the Queen's Gambit
where it can even be brought about
deliberately. (1 P–Q4 P–Q4 2 P–QB4
P×P 3 N–KB3 N–KB3 4 P–K3 P–K3 5
B×P P–B4 6 0–0 P×P 7 P×P!) The
various positions which have an
isolated pawn on Q4 can be
differentiated, depending on whether
the opposing QBP or KP has
disappeared in the process. The last
quoted sequence of moves gives us an
example of the first type, and the second
type is seen after the well-known
opening moves: 1 P–Q4 P–Q4 2 P–QB4
P–K3 3 N–QB3 N–KB3 4 B–N5 B–K2
5 P–K3 0–0 6 N–B3 QN–Q2 7 R–B1
P–B3 8 B–Q3 P×P 9 B×BP N–Q4 10
B×B Q×B 11 0–0 N×N 12 R×N P–K4
13 Q–B2 P×P 14 P×P.

Let us return to the first type

and consider its pawn skeleton (*48*):

48

Such a pawn structure is unfavourable in the endgame for the side with the isolated pawn, and this weakness can often lead to a loss. The situation is much more complex in the middle game, where the dynamic strength of the pawn can under certain circumstances come into effect. With well-placed pieces, the side with the pawn can carry out the advance P–Q5, often involving the sacrifice of this pawn. In addition the pawn supports good posts for the knight on K5 (if Black drives it away with ... P–B3 his KP is weakened) and QB5 (if Black has played ... P–QR3 and ... P–QN4, as he often does in order to fianchetto his QB). By exploiting the K5 square, White can often carry out a successful K-side attack. In general, we can say that, given the pawn structure of diagram 48, both sides should plan their play according to the following principles:

White
1. Avoid too much simplification.
2. Post the pieces in such a way that P–Q5 is possible at a suitable moment, or that Black's pieces are tied to preventing this move.
3. Either occupy K5 with a knight and attack on the K-side ...
4. Or operate on the QB-file, using QB5 as a strong-point.

Black
1. Prevent the advance of the QP by occupying the blockading square Q4 with a knight, or at least a bishop.
2. Tie down White's pieces to the defence of the isolated pawn by playing for example ... N–QB3 and ... B–KB3.
3. Strive for simplification and a transition to the endgame.

Let us now see how these principles are applied in actual games:

22 Szabo–Van Seters

Hilversum 1947, Nimzo-Indian Defence

1 P–Q4 N–KB3 2 P–QB4 P–K3 3 N–QB3 B–N5 4 P–K3 P–B4 5 B–Q3 P–Q4 6 N–B3 0–0 7 0–0 N–B3 8 P–QR3 BP×P 9 KP×P P×P 10 B×BP B–K2 (*49*)

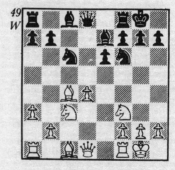

49
W

A typical position with an isolated pawn on White's Q4. It could also have been reached by the sequence: 1 P–Q4 P–Q4 2 P–QB4 P×P 3 N–KB3 N–KB3 4 P–K3 P–B4 5 B×P P–K3 6 0–0 P×P 7 P×P B–K2 8 N–B3 N–B3 9 P–QR3! 0–0 It is important to note the significance of P–QR3. The main purpose of this move is to prevent the possible manoeuvre ... N–QN5–Q4 blockading the QP. In addition it allows White to play Q–Q3 beginning a

K-side attack after moves like B–KN5, QR–Q1 and B–R2–N1. Nimzowitsch, among others, recommended an alternative set-up by 9 Q–K2 0–0 10 B–K3 followed by KR–Q1 and QR–B1, with White first developing all his forces and beginning a K-side attack at a suitable moment. Chess praxis, however, and in particular certain of Alekhine's games have demonstrated that the piece grouping adopted in the present game offers the best prospects, as it allows a speedy attack on the K-side.

11 R–K1   P–QN3

At all events, this is more solid than 11 ... P–QR3 12 B–KN5 P–N4 13 B–R2 B–N2, when the weakness of Black's QB4 quickly makes itself felt (e.g. after *14 Q–Q3 N–Q4 15 N–K4.*)

12 Q–Q3   B–N2
13 B–KN5   R–B1(?)

Black under-estimates the danger threatened by White's aggressively posted pieces and thinks he has sufficient time to complete his development. After 13 ... N–Q4 White has a choice between two good continuations:

a. 14 B×N P×B *(14 ... B×B 15 B–K4!)* 15 B×B N×B 16 N–KN5 N–N3 17 P–KR4! P–KR3 18 N–K6! P×N 19 Q×N Q×P 20 Q×KP+ K–R1 21 Q–K3 QR–K1! 22 Q–Q2! with a positional plus, for the knight is stronger than the bishop, and K5 is available for White's pieces.

b. 14 N–K4 R–B1 15 B–R2 followed by QR–Q1 and B–N1 with very good attacking chances.

14 QR–Q1   Q–B2 ?

Continuing the faulty strategic plan he began with his previous move. Black must aim for exchanges, so 14 ... N–Q4 was called for, even though White would then have the better of it.

15 B–R2   KR–Q1
16 P–R3

Preventing any tactical complications which might arise after ... N–KN5.

16 ...   R–Q2 *(50)*

Black's plan is too stereotyped. He now hopes to double rooks with pressure on the QP, but White has prepared a decisive breakthrough.

17 P–Q5!   N×P

If 17 ... P×P 18 B–N1! P–N3 19 R×B and 20 B×N wins.

18 B×N   Q–Q1

Perhaps Black had counted on this move to save him. He would lose the exchange after 18 ... P×B 19 N×P, and if 18 ... R1–Q1 19 R×P! follows, whereas now 19 R×P fails to 19 ... B×B and Black holds out.

19 Q–K4!

The point, as now 19 ... B×B allows 20 B×P! winning at least the exchange.

19 ...   P×B
20 N×P   B×B
21 N×B   P–N3

Not of course 21 ... Q×N 22 Q–K8+ and mate next move. There is nothing to be done.

22 Q–KR4   P–KR4
23 N–B6+   Q×N
24 R×R   N–Q1
25 R–K8+   K–N2
26 R×P+ !   1–0

After 26 ... N×R 27 N–K6+ wins the queen.

The decision in the above game was

brought about by the correctly timed advance P-Q5 which was of a definite tactical nature, as it was possible to calculate beforehand all the concrete variations leading to White's advantage.

This position (*51*) occurred in the 8th game of the 1968 match, Korchnoi-Tal. Black's position is extremely difficult. White is planning B-N1 followed either by Q-Q3 or by N-K5 and R-Q3. Black played the immediate **14 ... P-N3** to avoid all possible attacks on his KRP. Play went **15 B-QB4!** threatening both 16 P-Q5 and 16 B×P P×B 17 Q×P+ K-N2 18 P-Q5 followed by 19 N-K5, so **15 ... N-Q4** is forced. After **16 B×N!** Black should be satisfied with a slightly worse position by 16 ... P×B! (17 B×B R×B 18 Q-N5 R×R+ 19 R×R N-K2 or R4 20 N-K5). Instead he allowed White to carry out the advance of his isolated pawn under favourable circumstances by **16 ... B×B? 17 B-K4 B-B3** hoping for 18 P-Q5 P×P 19 N×P B-N2! with an adequate defence **18 N-K5! R-QB1** after 18 ... B×N 19 P×B Q-B2 20 N-N5! Q×P 21 R-Q7 etc. follows **19 N×N B×N 20 B×B R×B 21 P-Q5! R-Q3 22 N-K4! R-Q2 23 P×P R×P 24 N×B+ Q×N 25 R×R R×Q 26 R×R Q-B3 27 R-Q1.** White won two rooks for his queen which should have given him, in this position, a

comfortable victory. The game only ended in a draw as a result of later inaccuracies.

In both these games White had sufficient control over Q5 when he advanced his pawn, but this advance may often involve the sacrifice of a pawn, justified by the increased activity of the minor pieces and the opening of the K-file.

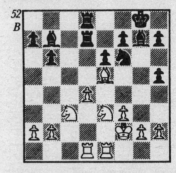

This position (*52*), from Kotov-Novotelnov in the 1947 Moscow tournament, offers equal chances to both sides, with the weakness of White's QP balancing out the weakness of Black's KRP. However, Black commits an instructive error with his next moves: he removes a piece which is controlling the vital blockading square Q4: **23 ... N-K1? 24 N-B2 N-Q3? 25 P-Q5! P×P 26 B×B!** but not 26 N×P? N-K5+! 27 R×N B×N, or here 27 P×N B×B. Black had probably planned for this contingency when he played ... N-Q3. **26 ... K×B 27 N-Q4!** The point, as 27 N×P this time fails to 27 ... N-B5. **27 ... K-B3 28 N3-K2 N-B4 29 N-B4** It is now clear that even in this simplified position the activity of White's pieces plays a vital rôle e.g. after 29 ... N×N 30 R×N Black's pawn on KR4 falls and his three isolated pawns on Q4, KB2 and KR2 place him at a serious disadvantage. **29 ... N-N2 30 P-KR4 R-K2 31 R×R**

K×R 32 R-K1+ K-Q2 Perhaps 32
... K-B3 33 P-KN4 P×P 34 P×P
P-KR3 gave better defensive chances,
but Black's king position is very
uncomfortable. 33 R-K5! P-B3 34
R-K2 R-QB1 35 R-Q2 This forces the
win of the QP, the first threat being 36
N-N5. 35 ... P-QR3 36 N.Q4-K2
K-K2 If Black tries to hang on to the
pawn by 36 ... R-B4 37 N-B3 K-Q3
then 38 N-K4+ wins the exchange. 37
N-B3 P-Q5 38 R×P White now stands
so much better that Black's next move,
which loses a pawn, only cuts short the
agony: 38 ... N-B4 39 R-N4 P-N4 40
P-R4! R-Q1 41 P×P P-R4 42 R-B4
R-Q7+ 43 K-K1 R-Q2 44 R-B5!
N-N6 if 44 ... N×P 45 R×P 45 P-N6!
K-Q3 46 R×QRP K-B3 47 N4-Q5
P-B4 48 P-N4 K-Q3 49 K-B2
N-R8+ 50 K-K3 R-N2 51 N-B4
R-K2+ 52 K-Q4 N-N6 53 N-N5+
K-B3 54 N-R7+! K-Q3 if 54 ... K×P
55 N-Q5+ B×N 56 N-B8+ 55 R-B5
N-K7+ 56 N×N R×N 57 R-B7 1-0.

Sometimes we find the positional
sacrifice P-Q5 occurring in true middle
game situations, with queens on the
board.

23 Petrosian-Spassky

Moscow 1971, Queen's Gambit

1 P-Q4 P-Q4 2 P-QB4 P×P 3
N-KB3 N-KB3 4 P-K3 P-K3 5 B×P
P-B4 6 0-0 P-QR3 7 P-QR4 N-B3 8
Q-K2 B-K2 9 R-Q1 P×P 10 P×P
0-0

    11 N-B3   **N-Q4**

Earlier experiences have shown that
the pawn must be blockaded as quickly
as possible. In the game Botvin-
nik-Petrosian (World Championship,
1963) Black continued less logically
with 11 ... N-QN5 12 B-KN5 B-Q2 13
P-Q5! P×P! (Black loses quickly after
*13 ... N3×P 14 B×B N×B 15 N-K5
N5-Q4 16 N×N N×N 17 B×N P×B 18*

R×P B-N5 19 Q-K4! winning a piece)
14 N×P N5×N 15 B4×N N×B 16 R×N
B×B 17 N×B (threatening *18 Q-Q3*) 17
... P-R3 18 Q-Q2 P×N 19 R×B
Q-B3 20 R×NP and White had won a
pawn, although this proved difficult to
convert into a win and the game ended
in a draw.

Later 12 N-K5 was suggested, but
after 12 ... B-Q2 the advance 13
P-Q5 leads to 13 ... P×P 14 N×QP
N5×N 15 B×N N×B 16 R×N B-KN5
17 Q-K4 Q×R! 18 Q×Q QR-Q1 with
equality. This variation confirms the
important principle that White should
not usually open up the position by
P-Q5 until he is fully developed.

    12 Q-K4

This move has no real significance in
itself, as Black could now invite
repetition of moves by 12 ... N-B3!
when White has nothing better than to
retreat his queen to K2. The usual
continuation here is 12 B-Q3 N3-N5 13
B-N1 when White has attacking
chances on the K-side and can even
bring his QR into the attack via QR3 if
need be.

    12 ...   **N3-N5(?)**

Black prevents the manoeuvre
B-Q3-N1 but grants his opponent a
much greater concession: White's
queen now becomes very active.

    13 N-K5   **R-R2**

An unnatural move, but Black was
already in difficulties because of
White's centralized queen. If 13 ...
P-QN3 14 N-B6! N×N 15 N×N is
possible, as 15 ... P×N 16 B×QP wins
a pawn, and after 15 ... B-N2 White
forces a serious weakening in Black's K-
side with 16 B-Q3! If 13 ... N-KB3
then 14 Q-B3 is possible, or White can
play as in the game 14 Q-R4 N3-Q4 15
Q-N3.

14 B-N3	**N-KB3**
15 Q-R4	**P-QN3**
16 Q-N3	**B-N2**

It was essential to play 16 ... K–R1, as Black's pieces now become even more unco-ordinated.

17 B–R6   N–K1
18 QR–B1   K–R1 (53)

19 P–Q5!

In the last resort this is a positional sacrifice of a pawn, but there is also the tactical point: 19 ... P×B? 20 P×P and Black's position collapses.

19 ...   P×P
20 B–K3   R–R1

After 20 ... B–B4 White cannot play 21 B×B P×B 22 N–K4? P–B5! (*23 R×P Q–K2!*) but 21 N×QP! N×N 22 R×B! P×R 23 B×P gives him a clear advantage.

21 N–B4!   N–Q3

Black prefers to give up his extra pawn rather than try to defend it by 21 ... B–B4 22 N–R5! e.g. 22 ... B×B 23 N×B Q–Q2 24 Q×B Q×N 25 N×P, or 22 ... P×N 23 B×B R–KN1 24 B×N (*24 R–Q4* or *24 Q–K3* are also strong) 24 ... P×B 25 N×P Q–R4 26 Q–B4 etc.

22 B×P

Not of course 22 N×NP? N–B4 23 Q–R3 N×B 24 Q×N P–Q5!

22 ...   Q–N1
23 N–R5   N–B4
24 Q×Q   QR×Q
25 N×B   R×N
26 P–R5

Now White has two active bishops and Black's QP is very weak. Spassky

has no way of avoiding a rapid defeat.

26 ...   B–N4
27 R–N1   P–Q5
28 N–Q5   N–B3

Black tries to complicate, as 28 ... N×N 29 B×N R–Q2 30 B–K4 wins the QP for White.

29 B–R4   R–B1
30 P–B4   N3–K2

No better is 30 ... B–B3 31 P–N4! N–K6 32 N×N P×N 33 P–N5, or here 31 ... N4–K2 32 N×N B×N 33 R.N1–B1 etc.

31 QR–B1!   R1–QN1
32 P×B   N×N
33 B–B6   R×B
34 P×R   N.Q4–K6

Or 34 ... N×P 35 B–K4 etc.

35 P–N7!   N×R
36 R×N   P–N3
37 P–KN4   N–N2
38 R×P   N–K3
39 R–Q7   1–0

All these examples, in which the advance P–Q5 is involved, clearly show us how important it is for the side with the isolated pawn to retain his 'good' bishop i.e. the bishop controlling the Q5 square. Without this bishop the pawn usually becomes a permanent weakness.

24 Portisch–Ivkov

Wijk aan Zee 1972, Queen's Gambit

1 P–Q4 N–KB3 2 P–QB4 P–K3 3 N–QB3 P–Q4 4 B–N5 B–K2 5 P–K3 P–KR3 6 B–R4 0–0 7 R–B1 P–QN3 8 P×P N×P 9 P×N N×N P×N 10 B Q×B 11 B–K2 P–QR4? correct is 11 ... R–Q1 followed by 12 ... P–QB4! 12 B–B3 Q–N5+ 13 Q–Q2 P–QB3 14 R–B3! Q–Q3 15 N–K2 N–Q2 16 0–0 B–N2 17 N–B4 KR–Q1 18 R1–B1 QR–N1

19 P–KR4

The black position is now somewhat cramped. Nevertheless, his best tactics are to wait with moves like ... P-N3 and ... K-N2. Instead, Black decides to become active on the Q-side, but in so doing creates a permanently weak QP with a strong-point for White on Q4 (a square not controlled by Black's 'bad' bishop). Under such circumstances the isolated pawn constitutes a grave disadvantage.

19 ...	P-QB4(?)
20 P×P	N×P
21 Q-Q4!	

This move seems to allow Black relief by 21 ... N-K3, but White then plays 22 N×N P×N 23 R-B7 P-K4 24 Q-KN4 Q-KB3 25 R-Q1! (threatening *26 R×B!* winning a pawn) and now 25 ... P-K5 loses to 26 B×P! P×B 27 R×R+ R×R 28 R×B.

21 ...	R-Q2
22 B-N4!	R-K2

This time 22 ... N-K3 fails to 23 B×N P×B 24 N-N6 and 25 N-K5 when Black's centre pawns are blockaded and he has a very passive bishop.

23 B-B5	R-Q1
24 R-Q1	R-K4
25 B-N1	(54)

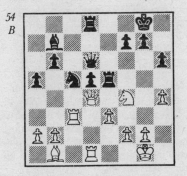

54
B

If we compare this position with the one in diagram 53, the difference is clear: the blockading square of the QP in the present game is under White's complete control. Once again 25 ...

N-K3 is bad, because 26 N×N P×N? 27 P-KN4 traps the black rook.

25 ...	Q-K2
26 N-K2	R-K1
27 P-R3	B-R3
28 N-N3!	

Surprisingly enough, White does not aim his pieces directly at the weak QP. In most cases, the plan of the active side is not to capture the QP by direct attack, as it can usually be defended as many times as it is attacked, but rather to blockade it, thereby tying down the enemy pieces and exploiting the greater activity of one's own.

28 ...	B-B5

The immediate 28 ... Q-B3 is better, although White can then play 29 P-N4 followed by R-B7. White now decides the game by a neat tactical sequence.

29 B-B2	

Threatening to win a pawn by 30 P-N4 P×P 31 P×P, as 31 ... N-Q2 loses to 32 R×B.

29 ...	P-R5
30 N-B5	Q-B3
31 N-Q6!	Q×N
32 R×B	

And now Black's QRP becomes his main weakness!

32 ...	Q-B2

Or 32 ... Q-K2 33 R-N4 and a pawn falls.

33 R-B3	Q-K2

Preventing 34 B×P R-K5 35 B×R.

34 P-KN3	Q-B3
35 Q-KB4!	

Now Black finds it impossible to defend all his own pawn weaknesses. If he exchanges queens, his position is hopeless after 36 NP×Q R-R4 37 R-Q4 R×RP 38 R×QP because his rook is out of play on KR5. In the game, White's rook on Q1 switches over to an attack on the QNP and QRP.

35 ...	Q-B3
36 R-Q4	Q-N4

| 37 R–N4 | Q–K7 |

The final despairing attempt to counter-attack

38 R×NP	N–K5
39 R–B7	R4–K2
40 R×R	R×R
41 R–N8+	K–R2
42 B×N+	1–0

If 42 ... P×B 43 Q–B5+ P–N3 44 Q–B6 wins.

In the following game White's attack succeeds without P–Q5, and the isolated pawn remains on the board until the very end.

25 Botvinnik–Vidmar

Nottingham 1936, Queen's Gambit

1 P–QB4 P–K3 2 N–KB3 P–Q4 3 P–Q4 N–KB3 4 N–B3 B–K2 5 B–N5 0–0 6 P–K3 QN–Q2 7 B–Q3 P–B4! 8 0–0 BP×P 9 KP×P if 9 KN×P? N–K4 9 ... P×P 10 B×BP

| 10 ... | N–N3 |

According to Botvinnik, 10 ... P–QR3 is better, intending ... P–QN4 and ... B–N2 (the weakness of Black's QB4 is not so critical here, as his knight is on Q2 rather than QB3). If White then plays 11 P–QR4 Black can continue as in the game ... N–N3–Q4, for White's QN4 square is weakened.

| 11 B–N3 | B–Q2 |
| 12 Q–Q3 | N.N3–Q4? |

Black neglects an important weapon in the fight against an isolated pawn: simplification. He could play 12 ... N.B3–Q4! when 13 B–B2 P–KN3 gives White nothing and ... N–N5 is threatened. After 13 B–K3 N×N 14 P×N B–QR5 or 13 N–K4 B–QR5!, Black advantageously exchanges pieces.

| 13 N–K5 | B–B3 |
| 14 QR–Q1 | (55) |

A typical set-up for both sides. White's pieces are posted so that they can switch to a K-side attack, whilst

55
B

being ready to support P–Q5 at a suitable moment. Black is blockading the QP and has placed a knight on the vital blockading square Q4. His QB would be better on QN2, for on QB3 it blocks the QB-file which is an important factor in Black's counter-play, and White can also exchange it at an opportune moment. Of course N×B at once would not be good, as it only strengthens Black's control of Q4, making it difficult for White to exploit the weak QBP.

| 14 ... | N–QN5? |

Once again Black loses in this game because he grossly under-estimates the dynamic possibilities of White's position. The following manoeuvre loses time which White uses to begin a direct attack. 14 ... Q–R4 or 14 ... R–B1 should have been played.

| 15 Q–R3! | B–Q4 |
| 16 N×B | N5×N? |

The final error, similar to his first one on move 12. It was essential to play 16 ... N3×N! 17 B–B1 R–B1, a typical continuation in which Black gains time by offering to exchange material, and compels the enemy pieces to give up their active posts.

17 P–B4!

This move deserves special mention. It is usually a poor move in positions with an isolated QP, as it weakens one's own king position. However, it is very strong here because it contains a concrete threat, P-B5, which cannot be prevented.

17 ...   **R-B1**

He cannot play 17 ... P-KN3 18 B-R6 R-K1 19 B-R4 winning the exchange, and after 17 ... N-K5 White has the elegant sacrifice 18 N×P!! R×N 19 Q×KP, or here 18 ... K×N 19 R.Q1-K1! and in both cases White regains his piece with a won position.

18 P-B5   **P×P**

After 18 ... Q-Q3 19 P×P P×P (*19 ... Q×P 20 Q-KB3*) 20 KR-K1, Black's KP is very weak.

19 R×P   **Q-Q3** (*56*)

Even the better 19 ... R-B2 is insufficient after 20 R1-KB1 giving the following variations:

a. 20 ... P-QR3 21 N×P R×N 22 B3×N N×B 23 R×R B×B 24 Q-K6!

b. 20 ... N-N3 21 Q-R4 (threatening *R×N*) 21 ... N.N3-Q4 22 N×P R×N 23 B3×N N×B 24 R×R B×B 25 Q×B (Panov).

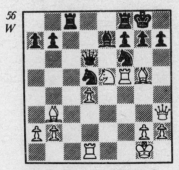

56
W

20 N×P!   **R×N**

Or 20 ... K×N 21 B3×N+ winning.

21 B5×N   **B×B**

If 21 ... N×B 22 R×N! and 23 Q×R+ wins

22 R×N   **Q-B3**

The last trap. If now 23 R-QB5? B×P+ etc.

23 R-Q6   **Q-K1**
24 R-Q7   **1-0**

A white knight often threatens to go to QB5 when Black has taken up an active position on the Q-side with ... P-QR3 and ... P-QN4 as we have already pointed out in game 22. This happened, for example, in the game Reshevsky-Stahlberg (Helsinki 1952) after the moves **1 P-Q4 N-KB3 2 P-QB4 P-K3 3 N-QB3 B-N5 4 P-K3 0-0 5 B-Q3 P-Q4 6 N-B3 P-B4 7 0-0 N-B3 8 P-QR3 QP×P 9 B×BP P×P 10 P×P B-K2 11 Q-Q3 P-QR3 12 B-R2 P-QN4 13 B-N1 B-N2 14 B-N5 P-N3 15 R-Q1 R-K1 16 B-R2! P-N5 17 N-QR4!** when Black could not play the natural 17 ... N-Q4 because of 18 B×B Q×B 19 N-B5 with advantage to White.

In the game Pachman-Golombek (Stockholm-Saltsjobaden interzonal 1952) White varied with **11 B-KN5 P-QR3 12 R-K1 P-QN4 13 B-Q3** So that after 13 ... P-N5 the RP is guarded. **13 ... B-N2 14 B-B2 R-B1 15 Q-Q3 P-N3 16 QR-Q1 P-N5 17 N-QR4 N-Q4 18 N-B5!** and White again stood better.

In our examples so far the possessor of the isolated pawn has succeeded in exploiting his better placed pieces and the strong-points created by the pawn, along with the dynamic possibilities connected with P-Q5. However, it would be wrong to assume from all this that it is in itself an advantage to have such a pawn. In most cases, and this applies to our examples too, the side with the isolated pawn only wins as a result of inaccurate defensive play. Nevertheless, it is worth noting that in positions arising from various lines in the Queen's Gambit or Nimzo-Indian Defence, White is in practice much more successful, despite his isolated pawn. This only serves to show that it is just as difficult to exploit this weakness as it is to bring about the necessary simplification.

Our next game is a good illustration of how to defend as Black when White has active piece play as compensation for his isolated pawn.

26 Botvinnik–Flohr

Groningen 1946, Queen's Gambit

1 P–Q4 P–Q4 2 N–KB3 N–KB3 3 P–QB4 P–K3 4 N–B3 P–B4 5 BP×P N×P 6 P–K3 N–QB3 7 B–Q3 P×P 8 P×P B–K2 9 0–0 0–0 10 R–K1 N3–N5 11 B–K4 11 B–N1 at once is better. 11 ...N–KB3 12 B–N1 P–QN3 13 N–K5 B–N2 (*57*)

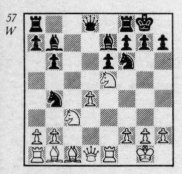

57
W

14 R–K3!?

In this situation, with White's bishop already on QN1 instead of on QB4 or QN3, Botvinnik decides to begin a direct attack before completing his development. White is two tempi behind the usual set up with pawn on QR3, bishop on KN5, and queen on Q3.

14 ...	N5–Q4
15 R–R3	P–N3

A move which will be forced sooner or later, as the pressure against Black's KR2 cannot be borne indefinitely.

16 B–R6	R–K1
17 Q–Q2	R–QB1
18 B–Q3	P–QR3!
19 R–K1	P–QN4

A good move in this position, as White cannot exploit his QB5 square

because he has now committed himself to the K-side. Attack and counter-attack on opposite wings just about balance each other out.

20 R–N3

Threatening to decide the game by the double sacrifice 21 N×KNP! RP×N 22 B×KNP!

20 ...	N–R4
21 R–R3	N.R4–B3
22 B–N1	

A logical conclusion to the game would have been a draw by repetition here, as Black's counterplay is fully adequate.

22 ...	R–B2
23 R–N3	N–R4
24 R–R3	N.R4–B3
25 Q–K2	N×N

Black meets the threatened 26 N×BP with an active defence, temporarily replacing the isolated QP by an isolated pawn couple on the QB- and Q-files. We shall deal later with this particular conversion of one weakness into another, but in this situation Black soon knocks out the support for the QP.

26 P×N   P–N5! (*58*)

58
W

Now 27 N×BP? loses to 27 ... Q–Q4! followed by 28 ... K×N

27 R–N3	R×P!
28 N×BP!	Q–Q4!
29 N–K5 ?	

The correct move is 29 R–N5! Q–B5 30 B×P! P×B 31 R×P+ K×N 32

R–N7+ K–Bl 33 R–N6+ with a draw
by perpetual check. Botvinnik either
missed this variation or was dissatisfied
with a draw. At all events his position
now becomes critical.

29 ...	R×R
30 BP×R	Q×QP+
31 K–R1	B–Q3

Black could have consolidated his
advantage much more simply by 31 ...
B–Q4.

32 B–B4	N–R4?

A serious mistake which loses a piece
but, surprisingly enough, not the game.
32 ... N–Q4 would have brought
about the logical result of a win for
Black.

33 R–Q1	N×B
34 P×N	Q×P

If the queen retreats to QB4 or QN3,
then 35 N–Q7! wins.

35 R×B	B–Q4

Threatening both 36 ... Q–QB8+
and 36 ... R–QB1

36 B–B2!	R–KB1

Here or on the next move, Black
could still try for a win with 36 ...
B×RP

37 P–KR3	Q–KB8+ ?
38 Q×Q	R×Q+
39 K–R2	R–B7
40 R×B!	P×R
41 B–N3	K–N2
½–½	

After 42 N–Q3 R–Q7 43 N×P
P–QR4 44 N×P P–R5 45 B–B4 R–Q5
46 N–N6 K–B3 White's slight
advantage is insufficient to win.

The side with the isolated pawn
frequently commits a grave strategic
error by blindly attacking on the K-side
without due regard to the correct
positioning of his pieces in relation to
his QP. The above game shows how
weak the pawn can become if White
tries to finish the game quickly by a
mating attack. Our next game
illustrates this point even more clearly.

Spassky attempts a risky pawn storm
against the castled king and it is only by
the skin of his teeth that he escapes
punishment for his romantic boldness.

27 Spassky–Flohr

22nd USSR Championship, Queen's
Gambit

1 P–Q4 P–Q4 2 P–QB4 P×P 3
N–KB3 N–KB3 4 P–K3 P–B4 5 B×P
P–K3 6 0–0 P×P 7 P×P N–B3 8 N–B3
P–QR3
   9 P–QR3

We are already acquainted with the
idea behind this move. White prevents
... N–QN5–Q4 and prepares Q–Q3,
B–KN5, QR–Q1 etc.

9 ...	B–K2
10 B–KN5	0–0
11 Q–Q3	P–R3!?

Clearly a two-edged continuation.
By driving back White's QB, Black
takes the pressure off his KN and so
anticipates the threat of B–R2–N1
(after QR–Q1), but his RP is now a
serious weakness. After the correct
reply 12 B–K3! Black will always have
to be on his guard against the B×KRP
sacrifice. Furthermore, once the KRP
has advanced, the useful defensive
move ... P–KN3 becomes practically
out of the question.

12 B–R4?	

This move, however, is a bad
strategic mistake. Not only does White
give up his pressure against the KRP,
but he also allows some simplification
which is, as we know, an important
weapon in the fight against the isolated
pawn.

12 ...	N–KR4!
13 B×B	N×B

It is more important to control Q4
than to maintain the attack on the
pawn. After 13 ... Q×B 14 P–Q5 is
possible, whereas now this is answered
by 14 ... N–B5

14 N-K5	N-KB3
15 QR-Q1	P-QN4
16 B-R2	B-N2 (59)

59
W

White should now be satisfied with 17 KR-K1, giving a position in which his active pieces just about compensate for the weak QP.

17 P-B4?

Beginning his faulty plan of a pawn storm on the K-side. However, as P-B5 is much more difficult to carry out than it was in game 25, this move and the next only serve to weaken White's own king position.

17 ...	Q-N3
18 P-KN4	

From an objective point of view, this move makes the situation even worse, as the long white diagonal is seriously weakened, giving Black an excellent basis for a counter-attack. However, without this advance, White's previous move would be pointless.

18 ...	QR-Q1
19 B-N1	

Threatening P-N5 winning a piece, but Black is now ready to begin his counter-measures.

19 ...	N-B3!

This knight has played a note-worthy rôle. Having helped to blockade the QP from move 13, it is now instrumental in eliminating White's well-placed knight on K5, as Black takes over the initiative.

20 N×N

After 20 N-B3 P-N3 21 P-R3 Black would have two good continuations:

a. 20 ... P-N5 21 N-QR4 Q-R2 when 22 N-B5 fails to 22 ... N×QP! White would be unable to exploit his QB5 square because his K-side is too exposed.

b. 20 ... R-Q2 followed by 21 ... KR-Q1 with more pressure on the QP.

20 ...	Q×N
21 Q-R3	

Not of course 21 P-Q5 P×P 22 P-N5 P-Q5! and Black's mating attack comes first.

21 ...	Q-N3!

Perhaps White had planned for 21 ... N×P 22 Q×N Q-R8+ 23 K-B2 Q×P+ 24 K-K1 Q×NP 25 Q-N3 (threatening *26 R-N1*) with advantage, as Black's three pawns are insufficient compensation for the piece in this position.

22 Q-Q3	P-N3
23 P-N5	

White has to push on with his plan now that he is committed, as after 23 P-R3 Black simply doubles rooks on the Q-file.

23 ...	P×P
24 P×P	N-R4!

This is more solid than 24 ... N-Q4 25 N-K4

25 Q-K3

To prevent ... P-K4, but Black still plays it, neatly opening a file for his rook and vacating K3 for his queen.

25 ...	P-K4!
26 Q×P	KR-K1
27 Q-QB5	Q-K3
28 P-Q5	Q-N5+
29 K-R1 (60)	

It is difficult to visualize that this position has arisen from an opening in which White had an isolated QP and so was attacking on the K-side. Admittedly he has managed to advance his pawn, but it is Black who has gone

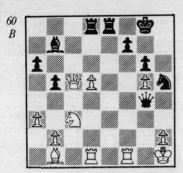

60
B

over to an attack which he should now conclude by the simple 29 . . . N–N6+ ! 30 P×N Q–R6+ 31 K–N1 Q×P+ 32 K–R1 K–N2 33 Q–Q4+ R–K4 etc. Instead of this, Black opts for a more complex, and indeed faulty combination. It is interesting that grandmaster Flohr, perhaps one of the greatest specialists of the fight against the isolated QP, should throw away the fruits of splendidly conducted games, both here and against Botvinnik, as a result of a tactical oversight.

| 29 ... | R×P? |
| **30 R×R!** | |

Not however 30 N×R? N–N6+ 31 P×N Q–R6+ 32 K–N1 Q×P+ 33 K–R1 R–K7 etc.

| 30 ... | N–B5 |
| **31 Q–N1!** | |

Black overlooked this simple defensive move. He had planned for 31 R×N? R–K8+ or 31 B–K4? R×B 32 R–Q8+ R–K1+ !

31 ...	Q×Q+
32 K×Q	N×R
33 B–R2!	R–K4

Not 33 . . . N×N? 34 B×P+

34 P–KR4	K–B1
35 B×N	B×B
36 R–B4	B–K3
37 K–B2	R–QB4
38 R–Q4	K–K2
39 K–K3	R–B1
40 K–B4	R–B4
½–½	

In game 26 we met an interesting stratagem when Black played 25 . . . N×N replacing the isolated QP with an isolated pawn couple. Admittedly, Black's next move in that game (26 . . . P–N5) forced the exchange of the QBP, but we often find that it is a good idea anyway to exchange weaknesses in this way. We shall be examining the isolated pawn couple in a separate section, but here is a simple example of how such a formation is brought about.

61
W

The usual continuation in this position (*61*) is 10 P–QR3 0–0 11 P–QN4 B–R2 12 B–N2. Black cannot then proceed in the same aggresive manner as Szabo in game 22, because he is two tempi down on the analogous position. with colours reversed. However, he has an even game after . . . B–K3, . . . Q–K2 and . . . KR–Q1. For this reason (against Sefc, Czechoslovak Ch 1953) I went in for a somewhat surprising manoeuvre: **10 N–Q4 0–0 11 N×N! P×N 12 P–QN3 R–K1** It is important to note that 12 . . . P–Q5 13 P×P leaves Black with a serious weakness on QB3. White's plan now is to blockade Black's QBP and QP in order to prevent . . . P–QB4 followed by . . . P–Q5. **13 B–N2 Q–Q3?** 13 . . . B–Q3 is correct. **14 R–B1 B–B4 15 N–QR4 B–R2 16 B–Q4! B–N1 17 P–N3 B–R6 18 R–K1 Q–K3 19 Q–B2** and White had a clear advantage. Black's desperate attempt at a counter-attack was contained and White won quickly as follows: **19 ... N–K5 20 Q×P B×P 21 BP×B! Q–B4 22 R–B1 B×R 23 R×B Q–N4 24 Q–B7 Q–N3 25 B–Q3 Q–R4 26 N–N6 QR–Q1 27 N×P! Q×N** if 27 ... R×N 28 B×N **28 B–B4 Q–KN4** if 28 ... R–Q2 29 R×P! **29 R×P K–R1 30 R×P 1–0.**

Let us now turn to positions of the second type in which the K-file is open and Black has a QBP rather than a KP.

62

This pawn structure (*62*) offers Black more chances to exchange the major pieces, because the K-file is usually less blocked than the QB-file on which both sides normally had knights at QB3. In the former positions K5 was a strong-point, whereas now the corresponding square QB5 is not as effective when occupied by a knight, as the latter only threatens the QNP as opposed to the dangerous threats to the king from a knight on K5. However, even in this case the side with the isolated pawn has good chances of piece play, utilizing his QB5 and K5 squares, as the following game shows. O'Kelly–Euwe, Amsterdam 1950 (*63*).

Theory had recommended Black's last move, ... Q–N3, on the assumption that, as White has an isolated QP, the exchange of queens should favour Black. However, this game refutes this assumption. After the exchange of queens, White has strong-

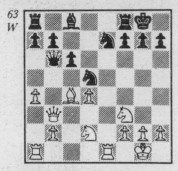

63
W

points for his knights on QB5 and K5 and the activity of his pieces more than compensates for his weak QP. Play went: **14 P–R5! Q×Q 15 N×Q B–B4** A little better is 15 ... R–Q1 16 N–B5 K–B1 17 N–K5, although even here White has a clear advantage. **16 N–K5 N–N5 17 QR–B1** not 17 N×KBP? N2–Q4 winning the exchange **17 ... N2–Q4 18 P–R6! P–QN4 19 B×N P×B 20 N–B6! N×N 21 R×N KR–K1** Here the game was surprisingly agreed a draw, although after 22 R×R+ R×R 23 P–B3 White has a big advantage in the endgame, as shown by the following variations from the tournament book:
a. 23 ... R–K8+ 24 K–B2 R–QN8 25 N–B5 R×P+ 26 K–N3 P–N4 27 R–B7 K–N2 28 R×RP R–R7 29 R–N7 B–B1 30 R×NP B×P 31 N×B R×N 32 R×P
b. 23 ... R–QB1 24 R–Q6 B–K3 25 N–B5 K–B1 26 N×B+ P×N 27 R×KP R–B7 28 R–Q6 R×QNP 29 R×P.

Our next game is a clear-cut example of effective play against an isolated pawn.

28 Botvinnik–Bronstein

World Championship 1951, French Defence

1 P–Q4 P–K3 2 P–K4 P–Q4 3 N–Q2 P–QB4 4 KP×P KP×P 5 KN–B3 N–KB3 6 B–N5+ B–Q2 7 B×B+

QN×B 8 0–0 B–K2 9 P×P N×P *(64)*

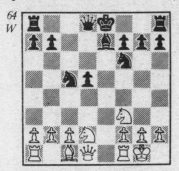

64
W

A position which occurs very often in this variation of the French Defence. In itself the exchange of the white-squared bishops was to Black's advantage but it has allowed White to speed up his development and at the same time to force Black's pieces onto unfavourable squares. For example, Black's bishop would be better on QB4, with his knight on QB3.

10 N–Q4!

This well-known blockade of the QP is linked here with the possible threat of N–B5.

10 ...	**Q–Q2**
11 N2–B3	**0–0**
12 N–K5	**Q–B1**
13 B–N5	**R–K1**
14 N–Q3	

A correct simplifying manoeuvre, but 14 P–QB3 was also good, strengthening the blockade of the pawn.

14 ...	**N×N**
15 Q×N	**Q–N5**
16 B–K3	**B–B4**
17 P–KR3	**Q–N3?**

A typical error in such positions. After the exchange of queens, Black relinquishes all the tactical possibilities of the middle game such as attack on the enemy king, and White has a permanent positional advantage. For these reasons 17 ... Q–R4 was

preferable, as White could not force the exchange of queens himself by 18 Q–B5 B×N 19 Q×Q N×Q 20 B×B R–K7 21 KR–B1 R–QB1 with adequate counterplay to Black.

18 Q×Q	**RP×Q**
19 QR–Q1	**R–K5**
20 P–QB3	**P–N3**
21 N–B2	**R–Q1**
22 R–Q3	**K–B1**

The exchange of the black-squared bishops often makes it more difficult to attack the isolated pawn, as White needs the bishop to exchange Black's knight, thereby eliminating the best protection of the QP. However, Black dare not exchange bishops, for he loses a pawn by force after 22 ... B×B 23 N×B P–Q5 24 R1–Q1, or here 23 ... R–Q2 24 R1–Q1 R–K4 25 P–QB4 etc.

23 R1–Q1	**K–K2**
24 K–B1	

24 P–KN4, followed by 25 K–N2, seems even stronger.

24 ...	**K–Q2**
25 B–N5	**K–B3**

Black has managed to bring his king over to protect his weak pawn, but his pieces are soon driven into most unfavourable defensive positions.

26 P–QN4!	**B–B1**

After 26 ... B–K2 both 27 N–K3 and 27 N–Q4+ K–N2 28 P–N5! followed by 29 N–B6 are to White's advantage.

27 N–K3	**R–K4** *(65)*

65
W

It is clear that Black's QP must succumb to the pressure of White's pieces. After the correct and logical 28 B×N! P×B White even has three ways of winning a pawn:

a. 29 P–QB4 P–Q5 (if *29 . . . B×P 30 N×P*) 30 N–B2

b. 29 P–R3 and there is no effective defence against the threat of P–QB4

c. 29 P–KB4! R–R4 30 P–B4 B×P 31 N×P B–Q3 32 N×BP R4–R1 33 N–K4 B–K2 34 R×R R×R 35 R×R B×R 36 K–K2 P–B4 37 N–N5 and the knight goes to K5 winning.

The text move is an oversight after which the game can no longer be won.

28 P–KB4?   R–K5
29 P–B5

Now 29 B×N fails to 29 . . . R×BP+ 30 K–N1 R×B

29 . . .   R–K4!
30 B–B4

Again 30 B×N does not work, in view of 30 . . . P×B 31 P–B4 B×P 32 N×P R×P+ 33 K–N1 B–B4+ or here 33 K–K2 R–K1+

30 . . .   R–K5
31 B–N5   R–K4
32 B–B4   R–K5
33 B–N5   ½–½

In these types of position, control of the open K-file is a very important strategic factor, as our next two games show. In the first game, the K-file helps the side with the isolated pawn to obtain good play for his pieces. In the second game, it allows the other side to simplify into a won endgame.

29 Pachman–Ojanen

Trencianske Teplice 1949, Queen's Gambit

1 P–Q4 N–KB3 2 P–QB4 P–K3 3 N–QB3 P–Q4 4 B–N5 B–K2 5 P–K3 QN–Q2 6 N–B3 0–0 7 R–B1 P–B3 8 B–Q3 P×P 9 B×BP N–Q4 10 B×B

Q×B 11 0–0 N×N 12 R×N P–K4 13 Q–N1 P×P 14 P×P N–QN3 15 R–K1 Q–B3 16 B–N3 B–B4 16 . . . B–K3! is better. **17 Q–B1 QR–Q1**

18 R–K5!

After 18 R3–K3? N–Q4 White cannot exploit the open K-file.

18 . . .   B–N5

No better is 18 . . . N–Q2 19 R5–K3 KR–K1 20 Q–K1 R×R 21 R×R with a clear advantage to White. Black cannot play 18 . . . N–Q4 19 B×N P×B when White has two open files at his disposal and his knight is superior to the bishop.

19 Q–K1!

Both increasing the pressure down the K-file and at the same time preventing 19 . . . B×N in view of 20 R×B Q–Q3 21 R×P! winning.

19 . . .   P–KR3
20 P–KR3   B–B1
21 R3–K3 *(66)*

66
B

A typical set-up in which White fully controls the only open file and is threatening the unpleasant 22 Q–R5

21 . . .   Q–Q3
22 Q–R5   Q–B2!

This is better than the passive 22 . . . Q–N1 when 23 N–R4 wins, e.g.

a. 23 . . . B–Q2 24 N–N6 KR–K1 25 N–K7+ K–B1 26 Q–B5

b. 23 . . . R×P 24 N–N6 R1–Q1 25 R–K8+

c. 23 . . . R–Q3 24 R–K8 N–Q4 25 N–B5! R–Q2 (if *25 . . . N×R 26 N–K7+*) 26 B×N etc.

23 Q×P

The strongest continuation is still 23
N–R4, as Black can answer the text-
move by 23 . . . B–K3! I had originally
planned the following combination: 24
B×B? R–R1 25 B×P+ R×B 26
R–K8+ R–B1 27 R8–K7, but as soon
as I had made my 23rd move I realized
that the whole plan fails to the simple 27
. . . R×Q 28 R×Q N–Q4. Fortunately
my opponent also thought the
combination was correct and selected
another move. After 23 . . . B–K3!
White would have to try other moves
such as 24 Q–R5! R–R1 25 Q–B3 B×B
26 Q×B N–Q4 when it is difficult to
utilize the advantage of an extra pawn.
If instead 24 R×B P×R 25 B×P+
K–R1 26 R–N3 Q–Q3! 27 R×N Q×B
28 R×NP R–R1, or here 27 Q×N Q×B
28 Q×NP R–QN1 29 Q×R R×Q 30
R×R+ K–R2, White has a material
advantage but the win is very difficult
to achieve.

**23 . . . R–Q3? 24 Q–R3 Q–Q1 25
Q–B5 N–Q4 26 B×N P×B 27 Q–N5
B–K3 28 R–N3 R–Q2 29 R5–K3
R–B2 30 R.N3–B3 R×R 31 R×R
Q–Q3 32 N–K5 R–R1 33 P–R3 R–N1
34 P–QN4 P–KN3 35 Q–B5 Q–Q1 36
Q–N5 K–N2 37 Q–K2 Q–Q3 38 Q–B2
R–QR1 39 R–B7 K–B3 40 Q–B1
P–KN4? 41 P–B4 R–R3 42 P–B5!
B×P 43 R×BP+ K–K3 44 Q–B8+
1–0.**

30 Capablanca–Rubinstein

Bad Kissingen 1928, Queen's Pawn
Game

**1 P–Q4 P–Q4 2 N–KB3 P–QB4 3
P×P P–K4 4 P–K4 B×P5 P×P P×P
6 B–QN5+ N–QB3 7 0–0 KN–K2 8
QN–Q2** We now have a position which
could have been reached via the 3
N–Q2 variation of the French Defence,
the important difference being that
Rubinstein is a tempo up on that line,

which should ensure him a comfortable
game. **8 . . . 0–0 9 N–N3 B–N3 10
R–K1 B–N5 11 B–Q3 N–N3** (67)

67
W

**12 P–KR3   B×N
13 Q×B   N.B3–K4?**

The first positional mistake. This
knight is well placed on QB3,
controlling the important blockading
square in front of his QP, so he should
move his other knight. After 13 . . .
N.N3–K4 14 Q–Q1 N×B 15 Q×N
Q–B3 Black has an even game (16
B–K3 P–Q5 17 B–Q2 KR–K1).

**14 Q–B5   N×B
15 Q×N.Q3   P–Q5?**

The second error, this time placing
Black at a clear disadvantage. His pawn
is in no way stronger here than on Q4,
and White now has time to seize control
of the K-file.

**16 B–Q2   Q–B3
17 R–K4!   QR–Q1
18 R1–K1** (68)

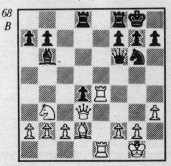

68
B

Threatening to win the exchange by 19 B–N4.

18 ...	Q–B3
19 P–N3!	

But not 19 B–R5? P–B4 20 R–K6 N–B5 winning.

19 ...	KR–K1
20 B–R5!	

This exchange of bishops lays bare the weakness of Black's QP.

20 ...	R×R
21 Q×R!	N–B1

If 21 ... Q×Q 22 R×Q B×B 23 N×B P–Q6 White replies 24 P×P R×P 25 N×P R–Q8+ 26 K–R2 R–Q7 25 N–B5 etc. After the text move, White completely changes the character of the position. He frees Black from the problem of his isolated pawn but reaches a won ending by playing his rook to the seventh rank. The game concluded: **22 Q×Q P×Q 23 R–K7 R–Q4 24 B×B P×B 25 R–N7 N–Q2 26 R–B7 R–Q3 27 R–B8+ N–B1 28 N–Q2! P–QB4 29 N–B4 R–K3 30 R–N8 R–K8+ 31 K–N2 P–KN4 32 P–QR4! R–QR8 33 N×P K–N2 34 R–B8 N–K3 35 N–Q7 R×P 36 N×P R–N5 37 N–Q3 R–N4 38 K–B3 P–R3 39 P–QN4 P–R4 40 P–N4 P×P+ 41 P×P P–B3 42 R–B4 K–B2 43 N–B5 N–Q1 44 N–N3! 1–0.**

For the major part of the above game, the isolated QP was on the fifth rather than the fourth rank. Such an advanced pawn has two main characteristics: on the one hand it cramps the opponent's position, and on the other hand it is more difficult to defend here than on the fourth rank. Our next two examples illustrate these points.

31 Lasker–Tarrasch

St. Petersburg 1914, Queen's Gambit

1 P–Q4 P–Q4 2 N–KB3 P–QB4 3 P–B4 P–K3 4 BP×P KP×P 5 P–KN3 N–QB3 6 B–N2 N–B3 7 0–0 B–K2 8 P×P B×P 9 QN–Q2 P–Q5!? 10 N–N3 B–N3

11 Q–Q3!	

This move threatens to win the QP by 12 R–Q1 so Black is forced to exchange his QB for White's QN, thus increasing the power of White's fianchettod KB.

11 ...	B–K3
12 R–Q1	B×N
13 Q×B	Q–K2
14 B–Q2	0–0 (69)

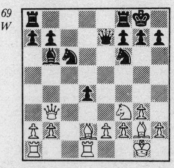

69
W

By his last move Lasker has indicated that a direct attack on the QP is not possible, and his next move reveals his plan. Utilizing the fact that Black's pieces are tied to the defence of the pawn, he sets out to undermine them, thereby significantly increasing the pressure along the KR1–QR8 diagonal and down the QB-file.

15 P–QR4!	N–K5

Not of course 15 ... Q×P? 16 R–K1 Q–R3 17 B–KB1 winning the queen. 15 ... B–B4 16 P–R5 P–QR3 was a little better than the text-move, but after 17 QR–B1 Black has an unenviable position.

16 B–K1	QR–Q1?

A mistake, losing material. 16 ... KR–Q1 was essential.

17 P–R5	B–B4
18 P–R6	P×P

Or 18 ... P–QN3 19 Q–R4! followed

by 20 P–QN4 and 21 P–N5 winning the QP. This variation serves to emphasize the point that it is really Black's advanced QP which is the cause of all his troubles.

19 QR–B1!	**R–QB1**
20 N–R4	

Threatening to win a piece by 21 B×N, and forcing the win of the exchange.

20 ...	**B–N3**
21 N–B5	**Q–K4**
22 B×N	**Q×B**
23 N–Q6	**Q×P**
24 N×R	**R×N**

The remainder of the game still presents White with a difficult technical problem, as Black has two pawns for the exchange, one of them being the strong QP. However, White must win if he succeeds in eliminating Black's rook, so that he can threaten the enemy king. The game ended: **25 Q–Q5 Q–K3 26 Q–B3 P–R3 27 B–Q2 N–K4 28 R×R+ Q×R 29 Q–K4 N–Q2 30 R–QB1 Q–B1** if 30 ... Q–Q1 31 Q–N7 or 31 Q–Q5 **31 B×P! N–B4** if 31 ... P×B 32 Q–N4+ **32 Q–N4 P–B4 33 Q–N6 Q–B2** the threat was 34 P–QN4 **34 Q×Q+ K×Q 35 B–N5 N–Q6 36 R–N1 K–K3 37 P–N3 K–Q4 38 P–B3 P–R4 39 P–R4 N–B4 40 P–R5 P–Q6 41 K–B1 P–R5 42 P×P N×P 43 B–B6! K–K3 44 B×P K–B2 45 B–K5 N–B4 46 R–Q1 1–0.**

70
B

This interesting position *(70)* was reached in Alekhine–Wolf, Pistyan 1922. It is essential for Black to eliminate White's QP, so the correct move is 9 ... P–K3! when 10 P–QN4 gives White no advantage after 10 ... N–R5 11 P×P B×NP+ 12 B–Q2 B×B+ 13 N×B P×P 14 N×P B×N 15 Q×B+ Q–K2. So White must quietly develop by 10 N–QB3 B–K2 11 B–B4 when he has somewhat the better of it, but his advantage is in no way as great as that obtained in the game (10 ... P×P 11 N×P N–B3!). Black may have thought that White's QP could be shown to be weak, as in the previous game, so he chooses another plan: **9 ... P–KN3(?) 10 N–KB3! Q–B2 11 Q–B3** threatening both Q×R and P–QN4 **11 ... R–N1 12 B–K3 P–N3 13 QN–Q2!** but not 13 P–QN4 B–N2 14 N–Q4 Q–R2 15 P×N P×P, or here 14 B–Q4 B×B 15 N×B Q–K4+ **13 ... B–N2 14 B–Q4 B×B 15 Q×B** Black already stands very badly. He now tries to develop his Q-side, but finally succumbs to the advance of White's QP which becomes a strong attacking weapon. **15 ... B–N4 16 B×B+ P×B 17 0–0 R–R5 18 P–QN4 Q–Q1 19 P–QR3 N1–Q2 20 KR–K1 K–B1 21 P–Q6! N–K3** or 21 ... P–K3 22 Q–K3 N–N2 23 Q–Q3 R–QR1 24 N–K4 winning the QNP **22 R×N! P×R 23 N–N5 Q–N1 24 N×KP+ K–B2 25 N–N5+ K–B1 26 Q–Q5 R–N2 27 N–K6+ K–N1 28 N×R+ K×N 29 P×P N–B3 30 Q×P** and White won quickly.

Our next two games also show the strength of an isolated pawn on the fifth rank.

32 Smyslov–Lilienthal

Moscow 1942, Grünfeld Defence

1 P–Q4 N–KB3 2 P–QB4 P–KN3 3 P–KN3 P–Q4 4 P×P N×P 5 B–N2

B–N2 6 N–KB3 0–0 7 0–0 N–N3 8 N–B3 N–B3 9 P–Q5 N–N1 10 N–Q4 10 P–K4 P–QB3 11 Q–N3 is better. **10 ... P–K3 11 P–K4 P×P?** A serious error; it was important to eliminate the QP by 11 ... P–QB3! **12 P×P** (*71*)

71
B

Black has apparently planned his game in the mistaken belief that White's QP is weak, but this is a wrong assumption in view of White's KB on KN2. On the contrary, the isolated pawn restricts the activity of the black pieces and fixes Black's QBP as an object of attack. In addition there is always the possibility of P–Q6 opening up the long diagonal for the white-squared bishop.

12 ...	**N1–Q2**
13 B–B4	**N–K4**
14 P–KR3	**N3–B5**
15 P–N3	

If 15 Q–B2 Black has a good game after 15 ... P–QB4! e.g. 16 P×Pep Q×N 17 P×P B×P 18 B×B QR–N1 etc.

15 ...	**N–Q3**
16 R–K1	**R–K1**
17 R–QB1	

Threatening 18 N3–N5

17 ...	**P–QR3**
18 N–R4	**N–N4** (*72*)
19 N–K6!	

A pretty tactical point made possible by the strong QP. Black cannot play 19 ... P×N in view of 20 B×N P×P 21

72
W

Q×P+ K–R1 22 B×B+ K×B 23 Q×Q R×Q 24 R–K7+ K–R3 25 N–B5.

19 ...	**B×N**
20 P×B	**R×P**
21 N–B5	**Q×Q**

Not, however, 21 ... R–Q3 22 Q–K2 N–Q5 23 Q–K4 P–B4 24 Q–K3 winning.

22 KR×Q	**R–Q3**
23 N×NP	**R×R+**
24 R×R	**R–N1**
25 P–QR4	**N–QB6**
26 R–Q2	**R–K1**
27 N–B5	**P–QR4**
28 R–B2!	**N–Q8**
29 B–Q2	**B–B1!**

In order to answer 30 B×P with 30 ... N×P obtaining counterplay (31 K×N? B×N+ 32 R×B N–Q6+).

30 N–K4	**R–N1**
31 B×P	**R×P**
32 B×P	

and White now converted his material advantage into a win as follows: **32 ... N–Q6 33 B–B1!** the threat was 33 ... R–N8 **33 ... N8–N7 34 P–R5 P–B4 35 N–Q2 R–R6 36 N–B4! N×N 37 R×N R–R8 38 B–N6 N–K4 39 R–B3 B–N5 40 R–B8+ K–B2 41 K–N2! 1–0.** White's powerful passed pawn quickly decides the game or else he wins a piece after 41 ... B×P 42 B–Q4 R–K8 43 R–B5.

33 Pachman–Uhlmann

Sarajevo 1963, English Opening

1 P–QB4 P–QB4 2 N–KB3 N–QB3 3 N–B3 P–KN3 4 P–K3 N–B3 5 P–Q4 P×P 6 P×P P–Q4 7 B–N5 P×P. 7 . . . N–K5 is better **8 B×P B–N2 9 P–Q5! N–QN1 10 0–0 0–0 11 R–K1** (73)

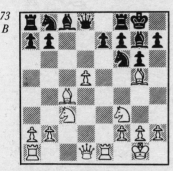

73
B

In such positions White's most important advantage is the pressure down the K-file, at the same time preventing the freeing move . . . P–K3, just as in the last game Black could not advance his QBP.

11 . . .	QN–Q2
12 Q–Q2	N–N3
13 B–N3	B–B4
14 N–Q4	B–Q2
15 QR–Q1	R–B1 ?

An instructive mistake, after which White's QP decides the issue. Black had

to play 15 . . . R–K1 but is still severely cramped.

16 Q–K2!

Not only threatening the KP but also 17 N–K6! P×N 18 P×P when the QP shows its strength.

16 . . . Q–B2

17 N4–N5!

Much stronger than 17 Q×P KR–K1 18 Q–N4 R×R+ 19 R×R B–B1 20 Q–R5 N–N5 followed by 21 . . . B–QB4

17 . . . Q–B4

Or 17 . . . B×N 18 N×B Q–B4 19 B–K3 Q–N5 20 N×P etc.

18 Q×P Q×Q

If 18 . . . B×N 19 B×N.

19 R×Q P–QR3

20 N–Q6 R–N1

Black has lost a pawn and also has a positional disadvantage. The remaining technical phase went as follows: **21 P–KR3 P–R3 22 B–KB4 N–B1 23 R×P! N×N 24 R×B.N7+ K×R 25 B×N R.N1–B1 26 B×R+ K×B 27 P–B4 P–QN4 28 R–Q4 P–QR4 29 P–R3 P–R4 30 K–B2 P–KR5 31 K–K3 N–R4 32 B–B2 N–N6 33 B–Q3 R–N1 34 P–Q6 K–B2 35 N–Q5 R–Q1 36 N–K7 N–B4+ 37 N×N P×N 38 R–Q5 K–K3 39 R×BP K×P 40 R–N5 R–K1+ 41 K–Q4 R–K8 42 B×P B×B 43 R×B R–K7 44 R–N6+ K–Q2 45 P–B5 R×KNP 46 R–N7+ K–K1 47 P–QN4 R–QR7 48 P–N5 1–0.**

5 The Backward Pawn

This section is directly linked with the previous one. By 'backward' we mean a pawn which has been left behind by the neighbouring pawns and can no longer be supported by them.

74

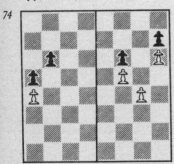

Black's QNP and White's KNP (74) are termed 'backward'. It is clear that certain methods of play against an isolated pawn will also apply here. Such a pawn is just as much of a disadvantage in the endgame, when it should be prevented from advancing. Again, as in the case of the isolated pawn, the backward pawn can rarely be captured by a direct attack. The next game is one of these rare cases, and it also shows us one of the most frequent ways in which a backward pawn is created.

34 Smyslov–Denker

USSR–USA 1946, Sicilian Defence

1 P–K4 P–QB4 2 N–QB3 N–QB3 3 P–KN3 P–KN3 4 B–N2 B–N2 5 P–Q3 P–K3 6 B–K3 N–Q5(?) 7 N3–K2 P–Q3 8 P–QB3 N–QB3 8 ... N×N is better. 9 P–Q4 P×P

10 N×P!

At first sight 10 P×P may seem more logical, forming a pawn centre, but it gives White nothing after both 10 ... P–Q4 11 P×P P×P followed by 12 ... KN–K2, and 10 ... N–B3 11 P–Q5 P×P 12 P×P N–K2. For this reason White aims to exploit the weakness of Black's QP

10 ...   N×N

White was threatening 11 N–N5

11 B×N   P–K4?

Exchanging bishops would weaken Black's K-side, but 11 ... N–B3! was much better than the text move which gives Black a permanent liability in the shape of his backward QP. Note that the backward pawn has arisen because Black wishes to drive an enemy piece away from a strong post in the centre. This often occurs when pieces are placed on K4 or Q4. At other times, threats of winning a pawn by an attack from a bishop or queen force the defence to accept a backward pawn as the lesser of two evils. Here is a simple example of this: 1 P–K4 P–QB4 2 N–KB3 N–QB3 3 P–Q4 P×P 4 N×P N–B3 5 N–QB3 P–K3 6 N4–N5 P–Q3(?) 7 B–KB4! P–K4 8 B–N5 and Black has a backward pawn.

12 B–K3   N–K2

13 N–K2   0–0

14 0–0   B–K3 (75)

75
W

It looks as though Black is going to eliminate his backward pawn and obtain good play for his pieces after . . . P–Q4. White must prevent this at all costs.

15 Q–Q2!   Q–B2

Black cannot play 15 . . . P–Q4 yet because of 16 B–B5! winning a pawn, so he plans to play . . . R–Q1 first. This means that White must prepare P–QB4, but he can only do this after the following subtle move, as an immediate 16 P–QN3? fails to 16 . . . P–QN4 with the better game to Black.

16 KR–B1!

The point is that now 16 . . . P–QN4 is answered by 17 P–QR4! P–QR3 18 R–Q1 when Black cannot avoid a serious disadvantage e.g. 18 . . . QR–Q1 19 P×P P×P 20 R–R7. Or 18 . . . KR–Q1 19 P×P P×P 20 R×R R×R 21 Q×P. Or 18 . . . B–N6 19 Q×P Q×Q 20 R×Q B×P 21 N–B1! threatening 22 P–N3

16 . . .   P–B4?

Black understandably does not want to be tied down to passive defence, so strives for counterplay. However, this move only helps White later to use his Q5 square to exchange bishops (see move 25) and his K4 square to attack the backward pawn (see move 29).

17 P–QB4   P×P
18 N–B3!   N–B4

The complications arising after 18 . . . B×P 19 N×P P–Q4 20 N–N5! are

favourable to White e.g. 20 . . . P–Q5 21 N–K6 P×B 22 Q×P Q–Q3 23 N×R B–B2 (*23 . . . B–Q4 24 B×B+ N×B 25 Q–B5 B×N 26 Q×Q B×Q 27 R–Q1*) 24 R–Q1 N–Q4 25 Q–N3 R–Q1 26 N×NP! P×N 27 B×N B×B 28 R×B Q×R 29 R–Q1! winning (Smyslov).

19 N×P   N×B

Black cannot shield his weak QP by 19 . . . N–Q5 when 20 P–B5! P–Q4 21 N–N5 B–B2 22 P–B4! wins

20 Q×N   P–KR3
21 R–Q1!   KR–Q1

In 21 . . . B×P 22 QR–B1 P–Q4 23 R×P Q–B2 24 N–Q6 wins.

22 QR–B1   QR–B1
23 P–N3   P–N3
24 N–B3!   Q–K2

Black could avoid the coming exchange of bishops by playing his king to R2, but he would still stand very badly after 25 B–K4 threatening Q–Q3, P–KR4–R5 and, if need be, N–N5.

25 B–Q5   K–R2
26 B×B   Q×B (*76*)

76
W

Certain features of this position remind us of Smyslov's game against Rudakovsky in volume 1. However, in that game he could not increase his pressure against the QP but won through a K-side attack backed up by a knight on Q5. In the present game, on the other hand, Black's king is well defended, but White's knight can occupy K4 with a direct attack on the QP.

27 R–Q3	R–B2
28 R1–Q1	R–B2
29 N–K4	B–B1
30 R–Q5	Q–N5

Attempting to complicate matters, as passive defence of the QP is futile after 30 ... R2–Q2 31 Q–Q3 followed by P–QN4 and P–B5.

31 R1–Q3

Not at once 31 N×P B×N 32 R×B Q×R+!

31 ...　　　　B–K2

Or 31 ... Q–K3 32 Q–Q2 R2–Q2 35 P–B5 NP×P 34 N×BP winning. After the text move both the backward pawn and the KP fall. The game ended: **32 N×P B×N 33 R×B R1–KB1 34 Q×KP R×P 35 R–Q7+ R7–B2 36 R×R+ R×R 37 R–Q8! R–KN2 38 Q–K8 P–KN4 39 Q–R8+ K–N3 40 R–Q6+ K–B2 41 Q×P Q–B4 42 R–Q1! Q–B4+ 43 K–N2 Q–K2 44 R–KB1+ K–N1 45 Q–KB6 Q–K1 46 Q–B5 P–N5 47 R–B2 Q–K2 48 Q–Q3 R–N4 49 R–K2 Q–B1 50 Q–K4 R–N2 51 Q–Q5+ Q–B2 52 R–K6! 1–0.**

It is more normal for the backward pawn to be exploited indirectly by driving the protecting pieces into passive positions.

77
W

This greatly simplified position (77) comes from Antoshin–Geller, 22nd USSR Championship 1955. It is clear that it would be hopeless for White to

try to win the QBP, and yet the weakness of this pawn is a vital strategic factor. As Black is forced to guard his pawn with his major pieces, these are compelled to remain in extremely passive positions, whereas White's pieces have much more room to manoeuvre. There are two reasons for this great difference in the activity of the pieces on either side:

1. Black's pieces only have two ranks (first and second) on which to move about, whilst White's have five ranks available to them.

2. White can choose to attack the QBP when he feels like it, whereas Black's pieces dare not wander too far away in case the pawn has to be defended.

As a result White has a permanent initiative and Black must remain passive. The remainder of the game, which was by no means faultless, went as follows: **29 Q–N4 K–B2 30 P–R5! Q–K2 31 Q–N3 Q–Q3** not 31 ... Q–B2 32 P–K4! Q×RP 33 P×P **32 Q–N7+ ?** A mistake; he should play 32 P–R6! when Black cannot reply 32 ... R–QN1 because of 33 R×P! Q×R 34 Q×R Q×P 35 Q–B7+ winning a pawn. Although Black then has a passed pawn in the queen ending, White's king is well placed enough for him to win. **32 ... Q–B2 33 P–R6? K–K3?** Black does not take the chance offered. The correct plan is 33 ... Q×P! 34 P×Q R–QN1 35 R×P R×P. If then 36 R–Q6 P–QR4 37 R×QP R–R2 Black draws comfortably, so White's best is 36 P–N4 K–K2 37 R–R6 when he has the better endgame, but the win is very difficult to achieve. **34 R–N1 K–Q2** Black must try to use his king to defend the QBP but this places it in a rather exposed position. **35 Q–N3 P–KB4 36 K–B1 P–R4 37 K–N1 R–KR1 38 Q–N4 R–QB1 39 Q–N2 R–KR1 40 Q–N7 R–QB1 41 Q–N3** White's last few pointless moves were merely to get him past the time-control, so that he could put in some high-powered adjournment analysis. **41 ... R–QR1 42 K–R2!** The king moves closer to Black's K–side pawns, so that any exchange of pieces will benefit him. **42 ... R–QB1 43 K–R3 Q–R4 44 Q–Q3?** Unfortunately yet another serious error. The logical and instructive way of winning quickly is as follows: 44 Q–N7+ Q–B2 45 K–R4 Q×Q 46 R×Q+ R–B2 47 R–N3 and 48 K–N5 with a won ending, or here 44 ... R–B2 45 Q–N8 Q×P 46. Q–N8 with a winning attack. **44 ... Q–R7 45 P–B3 R–B2 46 K–R2 Q–KB7 47 R–KB1 Q–N7 48 R–K1 P–R5!** This counter-attack should save Black. **49 Q–B1 P–R6?** And now White wins because after 50 K×P R–B1 he has the simple defence 51 K–R2 R–KR1+ 52 K–N1 which Geller probably saw too late. Instead, 49 ... P×P+ 50 K×P Q–R6 should draw. **50 K×P Q–N4 51 P–N4 R–B1 52 P×P P×P 53 K–N3 R–KN1+ 54 K–B2 Q–N1 55 P–B4 Q–N7+ 56 R–K2 Q–N4 57 Q–KR1 R–N2 58 Q–R5 K–B2 59 R–B2 Q×P 60 Q×P R–Q2 61 Q–K5+ R–Q3 62 Q–K7+ R–Q2 63 Q–B5 R–Q3 64 R–N2 Q–R5 65 P–N4 Q–R8 66 Q–N4 R–Q1 67 Q–N7+ K–Q3 68 R–B2 Q–R5 69 Q–R7 R–KR1 70 Q–N6+ K–Q2 71 K–N3 R–K1 72 Q–B5+ K–Q3 73 K–B3 R–K5 74 Q–KB8+ R–K2 75 R–B1 K–Q2 76 R–QN1 R–K1 77 Q–KB5+ R–K3 78 P–N5 Q–R6 79 Q–B7+ K–Q3 80 Q–B8+ R–K2 81 Q–QN8+ 1–0.**

In the next game the ex-World Champion based his whole strategy on Black's backward QBP, and when his opponent tried to eliminate this weakness, Fischer had a tactical refutation prepared.

35 Fischer–Barczay

Sousse interzonal 1967, Ruy Lopez

1 P–K4 P–K4 2 N–KB3 N–QB3 3 B–N5 P–QR3 4 B–R4 N–B3 5 0–0 B–K2 6 R–K1 P–QN4 7 B–N3 P–Q3 8 P–B3 0–0 9 P–KR3 N–N1 10 P–Q4 QN–Q2 11 N–R4 P×P 11 ... R–K1 is simplest, and also 11 ... N×P comes into consideration. **12 P×P N–N3 13 N–KB3! P–Q4?** 13 ... P–B4! **14 P–K5 N–K5**

15 QN–Q2   N×N

After 15 ... B–QN5 the exchange sacrifice 16 N×N!? is a serious possibility, but the positional continuation 16 R–K2 is good for White, as a double exchange on Q2 weakens the dark squares in Black's camp, making his QBP even more of a liability.

16 B×N   B–KB4
17 B–B2!   B×B
18 Q×B   R–B1 (78)

78
W

19 P–QN3!

An inexperienced player might consider preventing ... P–QB4 by the drastic 19 P–QN4? but this would be a serious positional mistake. After 19 ... N–B5 Black's weak QBP would be shielded from attack and he would have an excellent game. Another inaccurate move is 19 B–K3 N–B5! followed by ... P–QB4, whereas after the text-move 19 ... P–QB4 fails to 20 P×P B×P 21 Q–Q3 (threatening *22 N–N5*) 21 ... P–R3 22 B–R5! and this unusual pin

gives White a clear advantage. Or 20
... R×P 21 Q–Q3 threatening both 22
B–R5 and 22 B–K3.

19 ...   N–Q2
20 P–K6!

It was by no means easy for Black to
see that this is not the prelude to a direct
attack but a tactical means of
preventing ... P–QB4.

20 ...   P×P

Not of course 20 ... N–B3? 21 P×P+
R×P 22 N–K5 followed by 22 N–B6

21 R×P   P–B4?

Black cannot play 21 ... B–Q3? 22
N–N5 N–B3 23 R×N! winning. The
only possible defence is 21 ... N–N3
but 22 QR–K1 B–B3 23 B–R5! is very
strong, as White can then treble his
major pieces on the QB-file with
decisive pressure.

22 B–R5!

We now realize that the opening of
the K-file was a prophylactic measure
against ... P–QB4. Black's position is
hopeless.

22 ...   Q×B
23 R×B   Q–Q1

Or 23 ... P×P 24 Q–Q3 N–B4 25
Q×QP etc.

24 N–N5   1–0

Not only is mate threatened but also
25 R×P+ K×R 26 N–K6+ winning
the queen.

In the following game Black's
backward QBP is blockaded on QB3
and the defending pieces are forced into
passive positions, after which White
wins a pawn.

36 Hübner–Gligoric

Skopje Olympiad 1972, Grünfeld
Defence

**1 P–KN3 P–KN3 2 B–N2 B–N2 3
P–Q4 P–Q4 4 N–KB3 N–KB3 5 0–0
0–0 6 P–B4 P–B3 7 N–K5 B–K3 8
P×P P×P** 8 ... B×P is better. **9
N–QB3 N–B3?** And here 9 ... N3–Q2!

is the correct move. **10 N×N P×N
11 N–R4**

Immediately controlling the QB5
blockading square. However, the issue
is by no means clear, as in many similar
situations Black's strong bishop on KN2
gives him chances of playing ...
P–QB4 or ... P–K4 under favourable
circumstances.

11 ...   N–Q2´
12 P–N3!

Apparently allowing the freeing
move ... P–QB4. The expected 12
B–K3 is answered by 12 ... N–N3! 13
N–B5 B–B4 when the threat of ...
N–B5 forces 14 P–N3. White's KP is
then blocked so Black can prepare ...
P–K4 by 14 ... P–B3! without having
to fear P–K4.

12 ...   Q–R4

The trouble with the simple 12 ...
P–QB4 is that after 13 B–N2 the
opening up of the position clearly
favours White's active pieces e.g.

a. 13 ... P×P 14 B.QN2×P B×B 15
    Q×B N–B3 16 KR–B1 Q–Q3 17
    R–B3 and 18 QR–QB1

b. 13 ... R–B1 14 R–B1 Q–R4 (or *14
    ...P×P 15 R×R Q×R 16 B.QN2×P*
    threatening the QP and the QRP)
    15 B–QB3 Q–N4 16 P×P winning a
    pawn.

13 B–N2!

The direct blockade by 13 B–QR3
would not be so strong because after 13
... R–K1 Black is threatening ...
N–N3.

13 ...   QR–B1
14 R–B1 *(79)*

As 14 ... P–QB4 still fails to 15
B–QB3 and 16 P×P, Black now
prepares ... P–K4, but although this
removes the blockading QP his
permanently weak QBP still remains
blockaded by pieces.

14 ...   B–B4
15 R–K1   KR–K1
16 B–QB3   Q–N4

79
B

17 Q–Q2   Q–N1

We now see the difference between a white bishop on K3 and QB3. If Black tries to prepare ... P–K4 by 17 ... P–B3 then 18 P–K4! P×P 19 B×P B×B 20 R×B gives Black another serious weakness on the K–file (if 20 ... P–QB4 21 P–Q5 and 22 R1–K1).

18 B–N2   P–K4

If Black remains passive, then White establishes a full blockade by 19 N–B5 followed by doubling the rooks on the QB-file and pressure on the QBP.

19 P×P   N×P
20 B–Q4!   B–B1

Otherwise after 21 Q–B3 threatening P–B4 Black would be forced to play the passive 21 ... P–B3 when the opening of the game by 22 P–K4 would be highly unpleasant for him.

21 B–B5!

The exchange of black-squared bishops favours White, as it gives him more control over QB5. Black cannot avoid this exchange, as 21 ... B–N2 22 Q–R5 nets White a pawn.

21 ...   N–Q2
22 B×B   N×B

Or 22 ... K×B 23 N–B5 with a clear advantage to White. As we shall see in the next section, the isolated pawn couple on Black's QB3 and Q4 is a fatal positional disadvantage with white-squared bishops and major pieces on the board.

23 N–B5   Q–K4 (*80*)

80
W

24 P–K4!

It is much stronger to open up the game in this way rather than concentrate on the single weakness, as White can now combine the attack on the QBP with threats against the black king.

24 ...   P×P
25 B×P   B×B

Much worse is 25 ... QR–Q1 26 Q–R5! B×B 27 R×B Q–N4 28 Q–T followed by 29 R1–K1.

26 R×B   Q–Q4
27 Q–K3   R×R
28 N×R   Q–K4
29 R–B5!   Q–N2?

If 29 ... Q–R8+ 30 K–N2 and Black has in no way improved his position because 31 R–QR5 is threatened and 30 ... Q×P fails to 31 N–B6+ and 32 Q–QB3. However, the best defence is 29 ... Q–K2! when 30 Q–Q4 N–K3 31 Q–K5 P–B4! 32 N–Q6 R–B2 33 R–B3 N–Q1! 34 R–K3 Q×Q 35 R×Q R–Q2 36 N–B4 gives White an endgame advantage which is difficult to exploit. Instead, 32 N–N5! is an improvement in this line and after 32 ... R–K1! 33 N×N Q×N 34 Q–B4 White clearly stands better in view of Black's weak pawns and exposed king position. After the text move a pawn is lost immediately.

30 R–QR5	R–Q1
31 R×P	N–K3
32 K–N2	Q–K4
33 Q–KB3	P–KB4
34 N–B3	R–Q3

Threatening 35 ... N–N4.

35 P–KR4	P–R4
36 N–K2	R–Q7?

If 36 ... K–B1 37 Q–K3! Q×Q 38 P×Q R–Q7 39 K–B3 N–B4 40 N–B4 wins.

37 Q×QBP!	Q–K5+
38 Q×Q	P×Q
39 R–K7!	N–B4
40 N–B3	K–B1
41 R–QB7	N–K3
42 N×P	R×RP
43 R–B6	K–B2
44 R–N6	R–K7
45 N–B3	R–B7
46 N–Q5	P–N4
47 P×P	N×P
48 R–N7+	K–N3
49 N–B4+	K–B4
50 R–N5+	1–0

If 50 ... K–N5 51 N–Q5 wins.

As in the case of the isolated pawn, the backward pawn can be used indirectly as providing an excellent post on the blockading square for a piece, preferably a knight, which exerts a powerful influence over one wing and sometimes over the whole board.

37 Players in Consultation–Nimzowitsch

1921, Nimzowitsch Defence

1 P–K4	N–QB3
2 P–Q4	P–Q4
3 P–K5	P–B3
4 B–QN5	

4 P–KB4 B–B4 5 N–K2 is better.

4 ...	B–B4
5 N–KB3	Q–Q2
6 P–B4	B×N
7 R×B	0–0–0
8 BP×P	

If 8 P–B5 P–N4! 9 Q–K2 Q–K3 followed by ... N–R3–B2

8 ...	Q×P
9 B×N	Q×B
10 0–0	P–K3

White has mishandled the opening. Not only is his QP weak but he is left with a bad bishop. If he plays P×P now or on the next move, the open KN-file gives Black attacking chances. Nevertheless this was the lesser evil, as it would at least offer White some counter-chances against the KP.

11 B–K3	N–K2
12 Q–K2	N–Q4
13 KR–B1	Q–Q2
14 R–B4	K–N1
15 Q–Q2	R–QB1

In his annotations to this game Nimzowitsch praises the following grouping of his rooks on QB1 and Q1, but I feel it is too artificial and prefer the simple ... P–KB4 followed by ... B–K2.

16 N–K1	B–K2
17 N–Q3	KR–Q1
18 Q–B2	P–KB4 (*81*)

81 W

Black now has a markedly superior position and can advance his K-side pawns. White should at least go in for counter-chances on the Q-side by 19 P–QN4! when Nimzowitsch analyses as follows:

a. 19 ... P–QN3 20 N–B5! B×N (*20 ... P×N? 21 NP×P+ K–R1 22*

P–B6 Q–K1 23 R–R4 N–N3 24 P–Q5!
with a decisive attack) 21 NP×B
P–B3

b. 19 ... P–QN4 20 R–B6 K–N2 21
N–B5+ B×N 22 R×B N–N3
followed by 23 ... P–B3.

In both cases Black stands well.

19 R–QB1?	P–KN4
20 N–B5	B×N
21 R×B	R–N1
22 Q–K2	P–KR4!
23 B–Q2	

He cannot play 23 Q×P P–N5 when
the queen is in danger and Black's
attacking lines are opened.

23 ...	P–R5
24 P–R4	P–N5
25 P–R5	P–R3

Black's attack plays itself, whereas
White has no real counterplay. The
strong knight on Q4 supports the
advance of the K-side pawns and at the
same time effectively defends the Q-
side.

26 P–N4	P–B3
27 R–N1	Q–KB2
28 R–N3	P–B5
29 Q–K4	P–B6!
30 R–B1	P×P
31 K×P	QR–B1
32 R–B1	P–N6!
33 RP×P	P×P
34 P–B4	

White's king is in a mating net after
34 R×P R×R+

34 ...	N–K2! *(82)*

Suddenly White has yet another
backward pawn on KB4, so the black
knight immediately blockades it and
joins in the attack on the king. If now 35
R×P N–B4! 36 R–N5 R×R 37 P×R
N–R5+ wins.

35 B–K1	N–B4
36 R–R1	R–N5
37 B×P	Q–N3
38 Q–K1	N×B!

This leads to the capture of both
backward pawns, when the game is
soon over.

39 R×N	R1×P
40 R–R3	R×P
41 Q–B2	R×R+
42 R×R	Q–K5+
43 K–R2	Q×P

And now the pawn falls which had
been in turn guarded by both the
backward pawns.

44 K–N2	Q–Q4+
0–1	

The resulting space advantage is an
important factor in the exploitation of a
backward pawn. For instance, with
black pawns on Q3 and K2 and a white
pawn on Q5, White can double his
major pieces on the K-file, whereas
Black's lack of space makes it very
difficult for him to defend his KP. This
also applies if the black pawns are on
Q4 and K3 and the white pawn on Q4.
It is clear that the further back Black's
pawns are placed, the greater is White's
space advantage.

In contrast, with White's pawn on
Q2 and Black's pawns on Q6 and K5,
the backward pawn can be very strong
as it cramps White's position and there
are dynamic possibilities such as ...
P–K6 creating an advanced passed
pawn.

In many cases there is also another
method of utilizing our space
superiority in play against a backward
pawn. Once we have tied the enemy
pieces down to passive positions, we

choose the appropriate moment to exchange the backward pawn, so that our more active pieces can penetrate into the enemy position. This often lays bare the pawn previously guarded by the backward pawn. A simple example (*83*) will illustrate this:

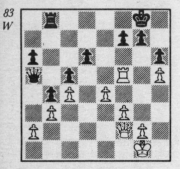

83
W

1 R–Q5 Q–B2 2 Q–Q2 R–N3 after 2 ... R–Q1 White wins by 3 P–K5, a common way of exploiting a pin **3 P–K5! P×P 4 R–Q8+ K–R2 5 R–Q7 Q–B3 6 Q–Q3+** winning e.g. if 6 ... P–K5 7 P×P Q–K3 8 P–K5+ P–N3 9 P×P+ Q×NP 10 R×P+, or 6 ... P–N3 7 R×P+ K–N1 8 P×P Q×NP 9 Q×Q+ R×Q 10 R–QB7 etc. If after Black's first move the white queen were on K3, then the immediate 2 P–K5 P×P 3 R×BP and R×KP is possible.

Just as in the case of the isolated pawn, we must stress that the backward pawn is not a disadvantage under all circumstances. Further examples will show that we can sometimes deliberately bring about a backward pawn and it can have important points in its favour. In specific instances this pawn can block an open file on which exchanges of major pieces might otherwise take place or along which enemy pieces might penetrate into our position. It can support important central squares and its tendency to advance at a given moment forces the enemy pieces to defend against this. For

the backward pawn to be acceptable, two conditions must usually be fulfilled:
1. The pawn must be protected in the simplest and most economical way.
2. Its own pieces must have effective control on the square in front of it.

For example, with white pawns on Q3 and K4 and a black pawn on K4, the backward pawn is best protected by a bishop on K2, with a knight on KB3 or QN3 and a bishop on K3 or QN2. Such a set-up keeps open the option of P–Q4 and makes it difficult for Black's pieces to occupy his Q5 square. A later ... N–Q5 is met by N×N or B×N forcing the pawn to capture, when White's QP is no longer backward and his K-side pawns become more mobile. Once the centre is stabilized in this way, White can often operate on one of the wings or even on both.

38 Smyslov–Suetin

20th USSR Championship, 1952, English Opening

1 P–QB4 P–K3 2 P–KN3 P–Q4 3 B–N2 N–KB3 4 N–KB3 P×P 5 Q–R4+ B–Q2 6 Q×BP B–B3 7 Q–B2 QN–Q2 8 0–0 P–K4 9 N–B3 B–B4 10 P–Q3 0–0 11 P–K4 (*84*)!

84
B

A very good positional move. White's KP controls the important Q5 and KB5 squares and, guarded by the backward QP, sets up a barrier to Black's QB.

White always has sufficient control of his Q4 square and in the further course of the game he operates both on the Q-side (QB-file) and on the K-side (P-KB4)

11 ...   **R–K1**

A prophylactic measure against a possible P–Q4. Black is apparently basing his whole strategy on the backward pawn, but White soon gives him other preoccupations.

12 B–K3   **Q–K2**
13 QR–B1   **QR–Q1**

Both 13 ... N–N5 and 13 ... N–B1 fail to 14 N–Q5. The tournament book recommendation is 13 ... B×B 14 P×B N–N5 15 Q–K2 QR–Q1, but after 16 N–KR4 Black's position is hardly inspiring. Both N–B5 and P–Q4 are threatened, and 16 ... Q–N4 17 N–B5 P–KN3? loses to 18 Q×N! Such an exchange on K3 is questionable on basic principles, as it strengthens White's control of Q4 and gives him attacking chances down the KB-file.

14 N–KR4   **Q–B1**
15 N–B5   **B–N3**
16 P–QR3

This prevents 16 ... N–B4 when 17 P–QN4! N×QP 18 R.QB1–Q1 traps the knight. Black can then obtain three pawns for the piece by 18 ... N×NP but White's pieces are very active and he has a winning attack on the king.

16 ...   **N–N5**

This forces the exchange of black-squared bishops, thus weakening White's control of Q4. However, this strategically correct plan gives White time to set up an immediate attack on the K-side.

17 B×B   **N×B**
18 P–R3   **N–B3**
19 P–B4   **P×P**

If 19 ... P–N3 White continues 20 P×P R×KP 21 P–Q4! R4–K1 22 P–Q5 with a strong attack.

20 P×P   **P–N3**

21 N–N3   **Q–B4+ ?**
22 K–R2   **K–N2**
23 P–N4   **Q–Q5**
24 R–B3   **P–QR3** *(85)*

85
W

White was threatening 25 P–N5. However, after the text move White manages to win a pawn and the game by a pretty combination. Admittedly, Black's faulty queen manoeuvre hastened his defeat, but even other moves would have hardly enabled him to defend for long against White's pressure on both wings.

25 N.B3–K2   **Q–Q2**
26 Q–N2!

Threatening both 27 N–B5+ ! P×N 28 R–N3+ and at the same time 27 P–K5 followed by 28 P–K6+

26 ...   **Q–K2**
27 N–Q4

Forcing the win of a pawn by the threat of 28 N–B5+ . The game ended as follows: **27 ... K–N1 28 N×B P×N 29 R×P R–Q3 30 R–QB2 R–Q2 31 B–B1 P–KR4 32 R–N2 K–R2 33 P–K5 N.B3–Q4 34 N–K4 Q–R5 35 Q–KB2 Q×Q 36 R2×Q K–N2 37 P–Q4 R–QR1 38 N–B5 R2–Q1 39 P–B5 P–N4 40 P–B6+ K–R3 41 N×P P–B3 42 R–B2 R.R1–B1 43 N–B5 N–KB5 44 R–Q2 N–Q2 45 N–K4 N–B1 46 P–KR4 N1–K3 47 N×P N×N 48 N×N N–K3 49 R–K4 R–QR1 50 R–Q3 R–R2 51 B–R3 N–B2 52 P–K6 P×P 53 B×P N–N4 54**

**P–B7 R–KB1 55 R–KN3 R×RP 56
R–N8 R6–R1 57 B–B4 N–B2 58 R–K7
N–Q4 59 R–K6+ 1–0.**

In the Sicilian Defence two systems are frequently used in which Black, as early as move 6, is willing to accept the risks connected with a backward pawn. Countless games have already demonstrated the vitality of both the Opocensky system (1 P–K4 P–QB4 2 N–KB3 P–Q3 3 P–Q4 P×P 4 N×P N–KB3 5 N–QB3 P–QR3 6 B–K2 P–K4!) and the Boleslavsky system (2 ... N–QB3 3 P–Q4 P×P 4 N×P N–B3 5 N–QB3 P–Q3 6 B–K2 P–K4!) In both cases the black set-up is so feared that White's 6 B–K2 has almost disappeared from practice to be replaced by 6 B–KN5 whose main purpose is to prevent 6 ... P–K4.

What ideas lie behind the advance of Black's KP in the above systems? The main point is that Black controls his Q5 and KB5 squares, preventing White from establishing a piece on Q4 which is such an important factor in, for example, the Dragon and Scheveningen variations. In addition, the move ... P–K4 blocks the centre, cutting out White's normal possibility of the powerful thrust P–K5 at some stage. It also allows Black to develop his pieces rapidly (B–K2, B–K3) whilst keeping an eye on his own weakness at Q4. He often succeeds in playing ... P–Q4, thus eliminating his backward pawn and obtaining a clear superiority in the centre. White must usually prevent this by playing a knight to Q5 and if Black can exchange this and force the recapture with the KP, he obtains a K-side pawn majority. A good example of how to exploit such a majority can be seen in the game Pilnik–Geller (volume 3, in the chapter 'Pawn Majority on the Wing')

Finally, the move ... P–K4 greatly restricts White's attacking chances on the K-side and makes it easier for Black to pursue his own attack on the other wing by exploiting his control of the QB-file. It is interesting to note that the latter is usually a more important factor than White's pressure down the Q-file. The reason for this is that Black's backward QP, guarded by his bishop on K2, represents a useful barrier to White's major pieces. As our next examples will show, the ... P–K4 systems of the Sicilian Defence contain a wealth of interesting strategic and tactical problems.

39 Unzicker–Bronstein

Göteborg interzonal 1955, Sicilian Defence

1 P–K4 P–QB4 2 N–KB3 P–Q3 3 P–Q4 P×P 4 N×P N–KB3 5 N–QB3 P–QR3 6 B–K2 P–K4
    7 N–N3

A move which is almost universally played today. After 7 N–B3 P–R3! (preventing 8 B–KN5 with pressure against Q5) White has fewer prospects of active play. If then 8 B–QB4 B–K3! (maintaining control of his Q4 square) 9 B×B P×B and Black has a good game in view of his strong central position (10 N–KR4 K–B2! followed by ... B–K2 and ... R–B1).

    7 ...   B–K2

Nowadays the usual continuation is 7 ... B–K3 8 0–0 QN–Q2. If then 9 P–B4 Q–B2 10 P–QR4 B–K2 11 P–B5 B–B5 12 P–R5 0–0 13 B–K3 P–QN4! 14 P×Pep N×NP 15 K–R1! KR–B1 16 B×N Q×B 17 B×B R×B, Black's QP is still backward but he has counterplay down the QN- and QB- files. After the text move Black reserves the possibility of developing his QB at QN2 if White plays P–KB4. The bishop would then not only control Q4 but also attack the

KP. For this reason, an early P–KB4 is unfavourable for White e.g. 8 0–0 0–0 9 P–B4? QN–Q2 10 B–K3 P–QN4 11 P–QR3 B–N2 and Black stands very well.

8 0–0   0–0
9 B–K3 *(86)*

86
B

9 ...   Q–B2!

The most exact move retaining the option of developing his bishop on K3 or QN2. 9 ... P–QN4 is shown to be bad after 10 P–QR4! P–N5 11 N–Q5. However, 9 ... B–K3 is a playable alternative. After 10 P–B4 Black has both 10 ... Q–B2 and the line 10 ... P×P 11 B×BP N–B3 12 K–R1 P–Q4! with only a minimal advantage to White

10 P–QR4   P–N3
11 Q–Q2   B–K3
12 KR–Q1   R–B1

By putting indirect pressure on the QBP, Black hopes to prevent N–Q5. However, White can now obtain an advantage by the interesting manoeuvre N–B1–R2–N4 increasing his control of Q5. So Black's best here is 12 ... QN–Q2 13 P–B3 KR–Q1! 14 N–B1 N–B4! threatening ... P–Q4. This forces 15 N–Q5 and after 15 ... N×N (worth consideration too is *15 ... B×N 16 P×B R.Q1–QB1! 17 P–B3 Q–Q1* followed by *... N–K1 ... P–R3* and *... B–N4*) 16 P×N B–Q2 with approximate equality.

13 Q–K1?   Q–N2!

Now Black's plan is clear. He has succeeded in controlling his Q4 with both queen and bishop which means that 14 B–B3 is White's only way of preventing Black's central breakthrough by ... P–Q4. However, this would mean disregarding his whole active plan of P–KB3 and Q–B2, and would reduce him to passivity after ... R–B2 and ... R1–QB1.

14 R–Q2   QN–Q2

Not of course 14 ... N×P? 15 N×N Q×N 16 B–B3, or 14 ... P–Q4? 15 P×P N×P 16 B–B3.

15 P–B3 *(87)*

If White tries instead to prevent ... P–Q4 by doubling rooks on the Q-file, 15 ... R×N! reveals the usefulness of Black's rook on the QB-file. After 16 P×R N×P 17 B–B3 P–Q4 18 B×N P×B followed by 19 ... P–B4 Black obtains excellent attacking chances.

87
W

Black can now carry out, under favourable circumstances, one of his main strategic goals in this system.

15 ...   P–Q4!
16 P×P   N×P
17 N×N   B×N
18 R1–Q1   N–B3

Threatening to win a pawn by 19 ... R×P! 20 R×R B×N

19 N–B1   P–K5
20 Q–B2   B–B4
21 B×B   P×B

Not only has Black a K-side pawn

majority to exploit but he can also attack down the QN-file.

22	Q–K3	R–K1
23	P–KB4	

White's queen now blockades the KP but we have already seen what a poor blockader this piece is, in our chapter on 'The Passed Pawn'.

23	...	P–B5
24	P–QN3	

The threat was 24 ... P–B6 25 P×P QR–B1, and after 24 P–B3 White's QRP is weakened and Black obtains a strong-point for his knight on Q6.

24	...	QR–B1
25	P–R3	B–K3
26	K–R2	Q–B2
27	R–Q6	

White's last two moves have not been good, as there is a half-pin exerted by Black's queen on the rook and KBP. However, it is well known that bad positions rarely produce good moves, and White has no active continuation at his disposal.

27	...	P–QR4
28	P×P	B×BP
29	N–N3	B×B
30	Q×B	P–K6!

Threatening 31 ... N–K5 winning the KBP.

31	R6–Q4	N–K5!
32	Q–B3	N–N4
33	Q–N4	N–K3
34	R–K4	P–R4!
35	Q–B3	N–N4

He could also win by the simple 35 ... N×P 36 Q×N R×R, or here 36 R×N P–N4.

36	R×R+	R×R
37	Q–N3	Q×QBP
38	R–Q5	P–K7!
39	R×N	P–K8=Q
40	R×NP+	K–R1
41	Q–N5	Q×P+ !
42	Q×Q	R–K7
	0–1	

The advance of his backward pawn is always an indication that Black's strategy has been successful, but sometimes it is only achieved at a very late stage of the game, as the culmination of Black's plan. This means that the backward pawn remains on Q3 for a long time, without White being able to exploit this fact.

40 Unzicker–Taimanov

Stockholm-Saltsjobaden interzonal 1952, Sicilian Defence

1 P–K4 P–QB4 2 N–KB3 N–QB3 3 P–Q4 P×P 4 N×P N–B3 5 N–QB3 P–Q3 6 B–K2 P–K4
7 N–B3

We shall deal more fully with the better retreat 7 N–N3 when we discuss the Pilnik–Geller game. Theory suggests the continuation 7 ... B–K2 8 0–0 0–0 9 P–B4(?) P–QR4! 10 P–QR4 (*10 B–K3 P–R5 11 N–B1 P–R6*) 10 ... N–QN5! with good play for Black. This last move has a double aim: to control Q4 and prepare action down the QB-file after ... B–K3 and ... R–B1 with pressure on the QBP.

7 ...   P–KR3!

Black must prevent 8 B–KN5 increasing White's control of Q5. Compare this with 7 N–N3 B–K2! 8 B–KN5 N×P equalizing at once.

8 0–0   B–K2
9 R–K1

After 9 B–K3 B–K3 White can no longer prevent ... P–Q4, whereas the text move is played in order to put indirect pressure on the KP after 9 ... B–K3 10 B–B1! The same prophylactic idea lies behind 9 P–QN3 and 10 B–N2, but although this prevents ... P–Q4, it is a typical example of a piece 'biting on granite', as Tartakower aptly put it. The disadvantage of the backward pawn is then more than offset by the passive placing of White's pieces.

9 ...	0–0
10 P–KR3	P–R3!

White's whole plan of development is based on the continuation 10 . . . B–K3 11 B–B1 R–K1 (preparing . . . *B–KB1* and . . . *P–Q4*) 12 N–Q5 B×N 13 P×B N–N1 14 P–QB4. He would then have better prospects than in similar positions, as he could exploit his bishop pair and Q-side superiority. However, Taimanov convincingly manages in this game to refute White's plan. He gives up the idea of an immediate . . . P–Q4 and first completes the development of his pieces in order to begin action on the Q-side. His QB goes to QN2 so as to be able to capture on Q4 with his knight after N–Q5, and also to put pressure on the KP in combination with his attack down the QB-file.

11 B–B1	P–QN4
12 P–R3	B–N2 (88)

88
W

Once again this is a typical position in which the backward pawn can hardly be classed as a liability. Black's plan of campaign is already clear: an attack down the QB-file. White, on the other hand, is not only embarrassed for a good plan but has difficulty completing his development. For instance, after 13 B–K3 R–B1 Black is already threatening . . . N–QR4–B5

13 P–QN3	R–B1
14 B–N2	R–B2
15 N–N1	

After 15 N–Q5 N×N 16 P×N N–N1 17 P–B4 P×P 18 P×P N–Q2 it is White who has the backward pawn. Black makes White's Q-side pawn majority useless by . . . N–B4 and can calmly prepare to advance his own K-side pawns. However, even this unattractive continuation would have been better than the blind alley in which White soon finds himself.

15 ...	Q–R1!
16 N1–Q2	N–Q1!

Beginning a series of manoeuvres which lead to a complete blockade of White's position.

17 B–Q3	N–K3

A splendid central post for the knight where it can move, if required, to QB4, Q5 or KB5.

18 R–QB1	R1–B1
19 N–R2	N–Q2!
20 N.R2–B1	N2–B4
21 N–N3	P–N3!

White's knights now have no strong-points from which they can exert any influence on the game.

22 N–K2

Hoping to persuade his opponent to win a pawn by 22 . . . N×KP? when 23 N×N B×N 24 B×B Q×B 25 N–B3 gives White's knight a strong blockading square at Q5.

22 ...	B–N4!
23 N–QB3	N–Q5
24 N3–N1	P–Q4!

89
W

The decisive culmination of Black's strategy. White cannot play 25 B×N because of 25 ... N×B.

25	P×P	N×B
26	P×N	R×R
27	B×R	B×P
28	P–B3	R–B7!

None of White's pieces has a reasonable move. If, for example, 29 R×P Q–B3 30 R–K1 R×B! 31 Q×R Q×Q 32 R×Q N–K7+ wins.

| 29 | P–QR4 | P–N5 |

| 30 | K–R1 | Q–B3 |
| | 0–1 | |

These last two games illustrated completely different plans by Black. In the first game an early ... P–Q4 opened up lines for an attack on the K-side. In the second game White managed to prevent an early... P–Q4, but in so doing he had to post his pieces so passively that Black was allowed to manoeuvre at will and to prepare an attack down the QB-file.

6 The Isolated Pawn Couple

Let us now have a deeper look at those positions in which an isolated pawn couple (QBP and QP) can be attacked down the open files in front of them. They usually arise when an isolated QP position is transformed by an exchange of knights on QB3. We have already mentioned this in our chapter on 'The Isolated Pawn', and the position Pachman–Sefc (diagram 61) illustrated the disadvantage of such a pawn couple blockaded on QB3 and Q4. Here is the characteristic pawn structure (90):

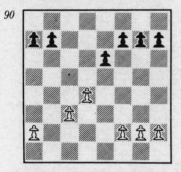

90

We know that White's QBP and QP can represent a serious weakness if they are blockaded then attacked e.g. by . . . P–QN3, . . . B–N2–Q4, . . . N–QB3–R4, . . . R–QB1, . . . Q–B2 etc. The QBP is backward and the opponent usually has a big space advantage on the Q-side, with control of the QB-file and occupation of the blockading squares. Note that the weakness of White's QRP is an extra

disadvantage, especially if it has already moved to R3, as it can then be attacked by moves such as . . . B–K2, . . . N–QB5 or . . . R–QB5–QR5.

The following example is a convincing demonstration of the weakness of an isolated pawn couple, even in a simplified position.

91
W

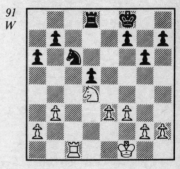

This endgame (91) occurred in Flohr–Vidmar, Nottingham 1936. Black's last move was . . . N–B3, probably played in the hope that the exchange of knights would solve his major problems. The game continued: **30 N×N! R–B1 31 R–B5! P×N** After 31 . . . R×N 32 R×R P×R 33 P–QN4! K–K2 34 K–K2 K–Q3 35 K–Q3 the pawn ending is won for White, as the black king must eventually give ground and allow the entry of White's king. The reader can easily verify this for himself. **32 K–K2 K–K2 33 K–Q3 K–Q3 34 R–R5 R–QR1 35 K–Q4 P–KB4** Anticipating White's intended break by P–K4 and hoping to simplify even more by a double exchange on this square. However, it would have been better to defend passively, perhaps with ... P–B3. **36 P–QN4 R–QN1 37 P–QR3 R–QR1** He cannot play ... R–N3, as it would tie his rook down and allow White to win by zugzwang. **38 P–K4!** It is clearly impossible to bring about a decision on the Q-side, so White opens up a second front in order to weaken Black's K-side pawns. He will finally gain the upper hand on this wing because Black's passively placed pieces are too far away from the future scene of action. **38 ... BP×P 39 P×P P×P 40 K×P R–R2 41 K–B4 P–R3** White was threatening K–N5–R6. **42 P–KR4! K–K3 43 K–N4 R–R1 44 P–R5! P–N4 45 P–N3 R–R2 46 K–B3 R–R1 47 K–K4 R–R2 48 K–Q4 K–Q3 49 K–K4 K–K3 50 R–K5+!** The decisive manoeuvre. If Black's king retreats, then 51 K–B5 wins, and otherwise White's rook penetrates to the eighth rank. **50 ... K–Q3 51 R–K8 P–B4** or 51 ... R–K2+ 52 R×R K×R 53 K–K5 wins **52 R–Q8+ K–B3** or 52 ... K–B2 53 R–KR8 etc. **53 R–QB8+ K–N3 54 R×P R–R2 55 R–K5 K–B3 56 R–K6+ K–N4 57 K–B5 R–KB2+ 58 R–KB6 1–0.**

The above example is a model of how to play against an isolated pawn couple, and our next two games are also classics in this respect.

41 Rubinstein–Salve

Karlsbad 1911, Queen's Gambit

1 P–Q4 P–Q4 2 P–QB4 P–K3 3 N–QB3 P–QB4 4 BP×P KP×P 5 N–B3 N–KB3 6 P–KN3 N–B3 7 B–N2 P×P 7 ... B–K2 is better. **8 KN×P Q–N3 8** ... B–QB4! **9 N×N! P×N 10 0–0   B–K2** 10 ... B–K3, aiming for ... P–QB4, is better. Then, according to Kmoch,

the following variation is possible: 11 N–R4 Q–N4 12 B–K3 P–B4 13 B–N5 B–K2 14 B×N B×B 15 B×P R–Q1 16 P–K4 0–0 with counterplay for the pawn. White has more prospects with the plan beginning 11 P–K4!

11 N–R4

This is the normal blockading procedure, but even better is the tactical 11 P–K4 P×P 12 B–K3! Q×P 13 N×P 0–0 14 B–Q4 Q–R6 15 B×N B×B 16 N×B+ P×N 17 Q–R5 with a dangerous attack.

11 ...   Q–N4
12 B–K3   0–0?

After this routine move Black has no chances of preventing the following deadly blockade. It was still essential to play 12 ... B–K3 e.g. 13 R–B1 N–Q2! 14 Q–B2 R–QB1!

13 R–B1   B–KN5
14 P–B3   B–K3 (92)

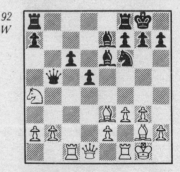

92
W

15 B–B5!

We saw a similar idea in game 36, but here White plans a systematic attack against Black's QBP.

15 ...	**KR–K1**
16 R–KB2!	**N–Q2**
17 B×B	**R×B**
18 Q–Q4	**R2–K1**
19 B–B1!	**R.K1–QB1**
20 P–K3	**Q–N2**
21 N–B5	**N×N**
22 R×N	**R–B2**
23 R2–B2	

Continuing his attack on the QBP. We now see the point of P–B3, R–B2 and P–K3, as the rook not only attacks the BP but also guards the QNP. If 23 ... QR–N1 White can simply play 24 P–QR3 and 25 P–QN4. Consequently, Black has no way of posting his pieces more actively and can only await events.

23 ...   **Q–N3**
24 P–QN4

Threatening 25 P–N5 R1–QB1 26 P×P R×P 27 R×R R×R 28 R×R Q×R 29 Q×RP.

24 ...   **P–QR3**

No better is 24 ... R1–QB1 25 P–N5! B–Q2 (if *25 ... P×P? 26 R×R R×R 27 Q×Q wins*) 26 Q–B3 followed by P–QR4–5.

25 R–R5   **R–N1**

Or 25 ... Q×Q 26 P×Q B–B1 27 R×QP!

26 P–QR3   **R–R2**
27 R×BP!

Finally the pawn is captured and White won quickly as follows: **27 ... Q×R.B3 28 Q×R R–R1 29 Q–B5 Q–N2 30 K–B2 P–R4 31 B–K2 P–N3 32 Q–Q6 Q–B1 33 R–B5 Q–N2 34 P–KR4 P–R4 35 R–B7 Q–N1 36 P–N5 P–R5 37 P–N6 R–R4 38 P–N7! 1–0.**

42 Thomas–Alekhine

Baden-Baden 1925, Alekhine's Defence

1 P–K4 N–KB3 2 P–Q3 P–B4 3 P–KB4(?) N–B3 4 N–KB3 P–KN3 5 B–K2 B–N2 6 QN–Q2 P–Q4 7 0–0–0 8 K–R1 P–N3 9 P×P? Q×P 10 Q–K1 B–N2 11 N–B4 N–Q5 12 N–K3 Q–K3 13 B–Q1 N–Q4 14 N.B3×N if 14 N.K3×N Q×N 15 Q×P KR–K1 16 Q–N5 N×N 17 B×N Q×Q 18 P×Q B×B 19 P×B R–K7 etc. **14 ... P×N 15 N×N Q×N 16 B–B3 Q–Q2 17 B×B Q×B 18 P–B4** otherwise the QBP would be very weak **18 ... P×Pep**

19 P×P   **QR–B1**

Black's first, none-too-difficult task is to force P–Q4.

20 B–N2?

A hopeless square for the bishop which is practically reduced to the status of a pawn, but White has a clearly inferior position even after the better 20 B–Q2.

20 ...   **KR–Q1**
21 R–B3   **B–B3**
22 P–Q4

White cannot avoid this move e.g. 22 Q–Q2 Q–B3 23 R–QB1 Q–R5 24 B–R1 R–Q4 with a tremendous positional advantage to Black. (25 P–B4? R×BP).

22 ...   **Q–Q4!**
23 Q–K3   **Q–QN4!**
24 Q–Q2   **R–Q4**
25 P–KR3   **P–K3**
26 R–K1   **Q–R5**
27 R–R1   **P–QN4**
28 Q–Q1   **R–B5** (*93*)

93 W

An excellent example of the successful blockade of an isolated pawn couple on QB3 and Q4. Once again Black plans to tie down White's pieces to defence of the Q-side, and then begin an action on the other wing. This means that an exchange of queens favours him, as it reduces White's tactical possibilities and allows the black king to support the action on the K-side. We can thus criticize Black's last move, for it was more exact to exchange queens first. Alekhine must now force queens off, which is not very difficult in view of his advantage in space.

| 29 Q–N3! | R–Q3! |

Beginning a splendid manoeuvre whereby the major pieces are to be regrouped (queen on QB5, rooks on QR5 and QR3) to attack the QRP and thus compel the exchange of queens.

30 K–R2	R–R3
31 R3–B1	B–K2
32 K–R1	R 5–B3
33 R.B1–K1	

A little trap. If 33 ... B–Q3? 34 R×P! P×R 35 Q×KP+ with swindling chances.

| 33 ... | B–R5! |

An excellent counter, for now 34 R–K5? fails to 34 ... Q×Q 35 P×Q R×R+ 36 B×R R–R3 37 B–N2 R–R7 38 R–K2 B–N6 winning, or 34 R–K2 Q×Q 35 P×Q R×R+ 36 B×R B–N6 etc.

| 34 R–KB1 | Q–B5 *(94)* |

94
W

| 35 Q×Q | |

Otherwise the above-mentioned manoeuvre ... R–R5 and ... R3–R3 will follow. Such a regrouping of the major pieces is typical of play against this weak complex of pawns.

35 ...	R×Q
36 P–R3	B–K2
37 R.B1–QN1	B–Q3
38 P–N3	K–B1

Black cannot yet win a pawn by 38 ... R5–R5, as his QNP would be

attacked, so he first brings his king across to QB3, forcing White's rooks into complete passivity on QR1 and QR2.

39 K–N2	K–K2
40 K–B2	K–Q2
41 K–K2	K–B3
42 R–R2	R5–R5
43 R1–QR1	K–Q4
44 K–Q3	R3–R4
45 B–B1	P–QR3
46 B–N2	P–R4!

The final phase, as in Flohr–Vidmar. Black is aiming to break through to the K-side by ... P–B3 and ... P–K4, but he first compels White to play P–R4 to prevent his threatened 47 ... P–R5, thus providing a square for his rook on KN5.

47 P–R4	P–B3!
48 B–B1	P–K4
49 BP×P	P×P
50 B–N2	

Or 50 P×P B×KP 51 R–KN2 R–KN5 wins.

50 ...	P×P
51 P×P	P–N5!
52 P×P	R×R
53 P×R	R×B
0–1	

In the following example *(95)* from Gligoric–Uhlmann, Hastings 1966–7, one of the isolated pawn couple was even a passed pawn, yet White could not avoid a clear positional disadvantage.

95
W

White should play an immediate 19 P–QR4! when after 19 ... P×P the removal of the blockade is more important than the fact that Black has an outside passed pawn. If Black does not capture the RP then 20 P×P P×P makes his QNP just as weak as White's QBP. This is a possibility worth noting for similar positions!

However, in the actual game White played **19 B×N** probably expecting 19 ... B×B 20 N–N4 Q–Q3 21 N×B+ Q×N 22 P–QR4! with full equality, but Black has a stronger move **19 ... P×B! 20 N–B3** or 20 Q–B3 Q×Q! 21 N×Q KR–B1 22 KR–B1 B–R3! 23 R–B2 R–B5! and 24 ... R1–QB1 **20 ... Q–B5 21 N–Q2 Q–R5** radically preventing P–QR4 **22 Q–Q3 QR–B1 23 KR–N1** if 23 KR–B1 B–R3 **23 ... KR–Q1 24 R–N4?** Better was 24 R–N3! and White might just hold the position. **24 ... Q–R4 25 N–B1 R–Q2 26 P–QR4** if 26 N–K3 R2–B2 27 N–Q5 R×P! wins **26 ... B–B1!** but not 26 ... R2–B2 27 Q–N1! and Black's advantage disappears! **27 R–N3 R2–B2 28 N–K3** The QBP is lost and with it the game. **28 ... R×P 29 R×R R×R 30 Q–K4 K–N2 31 N–Q5 R–B3 32 P–N4 R–K3 33 Q–B3 P×P** Now this outside passed pawn easily wins. **34 N–K3 P–R6 35 P–Q5 R–K1 36 Q–K2 B–B4 37 Q–Q3 Q–N5 38 K–N2 R×N! 0–1.**

For the player with the isolated pawn couple the most important strategic aim is to break the blockade, and in our next example, Taimanov–Karpov, Moscow 1973, Black thinks that it is even worth a pawn to maintain the blockade.

It seems that Black cannot prevent P–B4 after which he will even stand worse in view of the following threat of B–B4. So Karpov continued: **17 ... R–B5! 18 Q×P Q–B3 19 Q–R3 R–B1 20 P–R3 P–R3 21 R–N1 R–R5 22**

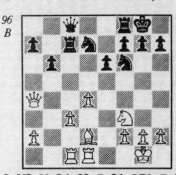

96 B

Q–N3 N–Q4 23 R.Q1–QB1 R–B5 Black has strong pressure for the pawn, and after 24 Q–N5 Q×Q 25 R×Q R–R1 26 R–N2 P–B3 followed by 27 ... K–B2 he would have a definite advantage despite his pawn minus **24 R–N2 P–B3** refusing to go in for the possible drawing line 24 ... N×P 25 B×N R×B 26 R×R Q×R 27 Q×Q R×Q 28 N–K5 N×N 29 P×N **25 R–K1 K–B2 26 Q–Q1 N–B1 27 R–N3 N–N3 28 Q–N1 R–QR1 29 R–K4** After 29 Q–Q3!? Black cannot play 29 ... R×RP? 30 R×KP! K×R 31 Q×N but he can choose between 29 ... N–B1 and 29 ... R5–R5. **29 ... R5–R5 30 R–N2 N–B1 31 Q–Q3 R–B5 32 R–K1 R–R6** Once again 32 ... N×P only draws after 33 B×N R×B 34 R×NP R×Q. **33 Q–N1 N–N3 34 R–QB1?** Better was 34 Q–Q3! when 34 ... N×P fails to 35 R–N3! **34 ... N×P 35 Q–Q3 N–K7+! 36 Q×N.K2 R×R+ 37 B×R Q×B+ 38 K–R2?** He had to play 38 N–K1 when Black obtains a positional advantage after 38 ... N–B5–Q4. **38 ... R×N!! 39 P×R N–R5!** and White lost on time in a position which surprisingly enough is a win for Black. Play might go 40 R–N3 Q–N4 41 Q–B1 Q–B5+ 42 K–N1 N×P+ 43 R×N Q×R and Black has a winning queen endgame.

So far we have only examined the isolated pawn couple on QB3 and Q4 in positions where the opponent has managed to prevent P-QB4. Such a configuration has been shown to be a clear disadvantage if the blockade is maintained and the resulting space advantage exploited. However, the side with the isolated pawn often succeeds in playing P-QB4, thus obtaining the so-called 'hanging pawns', as shown in diagram 97.

97.

From a strategic point of view this pawn structure (97) is much more complex than the previous one. Admittedly, these pawns can still be attacked along the open lines. For example, the QP can be attacked by moves such as ... N-QB3, ... B-KB3, queen or rook on Q1, and the QBP by ... B-QR3, ... N-QR4, ... R-QB1 etc. In compensation, however, the hanging pawns have real dynamic potential. Even in the case of the isolated QP, the threat of P-Q5 was always a vital factor, so one can easily imagine the latent strength of such an advance in the case of hanging pawns. In diagram 97, we can see the possibility of creating a passing pawn by P-Q5 or, more rarely, P-B5. As Black is forced to defend against these threats, his attack against the pawns is stopped or at least slowed down. Moreover, the hanging pawns control three important central points (QB5, Q5 and K5), and so constitute a definite

pawn centre. Let us consider the plans available to both sides:

White
1. He can post his pieces so as to threaten to create a strong passed pawn by advancing one of the pawns.
2. He can occupy the K5 strong-point with a knight and prepare a K-side attack. His KBP can support this attack by advancing to KB5, either weakening Black's KP or opening the KB-file and making the QP passed.
3. He can, if need be, advance his QRP to R5, either weakening Black's QNP or making the QBP passed and opening up an attack on Black's QRP.

Black
1. By effectively posting his pieces (e.g. bishops on QN2 and K2, knight on KB3) he can either prevent the advance of the hanging pawns or prepare to blockade any passed pawn that may be created (e.g. after P-Q5, Black can exchange pawns and play ... N-K1-Q3).
2. He can attack one of the pawns with his pieces at a suitable moment in order to tie down the opponent's pieces to defence.
3. He can meanwhile prepare a pawn attack by ... P-K4 or ... P-QN4. If the pawn is captured, this will isolate one of the hanging pawns, whilst if it is by-passed (P-Q5 or B5) the resulting passed pawn can be blockaded and an attack directed at his colleague which has now become backward.

The following examples illustrate the possibilities available to both sides in various positions.

43 Barcza–Golombek

Stockholm-Saltsjobaden interzonal 1952, Queen's Indian Defence

1 P–QB4 N–KB3 2 P–Q4 P–K3 3 N–KB3 P–QN3 4 P–K3 B–N2 5 B–Q3 B–K2 6 0–0 0–0 7 N–B3 P–Q4 8 P–QN3 P–B4 9 Q–K2 BP×P 10 KP×P N–B3

11 R–Q1

White is already preparing the P–Q5 break-through in case Black exchanges pawns. Golombek should play now or on the next move ... N–QN5 in order to force B–N1, temporarily shutting in the rook at QR1.

11 ...	**R–B1**
12 B–N2	**R–K1(?)**
13 QR–B1	**P×P(?)**

Black already stands worse, for 13 ... N–QN5 would now be pointless e.g. 14 B–N1 P×P 15 P×P B–R3 16 N–K4, or here 16 N–QN5 B×N 17 P×B when the strong-point on QB6 is more important than Black's blockading square on Q4. After the text move and Black's next careless move, White can begin a direct attack by a central break-through

14 P×P	**Q–B2** (98)

98
W

15 P–Q5!	**P×P**
16 N×P!	

A frequent method of play in such positions. Sooner or later Black is forced to exchange his valuable defensive knight on KB3 for White's knight on Q5, at the same time opening the long black diagonal for White's QB.

16 ...	**Q–N1**
17 Q–Q2	

Even stronger is 17 B–N1! threatening 18 B×N followed by 19 Q–Q3. After 17 ... N×N 18 P×N B–B3 White wins by 19 Q–B2 B×B 20 P×N! B×R 21 Q×P+ K–B1 22 Q–R8+ K–K2 23 R–Q7+ and mate in 3 moves.

17 ...	**N×N**
18 P×N	**N–N5**
19 B–K4	**R×R**
20 R×R	**R–Q1?**

Black could have put up longer resistance with 20 ... B–KB1 although he would be forced to sacrifice the exchange after 21 N–N5 (*21 ... R×B 22 N×R N×QP*) because 21 ... P–KR3 loses to 22 B–R7+! K–R1 23 B–B5! P×N 24 Q×P

21 Q–Q4	**P–B3**

Or 21 ... B–KB1 22 B×P+! K×B 23 Q–R4+ K–N1 24 N–N5 etc.

22 B×P+!	**K×B**
23 Q–K4+!	**K–N1**

Or 23 ... K–R1 24 N–N5! P×N 25 Q×B

24 Q×B	**N×QP**
25 Q–K6+	**K–R1**
26 Q–R3+	**K–N1** (99)

99
W

27 N–N5!	**P×N**
28 Q–K6+	**1–0**

If 28 ... K–R2 29 Q–B7 R–N1 30 Q–R5 mate.

This game was decided by the break-through beginning with P–Q5. In our next game the K-side attack is carried out without this thrust, but the hanging pawns prove their worth by controlling the central squares and restricting Black's activity because of the constant threat of P–Q5.

44 Botvinnik–Chekhover

Moscow 1935, Reti Opening

1 N–KB3 P–Q4 2 P–B4 P–K3 3 P–QN3 N–KB3 4 B–N2 B–K2 5 P–K3 0–0 6 B–K2 P–B3? 6 ... P–B4! 7 0–0 QN–Q2 8 N–B3 P–QR3 9 N–Q4 P×P? 9 ... P–B4! 10 P×P N–B4 11 P–B4! Q–B2 12 N–B3 R–Q1 13 Q–B2 N4–Q2 14 P–Q4 P–B4 15 N–K5 P–QN3 16 B–Q3 P×P 17 P×P B–N2 *(100)*

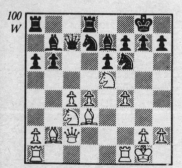

100
W

The hanging pawns very much favour White in this situation. Although Black's pieces effectively prevent P–Q5, White has K5 well under his control and P–KB5 represents a serious and permanent threat.

18 Q–K2   N–B1

To counter 19 P–KB5 with 19 ... R×P! 20 N–Q5 R×N giving up the exchange for both the hanging pawns.

White can now choose between the two following plans:

1. He can prepare P–KB5 by 19 QR–Q1 and B–N1.
2. He can leave his QBP, QP and KBP where they are for the moment and launch an attack with the pieces by bringing his QN over to KN5.

Botvinnik opts for the second plan, the strength of which is apparent within a few moves.

19 N–Q1   R–R2

This and Black's next move are very artificial. The probable intention is to play the queen to QR1 and use the rook to defend the second rank, but it is all too slow. However, even after more natural moves such as ... QR–B1 Black could not achieve much. If 19 ... N–N3 White can continue with his plan after 20 Q–K3 or can prepare P–KB5 by 20 N–K3, in both cases with the advantage.

20 N–B2   Q–N1
21 N–R3   P–KR3 *(101)*

There is no effective way of preventing White's next move.

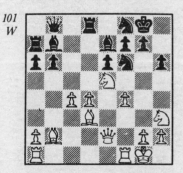

101
W

22 N–N5!   P×N
23 P×P   N1–Q2

He cannot play 23 ... N3–Q2 in view of 24 N×P followed by 25 Q–R5, but now White sacrifices another piece.

24 N×P!   K×N
25 P–N6+   K–N1

Or 25 ... K–K1 26 Q×P N–B1 *(26 ...R–B1 27 QR–K1)* 27 Q–B7+ K–Q2 28 B–B5+ etc. White now completed his splendid attack as follows: **26 Q×P+ K–R1 27 Q–R3+ K–N1 28 B–B5 N–B1 29 B–K6+ N×B 30 Q×N+ K–R1 31 Q–R3+ K–N1 32 R×N! B×R 33 Q–R7+ K–B1 34 R–K1 B–K4 35 Q–R8+ K–K2 36 Q×P+ ! K–Q3 37 Q×B.K5+ K–Q2 38 Q–KB5+ K–B3 39 P–Q5+ K–B4 40 B–R3+ K×BP 41 Q–K4+ K–B6 42 B–N4+ K–N7 43 Q–N1 mate.**

45 Botvinnik–Szabo

Groningen 1946, Queen's Gambit

1 P–Q4 P–Q4 2 N–KB3 N–KB3 3 P–B4 P–K3 4 N–B3 P–B4 5 BP×P N×P 6 P–K3 N–QB3

7 B–B4

In conjunction with move 11, this can be considered the loss of a tempo, but after 7 B–Q3 Black does not have to play ... N×N. He has 7 ... P×P 8 P×P B–K2 9 0–0 0–0 10 R–K1 B–Q2 followed by 11 ... R–B1. By putting pressure on Q5 Botvinnik wishes to force the exchange on QB3.

7 ...   N×N (?)

An imprecise move. It is important to delay this exchange for as long as possible, so that White must plan his development for an isolated QP and not an isolated pawn couple on QB3 and Q4. So Black should first play 7 ... P×P 8 P×P B–K2 9 0–0 0–0 and only after 10 R–K1 continue 10 N×N 11 P×N P–QN3

8 P×N   P×P
9 KP×P

Black has a comfortable game after 9 BP×P B–N5+ 10 B–Q2 B×B+ 11 Q×B 0–0 12 0–0 P–QN3.

9 ...   B–K2
10 0–0   0–0 (102)
11 B–Q3

White aims for a K-side attack as

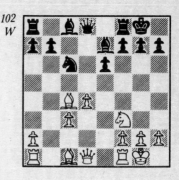

102
W

quickly as possible but he has insufficient resources for this, apart from the fact that this plan neglects his isolated pawn couple. Stahlberg found the correct method of play in his game against Szabo at Helsinki, 1952: 11 Q–K2! P–QN3 12 R–Q1 N–R4 13 B–Q3 B–N2 14 B–KB4 Q–Q4(?) 15 QR–N1! B–QB3 16 B–K5 B–QR5 17 P–B4 Q–Q2 18 R–Q2 and he succeeded in winning the game by the P–Q5 break-through.

11 ...   P–QN3
12 Q–B2   P–N3

It would be a gross error to play 12 ... P–KR3? 13 Q–K2 when 13 ... B–N2 loses a pawn to 14 Q–K4.

13 B–KR6

Too stereotyped! In a similar position (with White's rook on K1 and Black's bishop on QN2) Bronstein played against me (Göteborg interzonal 1955) 14 Q–Q2!? (threatening *15 Q–R6* and *16 N–N5*) 14 ... N–R4 15 N–K5. Now, after the correct 15 ... R–B1! Black obtains a very good game e.g. 16 Q–R6!? R×P 17 B–N2 B–N4! 18 Q×R+ Q×Q 19 B×R Q–R6. Or 16 B–N2 B–KB3 17 N–N4 N–B5! occupying an important blockading square. We can thus claim with good reason that in the given situation (especially after R–K1 and ... B–N2 which Black can force as we showed in our note to move 7) White's attacking chances offer insufficient compensation for his isolated pawn couple.

13 ...   **R–K1**
14 B–QN5

In this way White at least prevents his pawns being blockaded on QB3 and Q4, but the price is high: the exchange of his active white-squared bishop.

14 ...	**B–N2**
15 P–B4	**P–R3**
16 B×N	**B×B**
17 N–K5	**R–QB1**
18 Q–N2	**B–R1**
19 QR–B1 *(103)*	

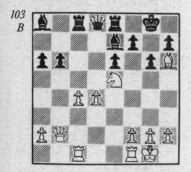

103
B

Black has without doubt achieved a strategic success. White has been compelled to defend his hanging pawns and has only limited chances of a K-side attack, mainly by preparing P–Q5 so as to open up the long black diagonal with N–N4.

19 ...   **P–QN4!**

From a strategic point of view, this is the decisive move of the game. If now 20 P×P Q–Q4! and if 20 P–Q5? P–B3 21 N–N4 P–K4 after which the hanging pawns quickly disappear.

20 P–B5   **Q–Q4**

Even better is 20 ... B–Q4 when Black's queen can go to QN2 to exploit his Q-side superiority.

21 P–B3   **P–B3?**

Black intends to cut off White's bishop on KR6, but this plan is

illogical. His bishop pair and blockade of the QP give him a clear positional plus, so it is pointless to indulge in tactical complications which offer White chances of an active game.

22 N–N4	**R.K1–Q1**
23 KR–Q1	**P–N4**
24 N–K3	**Q–B3**
25 P–KR4!	

Even though Black still has the advantage, the results of his faulty 21st move are already appearing. 25 ... P×P? fails to 26 P–Q5! P×P 27 Q–Q4! with a very strong attack e.g. 27 ... B×P 28 Q–KN4+ K–B2 29 Q–N7+ K–K3 30 Q×RP, or 27 ... Q–K3 28 Q×RP B×P? 29 R×B! R×R 30 Q–N3+ K–B2 31 Q–N7+ K–K1 32 Q–B8+ winning.

25 ...	**Q–K1**
26 P×P	**P×P**
27 N–N4	**Q–N3**
28 R–K1	**B–KB3**
29 R.B1–Q1	**R–Q4??**

A blunder after which the game is even lost. After 29 ... B–Q4 or, even better, 29 ... B–R1 the position is very complex, but Black has in my opinion the better chances. It is unnecessary for the purposes of our theme to analyse the complicated variations which could arise, as Black has already swerved from the logical path with his 20th and in particular his 21st move.

30 R×P!	**B×P+**
31 Q×B!	**1–0**

Black has completely overlooked this move, so he now resigned because he loses a piece after 31 ... R×Q 32 R×Q+, and after 31 ... Q×R? it is 32 Q–N7 mate.

This game shows how important it is to blockade the backward pawn that arises when one of the hanging pawns is forced to advance. However, it must not be overlooked that the advanced pawn becomes passed and this can prove a vital factor.

104
W

This position (*104*) occurred in Szabo–Pachman from the 1952 interzonal tournament. Black had adopted the Tartakower system of the Queen's Gambit, a line in which White can often successfully break up the hanging pawns by P–K4 e.g. 1 P–Q4 P–Q4 2 P–QB4 P–K3 3 N–QB3 N–KB3 4 B–N5 B–K2 5 P–K3 0–0 6 N–B3 P–KR3 7 B–R4 P–QN3 8 P×P N×P 9 B×B Q×B 10 N×N P×N 11 R–B1 B–K3 12 Q–R4 P–QB4 13 Q–R3 R–B1 14 B–K2 N–Q2 15 0–0 Q–B1 16 P×P P×P 17 N–Q2 QR–N1? (*17 . . . P–B4!*) 18 P–K4! P–Q5 19 P–B4 and White stands better. The knowledge of such a manoeuvre led my opponent astray in the above position. Play went: **20 P–K4? P–Q5 21 N.B3–K2** Black also has a good game after 21 N–QR4 N×N 22 Q×N P–KR4! **21 . . . P–KR4! 22 P–B3 KR–Q1 23 P–N3 N.B3–Q2!** White has no time to blockade on QB4 and Q3, and the advance of Black's passed QP is already in the air. **24 Q–Q2 N–K4 25 Q–R6** intending 26

N–B4 threatening both N×RP and N–Q3 **25 . . . R–B3 26 N–B1 R1–Q3!** threatening to trap White's queen by . . . P–N4! **27 Q–Q2 R–Q2 28 P–B4** if 28 N–B4 Black has the strong reply 28 . . . P–B5 **28 . . . N–N5 29 P–KR3 N–R3 30 Q–Q3 R–K3! 31 N–Q2 N–B4!** This knight penetrates into the heart of White's position, as 32 P×N loses to 32 . . . R–K6! followed by 33 . . . R×N. **32 R–K1 N K6 33 P–K5 N3–Q4 34 N–K4 R–B2** Threatening 35 . . . N×BP 36 N×N R×P and 37 . . . Q–N4, so White decides on a desperate piece sacrifice which is surprisingly successful. **35 N×QP!? P×N 36 Q×P R×R??** after 36 . . . Q–R5! White could resign at once e.g. 37 N–B6+ N×N 38 Q×N N–Q4 etc. **37 R×R N×BP** White's threats of N–B6+ or R–B8+ are so strong that Black must force the draw. **38 Q×N R×P 39 R–B8+** or 39 R–K1 K–N2! 40 Q×N P–B4 draws **39 . . . K–N2 40 Q×N R×N ½–½.**

What is the reason for the strategic (if not practical) failure of White's 20 P–K4 in the above game? After 20 . . . P–Q5 White's pieces are not active enough to blockade Black's QBP and QP and then attack them. Black on the other hand quickly succeeded in posting his pieces in such a way that . . . P–Q6 and . . . P–QB5 were always imminent, and in addition his knight occupied a very strong central square at K4. It is therefore important to weigh up the pros and cons of a threat like P–K4 before trying to break up the hanging pawns in this way.

7 The Doubled Pawn

During a game it often happens that two pawns end up on the same file, as a result of the exchange of a piece guarded by a pawn. The concept of the doubled pawn is well-known even to weak players who imagine that it always represents a disadvantage to be avoided at all costs. If such a pawn formation is a weakness, it is an important strategic problem to know how to exploit it. Equally we must be acquainted with those situations in which doubled pawns can be strong.

Every chess player knows that it is much more difficult to create a passed pawn from doubled pawns than it is from connected pawns.

105

This position (*105*), for example, is hopeless for White. Whereas Black can easily create a passed pawn on the K-side, White's doubled pawns always remain blocked on the Q-side. The less experienced player can easily convince himself of this by a little analysis.

White's defeat here is directly attributable to his doubled QNP which creates a situation in which Black is virtually a pawn to the good. If one pawn is moved from QN3 to QB3, the position is drawn.

If we were to add a black pawn on QB2 and a white pawn on KB2, the ending would again be drawn. The difference lies in the fact that the doubled pawn is just as effective as two connected pawns when preventing the advance of enemy pawns. We can draw an important conclusion from this: the disadvantage of the doubled pawn comes to the fore when it advances in an attacking situation, whereas in a defensive position it can be the equal of two connected pawns.

Of course the doubled pawn is at its weakest when isolated with an open file in front of it (e.g. if the pawn structure is: *White* QR2, QB2, QB3, K5, KB2, KN2, KR2. *Black* QR2, QN2, Q4, K3, KB2, KN2, KR2). We have already pointed out that an isolated pawn is a serious disadvantage, and in comparison the front pawn of an isolated doubled pair cannot be guarded or supported in its advance by a rook placed behind it.

Only the increased activity of our pieces can compensate for the clear strategic weakness of an isolated double pawn. In this chapter we shall mostly discuss positions in which the doubled pawn has at least some contact with the other pawns, with the result that its weakness is not so apparent.

The mobility of a doubled pawn is not necessarily limited in every case. With the support of pieces, it is often possible to exchange it off by advancing, and thus exploit our pawn majority. In the following two examples, both sides have a doubled pawn but the difference in mobility is a vital factor in any assessment of the positions.

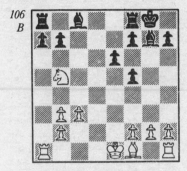

106
B

In the last few moves of this game (*106*), Alekhine–Tartakower, Vienna 1922, Alekhine deliberately allowed his opponent to give him a doubled QNP, apparently nullifying his Q-side pawn majority. Nevertheless, he rightly foresaw that this weakness could be eliminated much more easily than his opponent's doubled pawn complex. The game continued: **15 ... P–QR3 16 N–Q6 R–N1 17 P–QN4! R–Q1 18 0–0–0?** After this imprecise move Black could retain his bishop pair by 18 ... B–Q2! 19 P–N5 B–K4 with complications, so the correct move was 18 N×B at once, with a position similar to that of the game. **18 ... B–K4? 19 N×B R×R+ 20 K×R R×N 21 B–K2 K–B1 22 K–B2 R–B2 23 R–R1** If White immediately tries to eliminate his doubled pawn by 23 P–N5, the position is simplified so much after 23 ... P×P 24 B×P P–N3 that it would be

impossible to force a win. For this reason, Alekhine chooses a more subtle plan, keeping P–N5 in reserve and first attacking his opponent's weak pawns. **23 ... K–K2 24 P–R3 P–B5?** In his attempt to advance his pawns by ... B–Q3, ... P–K4, ... P–B4 and ... P–K5, Black seriously weakens his position. He should play 24 ... B–Q5! followed by 25 ... B–N3. **25 K–N3! R–Q2 26 R–R5! B–B2** 26 ... R–Q4 fails to 27 B–B3 R×R 28 P×R winning. After 26 ... P–B3 27 B–B3 K–Q1 28 P–N5 P×P 29 R×P K–B1 30 R–N6 R–K2 31 K–B4 followed by 32 K–Q3, the advance of White's Q-side pawns decides the issue. Black chooses an active defence to this threat, giving us a dramatic finish. **27 R–R5 R–Q7 28 B–B3 P–N3 29 R×P R×BP 30 B–R5! R×KNP 31 R×P+ K–Q1** Black naturally wishes to retain his connected passed pawns, as 31 ... K–Q3 32 R×P allows White to exploit his Q-side advantage without undue difficulty. **32 B–N4! P–K4 33 R–Q7+ K–B1 34 R–Q2+ R×B 35 P×R P–B6! 36 R–Q5!!** This beautiful move is the only way to win; after both 36 K–B2 P–K5 37 R–Q4! P–K6 38 K–Q1 B–N6 39 R–K4 P–K7+ 40 K–Q2 B–R5, and 36 P–KN5 P–K5 37 R–Q5 P–B7 38 R–KB5 P–K6 39 P–N6 P–K7 40 P–N7 P–K8= Q 41 P–N8= Q+ K–N2 the game is drawn, whilst Black even wins after 36 K–B4? P–K5 37 K–Q4 B–B5 38 R–KB2 P–K6 39 R×P P–K7. **36 ... P–K5** or 36 ... P–B7 37 R–Q1 P–K5 38 K–B2 and White wins by blockading the pawns on the white squares **37 R–KB5 B–N6 38 P–KN5 K–Q2** 38 ... P–K6 39 R×P P–K7 40 R–K3 wins **39 P–N6 K–K3 40 P–N7 K×R 41 P–N8=Q B–B5 42 Q–B7+ K–N5** or 42 ... K–K4 43 P–B4! **43 Q–N6+ B–N4 44 Q×KP+ K–N6 45 Q–N6 K–N5 46 Q×P 1–0.**

Our next game shows even more

clearly the difference in mobility of doubled pawns on each side. White's doubled pawn remains blocked until the end of the game and represents a decisive positional disadvantage.

46 Podgorny–Pachman

Czechoslovak Championship 1954, Grünfeld Defence

1 P–Q4 N–KB3 2 P–QB4 P–KN3 3 N–QB3 P–Q4 4 P×P N×P 5 P–K4 N–N3 6 B–K3 B–N2 7 Q–Q2(?) 0–0 8 R–Q1 P–K4 9 N–B3? 9 P×P Q×Q+ 10 R×Q B×P *9 ... B–N5 10 P×P Q×Q+ 11 R×Q N–B3 12 B–K2 B×N 13 P×B* 13 B×B N×P 14 B–K2 N4–B5 13 ... N×P 14 B×N RP×B (*107*)

Black's pressure down the QR-file will force White to play P–QR3 after which Black's doubled pawn can easily be eliminated by ... P–QN4–5. White, on the other hand, will find it almost impossible to create a passed pawn by advancing his K-side pawn majority. From a tactical point of view, it is important to note that White cannot play 15 N–Q5 P–QB3! 16 N×P R×P 17 P–B4? B–R3! 18 P×N B×R+ 19 K×B R×P+ winning.

15 0–0   P–QB3
16 R1–Q1

An immediate 16 P–B4 fails to 16 ... B–R3, but now this is a serious threat.

16 ...   P–KN4!

It was very tempting to blockade the pawns by 16 ... B–R3, but this bishop has a vital part to play on the KB1–QR6 diagonal, supporting the advance of the QNP.

17 P–QR3   P–N4
18 N–R2

Heading eventually for the strong-point at KB5, a weakness which Black had to take into account when playing ... P–KN4. As the further course of the game shows, the blockade of White's doubled pawns is a much more important factor than the weakness of this square.

18 ...	KR–K1
19 N–N4	B–B1
20 N–B2	B–B4
21 N–K3	K–B1!
22 N–B5	P–QN5

The first stage has been reached. Black must now improve the placing of his pieces before beginning the advance of his Q-side pawns.

23 P×P	B×NP
24 R–Q4	B–B4
25 R4–Q2	R–R7!

Now the importance of Black's 21 ... K–B1! is clear. His QR is freed from having to defend the back rank

26 P–R4!

Pursuing the correct strategic plan of lifting the blockade of his doubled pawns, a plan which Black refutes only by a hair's breadth.

26 ...   B–N5

Of course 26 ... P×P was out of the question, as White's whole position comes to life after, for example, 27 P–B4 N–N3 28 B–B4 R–R5 29 P–N3 R5–R1 30 R–Q7 etc.

27 R–B2	P–B3
28 P×P	P×P
29 N–N3	R1–R1
30 N–R5	R–R8!
31 R2–B1	

If 31 R×R R×R+ 32 K–N2 Black

admittedly cannot prevent P–B4, but after 32 ... R–R7 33 P–B4 P×P 34 N×P B–R6 35 N–K6+ K–K2 36 N–B5 B×N 37 R×B R×P! 38 R×N+ K–Q3 39 R–KR5 R×B 40 R×P P–N4 he wins the rook ending even though material is equal. It is clear from this variation that White's plan in the last moves was positionally justified, but as the logical P–B4 just fails, his position can be considered strategically lost from this point.

| 31 ... | R×R |
| 32 R×R | K–K2! |

Otherwise White could play 33 P–B4 P×P 34 N×P B–Q7 35 N–K6+ K–K2 36 R–Q1

| 33 R–Q1 | R–R7 |
| 34 R–N1 | B–Q7! |

Blockading the doubled pawn once and for all, so that Black is now virtually a pawn up. He does not even have to fear the exchange of knights, for his passed pawns on both wings would win for him even with bishops of opposite colour.

35 K–N2	P–N4
36 N–N3	K–B3
37 N–B1	B–B6!

Bringing about an advantageous simplification on the Q-side.

| 38 B×P! | B×P |
| 39 B–K2 | B–Q5 |

If now 40 N–N3 K–K3! followed by 41 ... P–R4 gives Black a quick win, so White comes up with another try.

| 40 R–Q1! | N–N3! |

After 40 ... P–B4 41 R–Q2 Black would of course still win but only after a long struggle. The text move, involving an original pawn sacrifice, wins much more speedily.

| 41 R×B | N–B5+ |
| 42 K–R1 | |

After 42 K–R2 R×B 43 R–Q6+ K–K4 44 R×P R×BP+ 45 K–N1 N–R6+ 46 K–R1 R×P Black is a pawn up and, despite the reduced material,

he wins the game because of the badly placed white king e.g.

a. 47 K–N2 P–N5 48 N–R2 N–B5+ 49 K–N1 R–KN6+ followed by ... P–R4

b. 47 R–KR6 R×N+ 48 K–N2 R–QR8! 49 R×N R–R7+ 50 K–N1 R–R2

c. 47 N–R2 R–KN6 48 N–B1 R–N8+ 49 K–R2 R×N 50 K×N P–R4

d. 47 R–B5+ K–Q5! 48 N–Q2 R–B7 49 R–Q5+ K–K6

e. 47 N–Q2 R–Q6 48 R–B5+ K–Q3 49 R–B2 P–R4 etc.

After the text move Black can reveal the main point of his combination.

| 42 ... | N×B! |
| 43 R–Q1 (*108*) | |

After 43 R–Q6+ K–K2 44 R×P R–R8 45 K–N2 N–B5+ 46 K–N1 P–R4 (*108*) an interesting position arises in which White is helpless despite his extra pawn.

108
W

The doubled pawn restricts the movement of White's king and his rook can undertake no effective action. Black would win by playing ... P–R5 followed by ... P–R6 and ... N–K7+ in any order, when the white knight is lost. Now back to the game:

43 ...	R–B7!
44 K–R2	N–B5
45 K–N3	P–R4!
46 N–K3	R–B8!
47 R–Q6+ ?	

Missing Black's mating idea, but the knight ending is lost after 47 R×R N-K7+ 48 K-N2 N×R

47 ...	**K-K4**
48 R-Q8?	**R-KR8!**
49 N-B4+	**K-K3**
0-1	

One of my best positional efforts whose interest lies in the logical exploitation of White's doubled pawn complex by means of a permanent blockade.

In Novak-Pachman, played at Solingen 1968, I based my whole plan on my opponent's doubled pawn which did not seem such a liability.

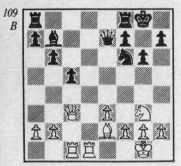

109
B

Is not this position (*109*) completely even? To be sure, Black has two small advantages: his minor pieces are more actively placed than White's and he has a Q-side pawn majority which is more mobile than White's central pawns. However, the position will become simplified after the exchange of the major pieces and what then? Play continued: **19 ... QR-Q1 20 R×R R×R 21 R-Q1 R×R+ 22 B×R** Now 22 ... P-KR4 comes into consideration, threatening ... P-R5-R6, and 23 P-KR3 fails to 23 ... N-K5! because White dare not exchange on K4, so his K-side pawns are shattered. However, White has a good defence in 23 B-B3! B×B 24 P×B when his position is by no means attractive but it

can be held, as the front BP is mobile and can threaten to go to B5 after P-B4. Finally I decided to go in for further simplification which seems to lead to a draw but in reality ensures Black a strategically won position. **22 ... N-K5! 23 Q-Q3** after 23 N×N? Q×N 24 P-B3 Q-N8 the QRP is lost **23 ... N×N 24 RP×N Q-K5! 25 Q×Q B×Q** Black has forced White into a bishop ending which is lost for two reasons: firstly Black has a mobile Q-side majority as opposed to the limited mobility of White's K-side pawns, and secondly White's pawns, especially his pawn on KN2, will be forced to remain on white squares. **26 B-K2 K-B1 27 P-B3 B-Q4 28 P-R3 P-B4!** A general rule can be applied to the bishop endings: you should not place your pawns on squares controlled by the enemy bishop. However, in this position we have an interesting exception to the rule, as Black's last move blockades White's doubled pawns, because 29 P-KN4? P×P 30 P×P would completely ruin his pawn structure. **29 K-B2 K-K2 30 K-K1 K-Q3 31 K-Q2 P-QB5! 32 K-B3 K-B4** even the QBP has gone onto a white square, but only because Black can now advance his Q-side pawns! **33 B-B1 P-QN4 34 B-K2 P-QR4 35 B-Q1 P-N5+ 36 P×P P×P+ 37 K-Q2 B-B3 38 B-K2 B-R5 39 B-B1** White cannot exchange bishops by 39 B-Q1 as the pawn ending is lost after 39 ... P-B6+ 40 P×P P×P+ 41 K-B1 B×B 42 K×B B-N5 43 K-B2 K-B5 44 P-K4 P×P 45 P×P K-Q5 etc. **39 ... P-N4!** the beginning of the end; Black will create an entry for his king on ... Q5. **40 B-K2 P-R3 41 B-B1 B-B3 42 B-K2 B-R5 43 B-B1 B-N4** threatening ... P-B6+ **44 K-B2 P-R4! 45 B-K2 P-R5 46 P×P P×P 47 B-B1 P-B5! 48 P×P B-Q2! 49 K-Q2 K-Q5 50 B-K2 P-B6+ 51 P×P**

P×P+ **52 K–B1 K–K6 53 B–B4 B–B4!
54 B–Q5 K–B7 55 B–K4 B×B 0–1.**

As we stated in our introduction, the doubled pawn is at its weakest when isolated on an open file, and this usually represents a decisive positional disadvantage, practically equivalent to a pawn minus.

47 Smejkal–Smyslov
Wijk aan Zee 1972, RuyLopez

**1 P–K4 P–K4 2 N–KB3 N–QB3 3
B–N5 N–B3 4 0–0 N×P 5 P–Q4 B–K2
6 P×P P–Q4**
   7 P–B4!?   P×P?

A serious error after which Black already stands positionally worse. It was essential to play 7 ... P–QR3! when 8 P×P P×B 9 P×N Q×Q 10 R×Q P×P is very good for Black, as his doubled pawn is mobile and his two bishops are strong after ... P–QB4 and ... B–N2. If instead 8 B–R4 then 8 ... P×P! is good, as White has difficulty regaining the sacrificed pawn without giving up his bishop pair e.g. 9 N–Q4 B–Q2 10 N×N P×N 11 Q–K2 N–B4 12 B–B2? B–K3. It is worth mentioning that even without the bishop pair, a strong-point in the centre can compensate for the weakness of a doubled pawn. For instance in the variation 1 P–K4 P–K4 2 N–KB3 N–QB3 3 B–N5 P–QR3 4 B–R4 N–B3 5 0–0 B–K2 6 R–K1 P–QN4 7 B–N3 P–Q3 8 P–B3 0–0 9 P–KR3 N–N1 10 P–Q4 QN–Q2 11 P–B4 P–B3 12 B–N5 Black has the interesting continuation 12 ... NP×P 13 B×P N×P 14 B×B Q×B and if now 15 R×N? (better *15 P×P*) then 15 ... P–Q4 16 R–K2 P×B 17 P×P N–B4 or here 17 N×P N×N 18 P×N B–K3 and he stands very well.
   8 N–Q4!   B–Q2

The sacrificial line 8 ... B–QB4 9 N×N B×P+ 10 K–R1 Q–R5 fails to 11 Q–Q8+! Q×Q 12 N×Q+ K×N 13 N–Q2 N×N 14 R×B N–K5 15 R×P with a clear advantage to White
   9 N×N   P×N

9 ... B×N is out of the question in view of 10 B×B+ P×B 11 Q–N4 etc.
   10 B×P.4   0–0 (*110*)

110
W

It is no exaggeration to state that White's position is already won and the rest is purely a matter of technique. He is virtually a pawn up, and to be frank his task would be harder if Black had a pawn on QN2 instead of the doubled QBP's!

11 Q–K2	**N–B4**
12 N–B3	**B–K3**
13 R–Q1	**Q–B1**
14 B–K3	**R–N1**
15 P–QN3	**R–N5**
16 R–Q4!	

A strategically important move, overprotecting his QB4 square in order to prevent the elimination of Black's doubled pawn. The rook move also threatens 17 B×B N×B 18 R×R B×R 19 Q–B4! forcing the exchange on QB3, when the weak pawns on the QB-file are quickly lost.

16 ...	**P–QR4**
17 R1–Q1	**B×B**
18 R×B	**R×R**
19 Q×R	**Q–K3**
20 Q×Q	**N×Q**
21 P–B4	**P–KB4**
22 P×Pep!	

The correct decision. Despite his passed KP, White would otherwise find it difficult to break through the blocked position. Now his pieces have more space to manoeuvre and Black is still tied to the defence of his weak pawns. The ending is easily won, although it takes a fair time to force resignation: **22 ... R×P 23 N–K4 R–B4 24 P–KN4 R–Q4 25 R–QB1 N–Q5 26 R–B4 P–B4 27 K–B2 K–B1 28 R–R4 N–B3 29 K–K2 K–K1 30 B–Q2 P–R4 31 P–KR3 N–Q5+ 32 K–B2 P×P 33 P×P P–N4** otherwise White wins the RP and then advances his K-side pawns **34 P–B5! R–K4 35 N–N3 N–B3 36 R–QB4!** better than 36 B×RP P–B5! followed by 37 ... B–B4+ **36...R–Q4 37 B–B3 N–N5 38 B×N RP×B 39 N–K4 K–Q2 40 K–K3 R–Q8 41 P–B6 B–Q3 42 N×NP R–K8+ 43 K–B2 R–QR8 44 R–B2 R–R8 45 R–K2 P–B5 46 P×P B–B4+ 47 K–N2 R–KN8+ 48 K–R3 R–KR8+ 49 K–N3 R–KN8+ 50 K–R4 R–KR8+ 51 N–R3 R–KB8 52 P–N5 B–Q5 53 K–N4 B×P 54 P×B R×P** and after a few pointless moves Black resigned.

Very often a doubled pawn seriously restricts the activity of one's own pieces. For example, the doubled pawn created on QB3 and QB4 (in modern openings usually the result of . . . B×N) can hem in White's QB.

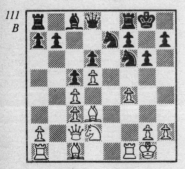

111
B

This position (*111*) occurred in Addison–Hubner, Palma de Mallorca interzonal 1970. White's pawns on QB3, QB4 and KB4 are a barrier to his QB, and this turns out to be the decisive factor. Play went: **13 ... B–B4!** Eliminating White's two bishops whilst maintaining the blockade of the KBP. Black's knights will now be very strong in this semi-blocked position. **14 B–N2** White intends to connect his rooks before returning his bishop to QB1, but it was better to simplify by 14 N–K4. **14 ... Q–Q2 15 QR–K1 QR–K1 16 R–B2 B×B 17 Q×B Q–B4! 18 Q×Q** Otherwise Black's queen can penetrate to QB7. The ending is very favourable to Black, but even the middle game would offer White no compensation for his weak pawns. How different the picture would look with a white pawn on QN3 instead of QB4, as P–QB4 would then give White a clear advantage! Even without his pawn on QB4 White would have better chances than in the game. **18 ... N×Q 19 R2–K2 R×R 20 R×R P–KR4 21 P–N3 K–N2!** After 21 ... R–K1 Black would stand better, but with rooks on he can work on both wings. **22 K–N2 P–R5! 23 N–B1 R–KR1 24 B–B1 K–B1 25 R–N2 P–N3 26 R–K2** essential to prevent the march of Black's king over to QR3 **26 ... P×P 27 P×P N–N5! 28 B–Q2 N–N2 29 R–K1 P–B4!** and now Black has created another strong-point on K5 for his knight. Once the knights are posted on K5 and KN5, Black's king will be free to cross the K-file and penetrate the Q-side. So White is forced to attempt counterplay along the QN-file, in the process giving Black a strong passed pawn. **30 P–R4 K–B2 31 P–R5 P×P! 32 R–R1.** White gets nowhere after 32 R–QN1 R–K1. **32... R–R1 33 R×P P–R3 34 K–B3 N–K1 35 R–R1 N–B2 36 R–QN1 K–K2 37 N–K3 N×N 38 B×N R–R1 39 B–N1 K–Q2 40 B–B2 P–R4 41 R–QR1 42**

P–N4 P–R5 43 P×P P×P 44 R–R3 R–R3 0–1 White resigned after the adjournment, as Black can simply play his knight to QN3 and his rook to K5, winning the QBP.

Our next game is an interesting illustration of the same theme.

48 Spassky–Fischer

World Championship 1972, Nimzo-Indian Defence

1 P–Q4 N–KB3 2 P–QB4 P–K3 3 N–QB3 B–N5 4 N–B3 P–B4 5 P–K3 N–B3 6 B–Q3 B×N+ 7 P×B P–Q3 8 P–K4

Already White is faced with problems, as this move restricts the activity of his KB whilst opening up a line for his QB. We may ask ourselves if the problem of the two bishops can be resolved with the given pawn structure. In the game Vaganian–Katalimov (1971) White played 8 Q–B2 P–K4(?) 9 P×BP P×P 10 N–N5! P–KR3 11 N–K4 P–QN3 12 0–0 B–N2 13 N×N+ Q×N 14 B–K4 N–R4 15 B–Q5 0–0–0 16 P–K4 B–R3 17 Q–R4 with a clear positional superiority. After Black's unsuccessful attempt at sacrificial counterplay 17 . . . R×B!? 18 KP×R B×P 19 R–Q1 R–Q1 20 B–K3 Q–N3 21 B×BP B×QP 22 P–N3 Q–B4 23 P–QB4!, White won quickly. This set-up of minor piece at Q5 (bishop or knight), following the exchange of the QP, is the ideal one with doubled pawns on QB3 and QB4, but in the above game Black's premature . . . P–K4 made it all possible. He should wait with . . . Q–B2, . . . P–QN3, . . . B–N2, until White has played P–K4, maintaining control of his Q4 square by leaving the KP on K3. Games 80 and 81 will illustrate these points further.

8 . . . P–K4
9 P–Q5 N–K2!

We shall see later that Black can

often attack the doubled pawn complex by . . . P–QN3 and . . . N–QR4 followed by . . . P–QN3 and . . . B–R3. However, such a plan is ineffective in this position, as White can protect his QBP comfortably, without limiting the activity of his pieces e.g. 9 . . . N–QR4 10 P–KR3! (to prevent . . . *B–N5*) 10 . . . P–QN3 11 B–K3! (but not *11 0–0? B–R3 12 Q–K2 Q–Q2 13 P–QR4 N–N6*) 11 . . . B–R3 12 Q–K2 Q–Q2 13 P–QR4! and Black's Q-side minor pieces are a long way from the main theatre of war on the K-side, where White will begin an immediate attack.

10 N–R4!

White must act at once on the K-side, as after 10 0–0 P–KR3! 11 N–K1 P–KN4! 12 P–N3 B–R6 13 N–N2 R–KN1, it is Black who has the attack.

10 . . . P–KR3!

Preventing B–N5, but not P–B4 as was once wrongly thought.

11 P–B4! N–N3!

Surprising moves in both attack and defence! If Black tries to win a piece by 11 . . . P+P 12 B×P P–KN4? then 13 P–K5 gives White the advantage e.g. 13 . . . N–R2 14 P×P N–N1 15 B–K5, or 13 . . . N–Q2 14 P×P N–KN1 15 Q–K2+ K–B1 16 B–K5 N×B 17 Q×N Q–B3 18 N–B3, or 13 . . . N–N5! 14 P–K6! (Black stands well after *14 P×P P×B! 15 P×N Q×KP+ 16 Q–K2 N–K6*) 14 . . . N–KB3 15 B×QP Q×B 16 0–0 with a winning attack.

12 N×N P×N
13 P×P?

This is surprisingly enough the decisive strategic mistake. Correct is 13 0–0 0–0 14 P–B5, or 14 P–KR3 followed by P–B5.

13 . . . P×P
14 B–K3 P–N3
15 0–0 0–0 (*112*)

At first sight it is scarcely credible that Black not only stands better but is winning, despite White's protected

112
W

passed QP and two bishops. Every static advantage must be evaluated according to concrete possibilities, or to express this in another way: a position is not advantageous purely because it looks good at a given moment, but only if it can look even better in the future. In the above position, White's game is totally lacking in possibilities. His bishops have no scope and his 'good' bishop on K3 is always threatened by ... N-N5 which cannot be prevented by P-KR3, as this allows Black to attack the king by ... P-KN4-5. The passed QP cannot be exploited, because Black can easily blockade it whereas White's pieces have no way of lending it their support. In the centre both sides must remain passive, and on the K-side only Black can undertake anything. But what about the Q-side?

16 P-QR4   P-QR4

This is the answer, after which the Q-side remains blocked. Admittedly Black's QNP is now backward, but it is no weaker than White's QRP!

17 R-N1   B-Q2

Another good set-up could be reached by 17 ... Q-Q3 followed by ... B-Q2 and ... QR-N1, but Black has other plans for his queen.

18 R-N2   R-N1
19 R2-KB2

This move was criticized after the game, as it leads unavoidably to the exchange of both rooks, after which

White must passively wait to see what Black undertakes. However, it is relevant to ask what else White can do with his rooks, as otherwise Black can always take over the KB-file by ... Q-K2 and ... N-N5.

19 ...   Q-K2
20 B-B2   P-KN4
21 B-Q2   Q-K1

The queen is heading for KN3, to attack the KP and prepare action on the K-side. Black could have played his queen to K1 two moves ago, but time is not an important factor in this position. Note that Black does not need to prevent P-Q6, as the bishop is a reserve blockader and the pawn would soon be lost.

22 B-K1

Aiming for KN3 to put pressure on the KP, although it never gets there.

22 ...   Q-N3
23 Q-Q3   N-R4!
24 R×R+   R×R
25 R×R+   K×R (*113*)

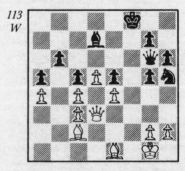

113
W

Imperceptibly but inevitably the end draws near. Apart from the line chosen which loses quickly, White has three possibilities:

a. 26 B-KN3 N-B5 27 B×N NP×B 28 P-Q6 (otherwise Black's blockades and his K-side pawns decide the issue) 28 ... Q-K3 followed by ... B-B3 and ... K-K1-Q2 winning the QP.

b. 26 P-N3 K-K2 followed by ...
K-Q3, ... N-B3, ... Q-R2 and
... B-K1-N3 winning the KP, a
plan which is normally unplayable
because of B-KN3 threatening
Black's KP.

c. 26 P-Q6 N-B5 27 Q-Q2 Q-K3 and
one of White's weak pawns must fall
sooner or later.

26 B-Q1   N-B5
27 Q-B2??

After this blunder Black wins
immediately. White had to play 27
Q-N1 when Black plays his king to QB2
then advances his K-side pawns. White
would be unable to ward off all the
threats on the K-side whilst at the same
time defending his weak pawns on
QR4, QB4 and K4.

27 ...   B×P!
0-1

If 28 Q×B Q×P forcing mate by ...
Q×NP or ... Q×B.

It is often so vital to rid oneself of a
doubled pawn, that a pawn sacrifice is
called for, in order to open lines for the
pieces. The following game is a simple
example of this.

49 Geller-Kramer

Amsterdam Olympiad 1954, Queen's
Indian Defence

1 P-Q4 N-KB3 2 P-QB4 P-K3 3
N-KB3 P-QN3 4 N-B3 B-N2 5 P-K3
B-N5 6 B-Q3 N-K5 7 0-0 B×N 8
P×B 0-0 9 N-K1 P-KB4 10 P-B3
N-KB3 11 P-QR4 N-B3 12 R-R2
N-QR4 13 R2-KB2 Q-K2 14 Q-K2
P-Q3 15 P-K4 P×P 16 P×P P-K4
    17 B-N5!

An extremely unpleasant pin which
gives White good K-side attacking
chances. It is worth noting that Black
cannot fix the doubled pawn by ...
P-B4, as this would allow White to play
his knight to Q5 or KB5 via QB2 and
K3.

17 ...   B-B3
18 N-B2   B-Q2

For the same reason, Black has no time
to capture the QRP.

19 N-K3   P-B3 *(114)*

114.
W

White has a clear positional
advantage, but he needs Q5 for his
knight. If at once 20 P-Q5 then 20 . . .
P-B4 follows. Moreover, the double
pawn limits White's Q-side activity. If
for example his pawn were on QN2
instead of QB3, it would be easy to
continue with P-QN4 followed by
P-N5 or P-R5, or to link P-B5 with
pressure down the KB-file. All this
means that the following break-
through is strategically well justified.

20 P-B5!   NP×P
21 P-Q5!

Black can no longer by-pass this
pawn immediately but must do
something about White's threat of P×P
obtaining either Q5 or KB5 for his
knight. Kramer rightly elects to give
back the pawn in order to keep the
centre blocked, but White has managed
to eliminate his doubled' pawn, so can
begin action on the Q-side.

21 ...   P-B5
22 B×P   N×B
23 Q×N·   P-B4
24 Q-R6!

With the strong threat of 25 N-B4,
against which there is no effective
defence.

24 ...	**B–B1**
25 **Q–B6**	**B–Q2**
26 **Q–B7**	**KR–B1**
27 **B×N**	**P×B**
28 **N–B5!**	

Forcing the win of a pawn, after which the game ended as follows: **28 ... R×Q 29 N×Q† K–B2 30 N–B5 B×N 31 R×B K–N2 32 R×BP R–Q2 33 R–K6 R–QN1 34 P–R4 P–KR4 35 R–B5 R–N6 36 R–N5† K–R2 37 R×RP† K–N2 38 R–N5† K–R2 39 R5–N6 R×P 40 P–KR5 R–B5 41 R–R6† K–N1 42 R.K6–N6† R–KN2 43 R×P R×RP 44 R–Q8† K–B2 45 R6–Q6 R–KN5 46 R6–Q7† K–B3 47 R–KB8† K–N4 48 R–KN7† K–R5 49 P–R6 R–R8† 50 K–R2 R–R3 51 P–R7 1–0.**

In our notes to the above game we did not mention that White even offered a pawn in the opening in order to rid himself of the doubled pawn which he could not avoid after 6 ... N–K5. The move 7 0–0!? offers a pawn and if Black replies 7 ... N×N 8 P×N B×P then 9 R–N1! gives White a dangerous initiative e.g. 9 ... B–R4 10 B–R3 P–Q3 11 P–B5 0–0 12 P×QP P×P 13 P–K4 R–K1 14 P–K5 P×P (if *14 ... P–Q4 15 P–R4!*) 15 N×P Q–N4 16 P–N3 P–N3 17 Q–R4 as in the game Denker–Fine, New York 1944. It was once thought that Black could draw by 7 ... B×N 8 P×B N×QBP 9 Q–B2 B×N 10 P×B Q–N4† 11 K–R1 Q–KR4 12 R–KN1 Q×BP† 13 R–N2 P–KB4 14 Q×N(?) Q–Q8† with perpetual check, but the improvement 14 B–R3! gave White an overwhelming attack in a match game Keres–Spassky, 1965.

Doubled pawns usually arise when a knight is exchanged at KB3 or QB3, so in the rest of this chapter we shall deal with various pawn formations all involving a doubled BP. First of all let us examine positions with pawns on

QB2, QB3 and Q3. Such a formation occurs frequently, as for instance in the Steinitz Defence to the Ruy Lopez (*115*).

115

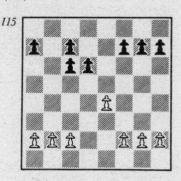

In our chapter on 'The Rooks' in volume 1, we gave a similar diagram, but with a black pawn on QN2 instead of QB3. It was shown there how White could exploit the Q-file by making use of his strong-point on Q5. In the above position, however, the black pawn on QB3 guards this vital square, so the Q-file loses a lot of its strength. Black on the other hand can under certain circumstances exploit the K-file by playing a knight to ... K4. If this is driven away by P–KB4, then White's KP becomes an object of attack. Black can also utilize the open QN-file by ... R–QN1 or ... Q–QN1 with pressure on the QNP. If White plays P–QN3, Black can attack this pawn by ... P–QR4–5 and, after careful preparation, ... P–QB4–5.

From the above explanation, it is clear that the main advantage of Black's doubled pawn complex lies in the control of his Q4 square. After ... P–QB4 he relinquishes this control and allows White to use the square as a strong-point. For this reason Black usually plays ... P–QB4 only when he has sufficient piece control of his Q4 square or when his Q-side action is so strong that White cannot exploit the weakness of this square.

The doubled pawn has its advantages, then, but White also has possibilities of effective play against it. He must strive to lay bare the intrinsic weakness of Black's pawn structure by preparing moves such as P–K5 or P–QB4–5. After ... P×KP or ... P×BP Black is left with an isolated doubled pawn, in the latter case on an open file. Let us consider a few games which illustrate the possibilities open to both sides.

50 Boleslavsky–Fine

USSR–USA Radio Match 1945, Ruy Lopez

1 P–K4 P–K4 2 N–KB3 N–QB3 3 B–N5 P–QR3 4 B–R4 P–Q3 5 P–B4 B–Q2 6 N–B3 P–KN3 7 P–Q4 P×P 7 ... B–N2 is safer, but after 8 B–KN5! White has a definite positional advantage. **8 N×P B–N2 9 N×N P×N** better is 9 ... B×N when White has only a slight edge.

10 0–0   N–K2 (*116*)

In the game Unzicker–Keres, Hastings 1955–6, Black played 10 ... N–B3 when again 11 P–B5! was possible e.g. 11 ... P×P 12 B–K3 Q–K2 13 P–B3 0–0 14 Q–Q2 R–K1 15 Q–KB2 B–KB1. Black retains his extra pawn but White's position is preferable. The

116
W

tripled pawns can scarcely be restrained indefinitely and White has the basis of an excellent Q-side attack.

11 P–B5!

A typical attack against the doubled pawn, in this case playable so early because White has already advanced his QBP on move five and is well developed. The tactical justification of the text-move lies not only in the variation 11 ... P×P 12 B–K3 followed by B3×P but also in the following line: 11 ... P–Q4? 12 P×P P×P 13 N×P N×N 14 Q×N B×B 15 Q–K4+ winning. This means that Black must defend passively, giving White a free hand to prepare action on the K-side.

11 ...   N–B1
12 B–K3   0–0
13 Q–Q2   Q–K2
14 QR–Q1   B–K1

14 ... R–Q1 is a little better, but even then Black stands very badly, as White's QBP exerts a crippling influence.

15 P–B4!   P–B4

Black can of course hardly go in for the win of a pawn as after 15 ... B×N 16 Q×B Q×P 17 B–QB2 followed by 18 P–B5 White's attack plays itself.

16 KP×P   NP×P
17 KR–K1   P×P

Black has no choice if he wishes to bring his knight back into the game, but now he will be left with an additional weakness in the shape of an isolated doubled pawn on the QB-file.

18 Q–KB2   N–Q3
19 B.K3×P   Q–Q1
20 B–Q4!

White could win a pawn by 20 Q–B3 but this would give Black a chance to exert some pressure down the QN-file with ... R–N1. The text move is a much surer way of consolidating his advantage. By eliminating his opponent's only active piece, the bishop on KN2, he forces Black into an ending which is hopeless in view of his weak Q-side pawns.

20 …	B×B
21 Q×B	Q–B3
22 B–N3+	K–R1
23 Q×Q+	R×Q
24 R–K7	R–QB1
25 R1–K1	

There was even a quicker win by 25 N–R4 N–K5 26 B–K6 R–N1 27 B×P, but even now Black has no chances. The game ended: **25 … B–N3 26 R1–K6 R×R 27 B×R R–K1 28 R×R+ B×R 29 N–R4 K–N2 30 N–B5 P–QR4 31 K–B2 B–B2 32 B×B K×B 33 P–QN3 P–R4 34 P–N3 K–K2 35 K–K3 N–N4** or 35 … K–B3 36 P–QR4 K–K2 37 K–Q4 and Black is in zugzwang **36 N–N7 P–B4 37 N×RP K–Q3 38 N–B4+ K–Q4 39 K–Q3 N–Q3 40 N×N P×N 41 P–QR3 1–0.**

Here is a position in which Black has played an early … P–QB4, from the 1954 World Championship Match. Smyslov–Botvinnik (*117*)

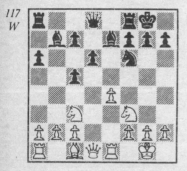

117 W

White must aim for P–K5, but this move does not work immediately because of 12 … N–Q2! 13 N–Q5 N×P 14 N×N P×N 15 R×P B–Q3, or here 13 B–B4 N–N3 followed by 14 … P–Q4. The game continued: **12 B–N5 P–R3 13 B–R4 R–K1** Again 13 … N–Q2! was playable e.g. 14 B×B Q×B 15 N–Q5 Q–Q1 16 P–K5 P×P 17 N×KP N–N3! 18 N–K3 Q–N4

followed by 19 … R–Q1 with active piece play compensating for his pawn weaknesses. Black probably wished to retain his two bishops so allows the exchange of queens. **14 P–K5! P×P 15 R×P!** and not 15 N×P Q–Q5! **15 … Q×Q+ 16 R×Q** An interesting position; after 16 … B×N 17 P×B B–Q3 18 R–B5! White has a clear advantage, for his own doubled pawn can be easily protected by the king, whereas Black's pawn on … QB4 remains weak e.g. 18 … N–Q2 19 N–K4. So Black plays for further simplification. **16 … B–Q3 17 R×R+ N×R** The alternative 17 … R×R!? 18 B×N P×B would give Black two pairs of doubled pawns, and his two active bishops would offer insufficient compensation. **18 N–Q2 B–K4!** The mobile bishops give Black an opportunity to weaken his opponent's pawns, thus achieving near equality. **19 N–N3 B×N 20 P×B P–B5 21 N–B5** or 21 N–R5 B–K5 22 R–Q2 R–N1 23 P–B3 B–B4 24 N×P B–K3 with an even game **21 … B–B3 22 R–Q8** otherwise the black rook occupies the important QN-file **22 … P–N4! 23 R×R B×R 24 B–N3 P–QR4 25 P–B3 P–B4 26 B–K5** Although Botvinnik actually went on to lose this game, he could now draw with 26 … P–B5 27 N–K6 K–N2, or here 27 N–R6 B–N2.

51 Tsvetkov–Pachman

Hilversum 1947, Ruy Lopez

1 P–K4 P–K4 2 N–KB3 N–QB3 3 N–B3 N–B3 4 B–N5 P–Q3 5 P–Q4 B–Q2 6 0–0 P×P 7 N×P B–K2 8 B×N P×B

9 P–B3

An unusual continuation. The best plan is to fianchetto the QB by 9 P–QN3 and 10 B–N2, for if Black later plays … P–QB4, then N–Q5 opens up the long diagonal for White's bishop.

Black's defence is at all events more difficult than after the customary 9 R–K1 0–0 10 B–N5 R–K1. Here are two examples from the Schlechter–Lasker match to show how play might go in this case.

a. 11 Q–B3 P–KR3 12 B–R4 N–R2 13 B×B Q×B 14 QR–Q1 N–B1 15 P–KR3 N–N3 16 Q–N3 Q–N4 17 Q×Q P×Q 18 P–B3 P–B3 19 K–B2 K–B2 20 N4–K2 P–QR4 21 P–QN3 R.K1–QN1 22 N–B1 B–K3 23 N–Q3 P–QB4 24 N–N2 (this knight admittedly prevents ... P–QB5 or ... P–QR5 but White cannot now use it for action in the centre and on the K-side) 24 ... N–K4 25 N–Q5 R–N2 26 R–K3 N–B3 with an even game.

b. 11 Q–Q3 N–N5 12 B×B Q×B 13 N–B3 QR–N1 14 P–QN3 N–K4 15 N×N Q×N 16 Q–K3 Q–QR4 17 Q–Q3 R–K2 18 R–K3 R1–K1 19 R1–K1 P–B3 20 P–KR3 B–K3 21 N–R4 B–B2 22 P–QB4 P–KR3 23 N–B3 K–R1 24 Q–Q2 B–N3 25 R1–K2 B–B2 26 Q–Q4 Q–N3 27 Q–Q2 Q–R4 and the game was drawn by repeating moves.

In the first example Lasker used his doubled pawn in an attacking position (QB2, QB4) and in the second he preferred the defensive formation (QB2, QB3).

9 ...   **0–0**
10 B–K3   **R–K1**

118 W

11 Q–Q2   **Q–N1!** (*118*)

Black begins to attack on the Q–side by forcing P–QN3 then preparing ... P–QR4–5 and ... P–QB4–5, whilst White's chances lie in the centre.

12 P–QN3   **P–QR4**
13 N4–K2   **Q–N5!**

After White's next move, this may seem like a loss of time. However, White's natural plan is 14 P–KN4 followed by 15 N–N3 which he now foregoes. The black queen is especially well posted on QN5, since after ... P–QB4 the move N–Q5 would allow the exchange of queens.

14 N–B4

This looks strong, as it threatens 15 N–Q3 followed by 16 P–K5, a logical thrust. Black's next move, however, prevents this idea.

14 ...   **Q–N2!**
15 QR–Q1

Black obtains good play after 15 N–Q3 B–K3 16 P–K5 N–Q2 17 B–B4 (*17 P×P P×P*) 17 ... P–Q4.

15 ...   **R.K1–Q1**
16 Q–B2   **B–KB1**
17 R–Q3   **P–B4**

Correctly timed, as ... P–B5 will gain a tempo by attacking the rock. White should now try to simplify with 18 N4–Q5.

18 R1–Q1   **R–K1**

This rook went to Q1 in order to prevent P–K5, but now that White's queen has left the Q–file and the rooks are doubled on it, the rook returns to its normal square on K1. White could still attain approximate equality after 19 N4–Q5 N×N 20 N×N P–R5. Instead he attempts a strategically unjustified attack on the king. As Black has no weaknesses on the K-side at the moment, White will require so much time to create serious threats, that his Q-side must in the meantime succumb to Black's attack.

19 P–KN4?   **B–B3**

20 P–N5	N–Q2
21 Q–N3	P–R5
22 R3–Q2	P× P
23 RP× P	R–R6! *(119)*

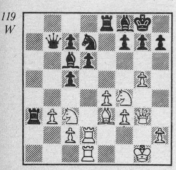

119
W

Black now threatens 24 ... P–B5

24 N4–Q5	R–K3

Preventing the possibilities arising after 25 N–B6+

25 P–R4	B× N
26 N× B	P–B5!

Winning a pawn, which should be enough to decide the game. White cannot play 27 P× P in view of 27 ... P–QB3 28 N–B4 R× B 29 N× R P× N 30 Q–N4 N–B4 winning.

27 B–Q4	P× P
28 P× P	R× NP
29 P–R5	N–K4??

This move cost me first place in the zonal tournament (the game was played in the last round), and with it the logical thread of the game is lost. The correct winning move is 29 ... R× KP! e.g. 30 N–B6+ N× N 31 P× N R× B 32 R× R R× P 33 Q–N2 Q–N6 etc. I had seen this variation clearly but at the last moment allowed myself to be intimidated by the line 30 B× P? B× B?? 31 N–B6+ winning, completely overlooking that I could simply capture the bishop with my king, after which White has nothing.

30 B× N	R× B
31 P–R6	R–N8

Or 31 ... R–K3 32 P× P B× P 33

N–B6+ K–R1 34 R–KR2! B× N 35 P× B R3× BP 36 Q–R4, or here 32 ... K× P! 33 N–B6, with a decisive attack for White in both cases.

32 P× P	B× P

Still overlooking the threat, but 32 ... K× P loses to 33 Q–R4!

33 N–B6+	K–R1
34 Q× R!	1–0

Similar strategic problems arise when the doubled pawn is on the K–side, with a pawn complex on K3, KB2 and KB3. If both players castle long, the situation is exactly the same as the one we have discussed, but if the king remains with the pawns, matters are more complicated. In certain circumstances the doubled pawn constitutes a serious weakening of the king's position, but there is also the possibility of using the open KN–file to attack the enemy king. Here are two examples of the doubled KBP when both sides castle short.

52 Smyslov–Stahlberg

Budapest Candidates' 1950, French Defence

1 P–K4 P–K3 2 P–Q4 P–Q4 3 N–QB3 N–KB3 4 B–N5 P× P 5 N× P B–K2

6 B× N	B× B

After 6 ... P× B we have a similar situation to the one with the doubled QBP e.g. 7 N–KB3 N–Q2 8 Q–Q2 *(8 B–B4 is more active)* 8 ... R–KN1 9 0–0–0 N–B1 10 P–B4 P–B3 11 P–KN3 Q–B2 12 B–N2 P–N3 13 KR–K1 B–N2 14 K–N1 0–0–0 15 N–B3 K–N1 16 Q–K3 N–N3 17 P–KR4 P–KB4! 18 N–K5 P–B5! 19 Q–B3 N× N 20 P× N P× P 21 P× P B–N5 22 P–R3 B× N 23 Q× B P–QB4 24 B× B Q× B 25 R–Q6 R× R 26 P× R R–Q1 27 R–Q1 Q–K5+ 28 K–R2 R–Q2 ½–½ (Nimzowitsch–Perlis, Ostend 1907). In this game Black had an easy time because White made no attempt to exploit the weakness of the doubled pawn by preparing P–Q5 or P–KB4–5.

7 N–KB3   N–Q2
8 B–B4   0–0
9 Q–K2   N–N3

It would be better to play 9 . . . P–B3 followed by . . . P–QN3 and . . . B–QN2 to prepare . . . P–QB4, but even the immediate . . . P–QB4 is not bad.

10 B–N3   B–Q2
11 0–0   B–QR5 ?

A tactical mistake after which Black must accept a doubled KBP in unfavourable circumstances. Three years after this game, the same players reached the same position in the 1953 Candidates' Tournament, when Stahlberg improved with 11 . . . Q–K2. However, after 12 KR–K1 QR–Q1 (*12 . . . KR–Q1!*) 13 QR–Q1 B–QR5 14 B×B N×B 15 Q–N5 N–N3 16 P–B4 P–B3 17 Q–N3 he again made the mistake of allowing his K–side to be weakened by playing 17 . . . Q–B2? (better *17 . . . R–N1* or *17 . . . R–Q2*) 18 N×B+ P×N 19 Q–K3! K–N2 (*19 . . . N×P? 20 Q–R6 Q–K2 21 R–K4 P–KB4 22 N–N5 P–B3 23 R×P*, or even better *21 N–R4!*) 20 N–K5!! Q–K2 (if *20 . . . P×N 21 Q–N5+ K–R1 22 Q–B6+ K–N1 23 R–K3 KR–K1 24 R–KN3+ K–B1 25 R–N7 Q–K2 26 Q–R6 Q–Q3 27 Q–N5* wins) 21 N–N4 R–KN1 22 N–R6! (Smyslov could also win by *22 Q–R6+* when the similarity between the two games would even more be striking, but he prefers to annex the exchange.) 22 . . . Q–B2 23 N×R R×N 24 P–QN3 K–R1 25 Q–R6 and White won on move 33.

12 N×B+ !   P×N

He cannot play 12 . . . Q×N 13 B×B N×B 14 Q–B4 winning a pawn.

13 P–B4!

White does not worry about accepting a doubled pawn, because he does not require mobile Q–side pawns in order to carry out his K–side attack.

Moreover, he can if need be use the open QR–file to transfer his QR to KR5.

13 . . .   B×B
14 P×B   P–B3 (*120*)

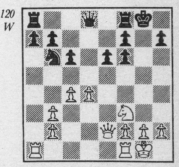

120
W

Black stands very badly, because he has no black-squared bishop to defend his K–side and his pieces are unfavourably posted for any action down the KN–file. White now pursues the following logical plan: by attacking the KBP he will try to force . . . P–KB4 with the consequential weakness of the K5 square. Black will eventually have to play . . . P–B3 to ward off the attack on his king, and this will seriously weaken his KP. This idea was also carried out in the game Pachman-Fichtl, Zlin 1945. After the same opening to Black's seventh move, play continued: 8 P–B3 P–QN3 9 B–N5 0–0(?) 10 B–B6 R–N1 11 Q–K2 B–N2 12 B×B R×B 13 0–0–0 P–B3 14 N–K5 Q–B2 15 N×N Q×N 16 N×B+ P×N 17 R–Q3 K–R1 18 Q–B3! P–KB4 19 Q–K3. It was now essential to play 19 . . . P–B3 when White was hoping to exploit the weakness of the KP, no easy task with major pieces on the board. However, Black lost quickly after 19 . . . Q–Q4? 20 Q–R6 Q–Q1 21 R–R3 P–B3 22 R–K1 R–K1 23 R3–K3.

15 Q–K3!   K–R1
16 N–Q2!   R–KN1
17 N–K4   N–B1 ?

It is understandable that Black wishes to improve the placing of his knight as quickly as possible, and 17 . . . N–Q2 loses a pawn after 18 N–Q6. However, he should play 17 . . . Q–K2 followed by 18 . . . N–Q2, as his intention of playing the knight to Q3 cannot be realized.

18 Q–B4!   R–N3

Perhaps Black had overlooked on his previous move that he cannot play 18 . . . Q×P in view of 19 KR–Q1 Q–K4 20 Q×P+ Q×Q 21 N×Q R–B1 22 R–Q7 winning.

19 KR–Q1   N–K2

Black offers a pawn in order to get his pieces into play, but he has insufficient compensation. He had to play 19 . . . P–KB4 e.g. 20 N–B5 Q–K2! but not 20 . . . P–N3 21 N–Q3 P–B3 22 Q–K3, or 20 . . . Q–Q3 21 Q–K5+! Q×Q 22 P×Q etc., both winning for White. Smyslov would then have to exploit the weakness of the K5 square, but this would not be easy.

20 N×P   N–B4
21 N–R5?

This makes it very difficult for him to exploit his extra pawn. The correct move is 21 N–K4 e.g. 21 . . . Q–R5 22 Q×Q (*22 Q–K5+? P–B3 23 Q×KP? R×P+!*) 22 . . . N×Q 23 P–N3 N–B4 24 N–B5 etc.

21 . . .   Q–N4
22 Q×Q   R×Q
23 N–N3   N×N

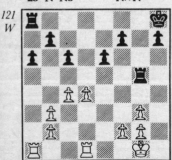

121
W

24 RP×N   P–QR3 *121*

We now have a very interesting double rook ending. White has an extra pawn but the mobility of his pawns is restricted by the fact that he has a doubled QNP and KNP. For this reason the win is extremely difficult to achieve. However, Black now adopts a faulty plan which finally allows White to eliminate his doubled pawns. Even though Black rids himself of his weak KRP by exchanging it for the KNP on move 36, his whole manoeuvre from move 27 to 33 is based on the erroneous assumption that he should try to exchange as many pawns as possible. His best chances of a successful defence lay in posting his pieces as actively as possible in order to prevent a breakthrough on the K-side or in the centre.

The game continued: **25 R–Q3 R–Q1 26 R1–Q1 K–N2 27 K–B1 R–QR4 28 K–K2 R–R7 29 R1–Q2 R–R8 30 R–Q1 R–R7 31 R3–Q2 P–R3 32 P–KN4 P–QR4? 33 K–Q3 P–R5 34 P×P R×RP 35 P–QN3 R–R4 36 K–B3 P–R4 37 P×P R×RP 38 R–QR1 K–B3 39 P–N3 K–K2 40 R–R7 R–Q2 41 R–K2 K–Q1 42 R–K4 R–R8 43 R–R8+ K–K2 44 R–QN8 R–KB8 45 R–B4 R–B8+ 46 K–N4 R–Q8 47 P–N4!** P–N4! if 47 . . . R8×P 48 R×R R×R 49 K–B5! R×NP 50 R×P+ K–B3 51 R–QR7 R–B5 52 R–R2 R–B6 53 P–N4 wins **48 K–B5 R–QB8 49 R–QB8!** 49 K×BP? P×P 50 R×P+ K×R 51 K×R R–Q8 draws **49 . . . P×P 50 P×P R–Q4+ 51 K–N4 R–QN8+ 52 K–B3 R–QB8+ 53 K–Q3 R–Q2 54 R×QBP P–K4 55 R–K4 R×QP+ 56 R×R R–Q8+ 57 K–K4 P×R** or 57 . . . R×R+ 58 K×P R×NP 59 R–B7+ K–K1 60 P–B4 **58 R–QR6 P–Q6 59 R–R2!** K–Q3 if 59 . . . P–Q7 60 K–Q3 R–KN8 61 R×P R×P 62 K–B3 **60 K–Q4 P–Q7 61 K–K3 R–K8+ 62 K×P R–K5 63 R–R4! K–B4 64 P–B3 R–B5 65 K–K3**

R–B3 66 K–K4 R–K3+ 67 K–B5 1–0

We have thus seen the disadvantage of the doubled KBP, but what about the compensation of the open KN-file? Our next game illustrates the successful exploitation of this file by the rooks supported by well-placed minor pieces. Black's task is facilitated by the fact that the KN-file is opened before he has castled. However, even after castling there are many games in which the KN-file has been used for attacking purposes after K–R1 and R–KN1.

53 Szabo–Euwe

Groningen 1946, Queen's Gambit

1 P–Q4 P–Q4 2 P–QB4 P×P 3 N–KB3 P–QR3 4 P–K3 N–KB3 5 B×P P–K3 6 0–0 P–B4 7 Q–K2 N–B3 8 R–Q1 P–QN4 9 B–N3 P–B5 B–B2 N–QN5 11 N–B3 N×B 12 Q×N B–N2 13 P–K4 13 P–Q5! P–N5 14 P–K5 P×N 15 P×N NP×P *(122)*

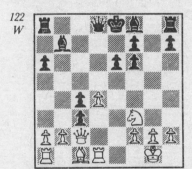

122
W

Black has obtained a doubled pawn under particularly favourable circumstances. He has the two bishops, his QB being especially powerful, bearing down as it does on White's KNP, and his king can remain in the centre, allowing his rooks to seize the KN-file without any loss of time. White should take immediate measures to neutralize the pressure down the KN-file by playing 16 Q×BP R–KN1 17 B–B4

Q–Q4 18 B–N3. He still has a poor position but with more defensive chances than in the game continuation.

16 Q–R4+   Q–Q2
17 Q×BP

The game is strategically hopeless for White after 17 Q×Q+ K×Q 18 P×P R–KN1 19 K–B1 B–Q3, or here 19 N–K1 B–Q4, when he has no counterplay at all.

17 ...	R–B1
18 Q–K2	R–KN1
19 N–K1	Q–Q4
20 P–B3	B–Q3
21 K–R1	Q–KR4

Black has an even more energetic continuation in 21 ... P–B7! when 22 N×P? fails to 22 ... R×N! e.g. 23 Q×R Q×BP 24 R–KN1 Q–KR6 25 Q–B8+ B×Q 26 P×Q B–N2+ etc., and after 22 R–Q3 Q–KR4 23 P–KR3 R–N6 Black has a strong attack because his QBP hinders White's defence.

22 P–KR3   R–N6

He could still interpose 22 ... P–B7!

23 B–K3   K–K2
24 Q–B1   R1–KN1! *(123)*

Black does not worry about his QBP, as the pressure down the KN-file will be too much for White.

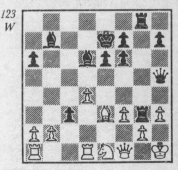

123
W

25 P×P   R×NP!

The simplest winning method. Although White temporarily obtains two rooks for his queen, the exposed position of his king will soon lead to material loss. He cannot of course play 26 N×R Q×RP+ 27 K–N1 B×P 28 R–Q2 B–R7+ etc.

26 Q×R	**R×Q**
27 K×R	**Q–N3+**
28 K–B2	**B–N6+**
29 K–K2	**B×N**
30 R×B	**Q–N7+**
31 K–Q3	**B×P**
32 P–QR4	**B–K5+**
33 K–B4	**Q–QB7**
34 P–Q5	**B×P+**
35 K–N4	**K–Q2**
36 P–B4	

A desperate attempt to ward off the mating threats by giving his pieces more room. The game ended: **36 ... Q×BP+ 37 K–R5 Q–B6+ 38 K×P B–B5+ 39 K–N7 Q–N6+ 40 B–N6 Q–KB6+ 41 K–N8 B–R3 42 R.K1–Q1+ K–K1 0–1.**

Let us now examine positions in which the pawn on the file adjacent to the doubled pawn stands on the 4th instead of the 3rd rank, giving the following kind of pawn structure.

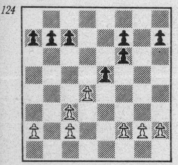

124

For the sake of simplicity, our illustration (*124*) shows the same pawn complex on both wings. Of course, such a situation is extremely rare in practice, but is possible after the moves: 1 P–K4 N–KB3 2 N–QB3 P–Q4 3 P–K5 P–Q5 4 P×N P×N 5 NP×P (*5 P×NP!*) 5 ... NP×P 6 P–Q4 P–K4? (*6 ... B–B4!* followed by *7 ... P–K3*). As a rule it is

only one side which has this doubled pawn complex. A glance at the diagram should tell us that the doubled pawn is more vulnerable here, with particularly weak squares on White's QB4 and Black's KB4. When an enemy blockading piece occupies such a square, it cripples the whole pawn complex, as the following game shows.

54 Fischer–Addison

Palma de Mallorca Interzonal 1970, Centre Counter

1 P–K4 P–Q4 2 P×P Q×P 3 N–QB3 Q–Q1 4 P–Q4 N–KB3 5 B–QB4 B–B4 6 Q–B3 Q–B1 7 B–KN5! B×P 8 R–B1 B–N3 9 KN–K2 QN–Q2 10 0–0 P–K3 11 B×N!

White has offered a pawn for the sake of speedy development, and now he begins operations in the centre with this far from obvious exchange. If Black replies 11 ... N×B then 12 P–Q5! puts him in serious difficulties e.g.

a. 12 ... P×P? 13 N×P N×N 14 B×N R–QN1 (if *14 ... P–QB3 15 R×P!*) 15 N–B4 with a decisive attack.

b. 12 ... B–Q3 13 P×P 0–0! (if *13 ... P×P? 14 N–B4*) 14 N–N5! P×P 15 N2–Q4! etc.

c. 12 ... P–K4 13 B–N5+ N–Q2 14 P–KR4 P–KR3 15 P–R5 B–R2 16 Q–N3, or here 14 ... P–KR4 15 N–N3 followed by 16 KR–K1 etc.

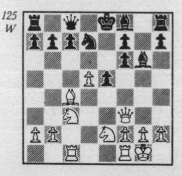

125
W

| 11 ... | P×B |
| 12 P-Q5 | P-K4 (*125*) |

In this way Black retains his extra pawn and the two bishops, but he still has a very bad game, as his KP and KBP offer White excellent blockading chances.

13 B-N5!

Threatening 14 Q×BP, and if now 13 ... P-KB4 then White has a clear advantage after 14 N-N3 P-B5 15 N.N3-K4 B-K2 16 P-Q6! or here 14 ... P-K5 15 KR-K1 B-K2 16 N×BP! P×Q 17 N×B.

13 ...	B-K2
14 N-N3	P-QR3
15 B-Q3!	Q-Q1

After 15 ... B×B 16 Q×B N-B4 17 Q-B3 Black has a hopeless game.

16 P-KR4! **P-KR4**

Otherwise White will force the exchange of bishops by 17 P-R5, giving his knights the use of K4 and KB5.

| 17 B-B5 | N-N3 |
| 18 N.B3-K4! | |

A pretty pawn sacrifice. Relatively best for Black is now 18 ... N-B1 when White can build up pressure by R-B3 and KR-B1. Not of course 18 ... Q×P? 19 R×P threatening 20 R×P+ ! K×R 21 B×B.

18 ...	N×P
19 KR-Q1	P-B3
20 N-B3	Q-N3
21 R×N!	P×R
22 N×QP	Q×NP
23 R-N1	Q×RP
24 R×P	1-0

if 24 ... B-Q1 25 B×B P×B 26 N×BP+ wins.

Such a weak pawn complex can also be blockaded by a pawn, although it is then more difficult to launch a direct attack against the doubled pawn.

55 Janowski-Lasker

World Championship 1909, Four Knights Game

1 P-K4 P-K4 2 N-KB3 N-QB3 3 N-B3 N-B3 4 B-N5 B-N5 5 0-0 0-0 6 P-Q3 P-Q3 7 B-N5 B×N 8 P×B N-K2 9 B-QB4 N-N3 10 N-R4 N-B5 11 B×N.B4 P×B 12 N-B3 The threat was 12 ... N×P. **12 ... B-N5 13 P-KR3 B-R4 14 R-N1 P-QN3 15 Q-Q2?**

A serious positional error, over-estimating the importance of the KN-file and the strengthening of his pawn centre. The correct move was 15 P-N4!, as the piece sacrifice 15 ... N×NP 16 P×N B×P fails to 17 P-Q4. After 15 ... B-N3 Black's bishop is badly placed and if 15 ... P×Pep 16 P×P followed by K-R2 and White can exploit the open KB-file.

15 ...	B×N
16 P×B	N-R4
17 K-R2	Q-B3
18 R-N1	QR-K1
19 P-Q4	K-R1 (*126*)

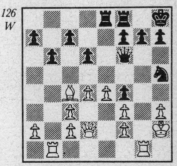

126
W

This position is an excellent illustration of our theme. White has two sets of doubled pawns with the adjacent pawns on the fourth rank constituting an impressive looking pawn centre (Q4 and K4). Furthermore, he controls the KN-file and his bishop is more active than the knight. Nevertheless, it is Black who already has a clear positional advantage, although the reader may find this improbable. Even Janowski felt that the position was so much in his favour that he was ready to repeat the experiment in a later game of the same match, despite his poor result in this game. He achieved the same result! White's advantages are only apparent; not real. Consider his centre which looks so imposing. We shall later point out that the strength of a pawn centre depends upon its mobility, and here the doubled pawns render White's entire central pawn structure immobile. In this connection it is worth noting that when White later advances his QBP (24 P–B4) he lacks a QNP which could go to QN4 to support the advance P–QB5. In addition, the P–K5 thrust, which could prove a useful threat under normal circumstances, does not come into consideration here in view of the two sets of isolated doubled pawns which remain after . . . P×P, P×P. In contrast to White, Black has a positive plan available. He can prepare an attack against White's weakened K–side.

20 R–QN5   Q–R3

It would be a grave strategic mistake to play 20 . . . P–QB4, as this would give White an object of attack on the QN–file, and after P–QR4–5 he would have the advantage.

21 R5–N5   P–KB3
22 R5–N4   P–N3!

Weaker is 22 . . . P–KB4 23 R4–N2! P×P 24 P×P R×P 25 B–K2! with counterplay e.g. 25 . . . P–B6? 26 Q×Q P×Q 27 B×P, or 25 . . . N–N6 26 B–B3, or 25 . . . R×B 26 Q×R P–B6 27 Q–K7 Q–B5+ 28 R–N3. This is another example of eliminating a doubled pawn by sacrificing a pawn.

23 B–Q3   R–K2
24 P–B4?

In bad positions it is often difficult to wait patiently for whatever our opponent has in store for us. This move gives Black an opportunity to bring his knight into an attacking position without loss of time.

24 . . .   N–N2!

Now 25 Q×P Q×Q 26 R×Q N–K3 27 R4–N4 N×P gives Black an easily won ending in view of White's pawn weaknesses.

25 P–B3   N–K3

Threatening . . . N–N4 with an attack on the KBP and KRP.

26 B–B1   P–KB4
27 R4–N2   R–B3
28 B–Q3   P–KN4!

Threatening 29 . . . Q×RP+ ! 30 K×Q R–R3 Mate.

29 R–KR1   P–N5!

Once again threatening . . . N–N4, but this time there is no defence. If instead 29 . . . Q×RP+ 30 K–N1 Q×P 31 P×P White could fight on.

30 B–K2   N–N4!
31 BP×P   P–B6
32 R–N3   P×B
         0–1

Most of our examples have shown us that it is unfavourable to advance the doubled pawns, as this makes them even weaker. There are of course exceptions, as in game 39 from volume 1 where Botvinnik made active use of his doubled KP in the pawn complex on K3, K2 and KB3. By advancing all three pawns, he won the game, but such cases are rare and usually depend upon the superior placing of one's pieces. With the pawns on QB2, QB3 and Q4, it is generally a serious error to advance any of the pawns, so White must strive to keep the structure intact. Our next diagram (*127*) will illustrate this point more clearly.

White can hardly play P–QB4, as he is left with an isolated doubled pawn after . . . P×P, just as he is if he ever plays P×KP. The case of P–Q5 requires a little more explanation. When we deal with the concept of the pawn-chain, we shall point out that when

127

White has pawns on Q5 and K4 facing black pawns on Q3 and K4, then P-QB5 is the correct way of breaking through. However, with doubled pawns on QB2 and QB3, this advance cannot be carried out because after . . . P-QN3 White has no QNP available to lend its support on QN4. In addition Black has two advantages after P-Q5:

1. He can post a piece on QB4 (usually a knight) and White cannot drive it away with P-QN4.

2. He can frequently play a rook to QB1, then attack White's pawns by opening the QB-file with P-QB3. It is usually irrelevant then if White plays P-QB4 and after . . . P×P recaptures with the BP in order to eliminate his doubled pawn. Black still exerts uncomfortable pressure against White's backward QBP.

However, the situation is very difficult when Black has played . . . P-QB4 to force P-Q5, as neither of the above methods is then available. This means that the weakness of the doubled pawns is not so easy to exploit and action on the other wing usually takes precedence. If Black does not play . . . P-QB4, White must strive to maintain the pawns on QB3, Q4 and K4, when his active position in the centre normally compensates for the weakness of the doubled pawn. Our next game is a good example of this.

56 Botvinnik–Reshevsky

World Championship 1948, Four Knights Game

1 P-K4 P-K4 2 N-KB3 N-QB3 3 N-B3 N-B3 4 B-N5 B-N5 5 0–0 0–0 6 P-Q3 B×N 7 P×B P-Q3 8 B-N5 Q-K2 9 R-K1 N-Q1
 10 P-Q4   N-K3

The move 10 . . . B-N5 is best suited to the plan of inducing P-Q5. The tactical disadvantage of the move is that Black's bishop can be driven back by 11 P-KR3 B-R4 12 P-N4 B-N3. However, if White continues 13 N-R4 P-KR3 14 B-QB4!, Black has no problems after 14 . . . B-R2! In books on opening theory, including my own, the reader is informed that 13 P-Q5 gives White an advantage. As an example they quote the game Wolf–Cohn (Nuremberg, 1906) which continued: 13 . . . P-B3! 14 B-KB1 P×P 15 P×P R-B1 16 P-B4 P-N3 17 P-QR4. White's clearly anti-positional move 13 P-Q5 is partly justified by the unfavourable posting of Black's bishop and the restriction placed on his knights. However, a thorough examination of the position reveals that Keres is right in his claim that Cohn only lost the above game as a result of further mistakes, the position at move 17 being in no way good for White. Furthermore, Keres improves for Black with 14 . . . R-B1 15 P-B4 P-N3 followed by 16 . . . N-N2, depriving White of all the tactics based on N-Q4. We can therefore conclude by reaffirming that 10 . . . B-N5! is Black's best chance against this doubled pawn formation, and improves upon the usual plan adopted here by Reshevsky.

 11 B-QB1   R-Q1

As Black cannot force P-Q5 without playing . . . P-B4, he should do this at once, achieving approximate equality

after 11 ... P–B4 12 P–Q5 N–B2 13
B–Q3. There is an interesting
alternative for White in 12 P×KP!?
P×P 13 B–QB4! followed by 14 B–Q5,
when despite his isolated doubled pawn
he has good compensation in the vital
strong-point on Q5. It also is worth
noting that after 11 ... P–B4 12 B–B1
Black's best is 12 ... BP×P! 13 P×P
Q–B2, eliminating White's doubled
pawn but obtaining good chances down
the QB-file.

For this reason, the text move is
weaker as it only protects the KP
without forcing White to change his
pawn structure. Another example of
faulty strategy was seen in the game
Spielmann–Rubinstein, Karlsbad
1911, which continued: 11 ... P–B3? 12
B–B1 R–Q1 13 P–N3 Q–B2 14 N–R4!
P–Q4 15 P–KB4! P×BP 16 P–K5 N–K5
17 P×P P–KB4 18 P×Pep! N×P.KB3 19
P–B5 N–B1 20 Q–B3 Q–B2 21 B–Q3
B–Q2 22 B–KB4 R–K1 23 B–K5 P–B4
24 K–R1 P–B5 25 B–K2 B–B3 26 Q–B4
N1–Q2 27 B–B3 R–K2 28 R–K2
R–KB1 29 R–KN1 Q–K1 30 R2–N2
R1–B2 31 Q–R6! K–B1 32 N–N6+!
P×N 33 Q–R8+ N–KN1 34 B–Q6
Q–Q1 35 R×P N2–B3 36 R×N R×R 37
R×P! 1–0. In the present game, too,
Botvinnik manages to maintain his
pawns on QB2, QB3 and Q4 and to
carry out a K-side attack.

12 B–B1   N–B1 ? (128)

He should still play ... P–B4, but
this makes his previous move
superfluous and gives White the better
prospects.

13 N–R4!

Planning to answer 13 ... N–N3
with 14 N–B5 B×N 15 P×B. Black
should settle down to solid defence with
13 ... N–K1 14 P–N3 P–KN3!, but not
13 ... N×P 14 R×N P–KB4 15
B–QB4+ K–R1 16 Q–R5! P×R 17
B–KN5 with a winning attack.

13 ...   N–N5(?)
14 P–N3   Q–B3
15 P–B3   N–R3
16 B–K3

But not 16 B×N? P×B and after the
disappearance of White's strong
bishop, his doubled QBP is surprisingly
just as disadvantageous as Black's
KRP.

16 ...   R–K1
17 Q–Q2   N–N3

In order to answer 18 B–KN5 or 18
B×N with 18 ... N×N!

18 N–N2!   B–R6

It would be dangerous to play 18 ...
Q×P 19 B–K2! Q–B3 (*19 ... Q×KP? 20
B×N P×B 21 B–N5*) 20 B–QB4 Q–K2
21 B×N P×B 22 Q×P followed by 23
R–KB1 with a mighty attack. White
was threatening 19 B–KN5 winning a
pawn, but now this fails to 19 ... Q×P
(20 B–K2?? Q×N mate).

19 B–K2   B×N
20 K×B

Suddenly Black's position has
become hopeless. For example, White
has a winning attack after 20 ... N–B1
21 P–N4! Q–N3 22 P–KR4 etc. So
Reshevsky tries to complicate matters
with a pawn sacrifice, but this proves
insufficient to save him.

20 ...   P–Q4
21 KP×P   P×P

Or 21 ... N–B4 22 B–KN5 Q–Q3 23
B–N5 P–QB3 24 P×BP NP×P 25 B–Q3
etc.

22	P×P	N–B4
23	B–B2	R.K1–Q1
24	P–QB4	P–KR4
25	P–KR4	P–N4
26	Q–N5	Q×Q
27	P×Q	P–R5 ?

Better is 27 ... P×P 28 B×P N4–K2 29 QR–B1 N×P 30 B–N3 followed by 31 R–B5 with a plus to White. The game now finished: **28 B–Q3 RP×P 29 B×P N×P? 30 QR–Q1! P–QB4 31 QP×Pep N×QBP 32 B–K4 QR–B1 33 R×R+ N×R 34 B–B5! R–R1 35 R–K8+ K–R2 36 P×P P–B3 37 B–B7 N–K3 38 R×R N×B 39 R×P N×P 40 R–Q7 P×P 41 P–R4 1–0.**

In the above game White succeeded in maintaining his formation of pawns on QB2, QB3 and Q4, and this is why Black could not obtain any effective counterplay. Our next game shows how such a formation becomes weak once the pawns are forced to advance.

57 Szabo–Kotov

Budapest Candidates' 1950, Sicilian Defence

1 P–K4 P–QB4 2 N–KB3 P–Q3 3 P–Q4 P×P 4 Q×P N–QB3 5 B–QN5 P–QR3 6 B×N+ P×B 7 0–0 P–K4 8 Q–Q3 B–K2 9 R–Q1 N–B3 10 B–N5 0–0 11 B×N! P×B

12 N–R4

In the further course of the game White intends to exploit the weakness of Black's doubled KBP by the logical plan of blockading on KB5 with a knight. However, we must ask ourselves whether it would be better to play 12 P–QB4 before posting the knights on KR4 and K3. Black would then have great difficulty in carrying out ... P–Q4, although he would have pressure down the QN-file (... Q–N3 and then ... P–QR4 if White plays P–QN3). If White tries to prevent ... P–Q4 by playing his knight to QB3, this knight can no longer help in the blockade of the doubled pawn.

12 ...		K–R1
13 N–Q2		B–N5!
14 R–K1		

After 14 P–KB3 B–K3 Black would be threatening both ... P–Q4 and ... Q–N3+ .

14 ...	P–Q4
15 N–B1	R–KN1
16 N–K3	B–K3
17 P–QB3	

White is intending to maintain one knight on K3 and play the other to KB5, so he can later attack the KBP with N–N4. For this reason he has to prevent any chances Black may have with a subsequent ... P–Q5.

17 ...	Q–R4
18 N4–B5	B–KB1 *(129)*

129
W

So White has managed to blockade the doubled pawn in typical fashion by putting a knight on KB5. Black on the other hand has compensation in his two bishops which can later become active, and above all he has an attacking position in the centre (the threat against White's KP). The game is approximately even.

19 R.K1–Q1	Q–N4
20 Q–B2	Q–N2
21 R–Q2	B–B4
22 R1–Q1	QR–Q1
23 K–R1	R–Q2
24 P–B3	R1–Q1 ?

There are two reason why this move is wrong:

1. Black overlooks the threat of a direct attack against his weak pawns.
2. He had a good opportunity to simplify here by 24 . . . B.B4×N (one of the advantages of the two bishops is that they can always be exchanged at the appropriate moment!) 25 N×B R1–Q1. White would then hardly be able to exploit the weakness of the doubled pawn, and he would have to watch the enemy centre very carefully.

25 P×P!   P×P

It is already too late to simplify, as 25 . . . B.B4×N? fails to 26 P×P! as the pawn cannot be stopped after 26 . . . R×R 27 R×R R×R 28 Q×R B×Q? 29 P×Q. Even more beautiful is the variation after 25 . . . B.K3×N? 26 Q×B! B×N 27 Q×BP+ K–N1 28 P×P! R×R 29 Q×R+ ! winning.

26 N–N4!   P–K5
27 N–Q4   P–B4

Black's last two pawn moves were played to save his pawn on KB3, but it would have been better to eliminate the knights by 27 . . . B.K3×N 28 P×B B×N 29 R×B. White still has a clear advantage with play down the open files against the backward QP and the doubled KBP, but Black's passed KP would give him some drawing chances.

28 N–KB6   R–Q3

Now the advance of Black's pawns has compromised his position so much that a combination is in the air.

29 N–N3!   B–K6
30 P×P!   B×R

Forced, as 30 . . . BP×P fails to 31 N×KP.

31 Q×B   BP×P

And now 31 . . . QP×P is answered by 32 N–Q4 when Black is helpless against the mating attack by Q–R6 e.g. 32 . . . R–KN1 33 Q–R6 R–N2 34 N–R5 etc.

32 Q–Q4!   B–B4
33 R–KB1!

The quickest way to win. If now 33 . . . B–N3 34 N–K8+ P–B3 35 R×P clinches matters.

33 . . .   Q–B1
34 N×KP+   K–N1
35 N×R   R×N
36 Q–K5!   B–Q6
37 Q–N3+   1–0

To conclude this chapter we shall examine positions in which the doubled pawn complex is further advanced. In practice this means the formation of pawns on QB3 and QB4 which often occurs in modern openings, especially in various lines of the Nimzo-Indian Defence. Consider our next diagram (*130*):

130

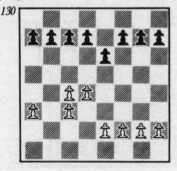

White's plan in such positions is to play P–K4 and P–KB4–B5 with an attack on the K-side. Black, on the other hand, will try to exploit the weakness of White's doubled pawn. It would be very good for him if he could induce White to play P–Q5 without having to play . . . P–QB4 himself For example, if Black plays . . . P–Q3 and . . . P–K4 and White answers with P–K4 and P–Q5? we have reached a position we know well, in which Black can post a knight on QB4 and exert pressure down the QB-file after . . . P–QB3. However, experience teaches us that after . . . P–K4 Black can hardly ever force White to play P–Q5. Once again White tries to maintain his pawn complex on QB3, QB4, and Q4 whilst aiming for a K-side attack, just as he did with his pawns on QB2, QB3 and Q4. If Black plays both ... P–K4 and ... P–QB4, White can usually play P–Q5 without serious disadvantage, as the position remains blocked. For this reason Black usually chooses a different plan:

1. He leaves his KP on K3
2. He blockades White's doubled pawn with ... P–QB4
3. He launches an attack against White's pawn on QB4 by playing ... P–QN3, ... B–R3 and ... N–QB3–R4, with the constant threat of increasing this pressure by ... R–QB1 and ... P×QP.
4. He counters White's threatened attack on the K-side by one of two methods: either he castles long, which does not occur very often, or else he castles short then blockades by ... P–KB4! once White has played P–K4 and P–KB4.

We can thus state that the pawn structure in diagram 130 is unfavourable for White. However, he usually has counter-chances in piece play especially if he can exploit his two bishops (the position normally arises after Black has played ... B×N+ in the Nimzo-Indian Defence). He can also frequently sacrifice his QBP for the attack, as Black may lose time and decentralize his pieces in winning the pawn. The Sämisch variation of the Nimzo-Indian Defence (1 P–Q4 N–KB3 2 P–QB4 P–K3 3 N–QB3 B–N5 4 P–QR3 B×N+ 5 P×B) well illustrates the strategic and tactical problems arising from such a pawn formation.

Our first example is taken from Nimzowitsch's *My System*. It shows a successful exploitation of the disadvantageous pawn complex with Black pawns on QB3, QB4 and Q5, allowing White to post a knight on QB4.

58 Nimzowitsch–Rosselli

Baden-Baden 1925, Nimzowitsch–Larsen Opening

1 N–KB3 P–Q4 2 P–QN3 P–QB4 3 P–K3 N–QB3 4 B–N2 B–N5 5 P–KR3 B×N 6 Q×B P–K4 7 B–N5 Q–Q3 8 P–K4!

After 8 B×N+ P×B 9 P–K4 White cannot force Black to weaken his pawns by ... P–Q5, so Nimzowitsch goes in for an original plan: he first forces ... P–Q5, then hopes that piece manoeuvres will compel Black to double his QBP.

| 8 ... | P–Q5 |
| 9 N–R3! | |

Threatening 10 N–B4 Q–B2 11 B×N+ when Black is forced to retake with the pawn.

| 9 ... | P–B3! |
| 10 N–B4 | Q–Q2 |

Black plans to castle long, so that he can then exploit the unfavourable placing of White's bishops. White's next manoeuvre is designed to prevent this.

| 11 Q–R5+ ! | P–KN3 |

Not of course 11 ... Q–KB2? B×N+ and White has managed to double the pawns.

| 12 Q–B3 | Q–QB2 |

The point of White's plan is that 12 ... 0–0–0 allows 13 N–R5 when 13 ... KN–K2 would lose a pawn.

| 13 Q–N4 | K–B2 |

After 13 ... Q–Q2 14 Q×Q+ K×Q 15 N–R5 R–QN1 16 B×N+ Black's doubled QBP would be a grave disadvantage in the ending. White was threatening 14 Q–K6+.

14 P–B4!	P–KR4
15 Q–B3	P×P
16 B×N!	P×B (131)

If Black tries to avoid the doubled pawn by 16 ... Q×B then White continues 17 Q×BP R–K1 18 0–0! when both 18 ... R×P 19 N–K5+! and 18 ... Q×P 19 Q–B7+ Q–K2 20 N–Q6+ win for White.

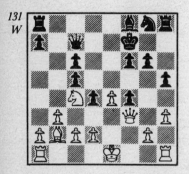

131
W

At the cost of a pawn White has achieved his basic aims of doubling the QBP and obtaining a strong post for his knight on QB4. However, as Black has in addition a weakened king's position the game is over in a few moves.

17 0–0   P–N4

Black would have a good position if he had time to bring his knight to K4. However, as things stand, White has three possible ways of achieving a break-through:

1. P–B3 which is, as we know, a standard method of play against the doubled pawns.
2. P–K5, a central break-through.
3. P–KR4, opening up the K-side.

Within a short space of time Nimzowitsch manages to carry out all of these!

18 P–B3   R–Q1

Exchanging pawns is out of the question, as it not only lays bare the weakness of the doubled pawn but, more seriously, it opens up the long black diagonal onto the enemy king. Now Black's rook is tied to the defence of the QP, making a further break-through easier for White.

19 QR–K1   N–K2
20 P–K5   N–B4
21 BP×P   N×P

Or 21 ... P×QP 22 P×P K×P 23 Q–K4

22 Q–K4   B–K2

In reply to 22 ... P–B4 Nimzowitsch gives the interesting continuation 23 Q–N1 K–K3 24 Q–Q3! followed by 25 N–Q6, but the immediate 23 Q–Q3 is also very strong.

23 P–KR4!   Q–Q2
24 KP×P   B×P
25 P×P   1–0

After 25 ... B–N2 26 N–K5+! B×N 27 Q×B Black is helpless against the many threats.

Two further examples illustrate the problems arising from the Sämisch variation that we have already mentioned. In the first game Black is successful in his fight against the doubled pawns, whereas in the second White manages to avoid a positional struggle by obtaining tactical chances with a neatly timed pawn sacrifice.

59 Botvinnik–Reshevsky

World Championship 1948, Nimzo-Indian Defence

1 P–Q4 N–KB3 2 P–QB4 P–K3 3 N–QB3 B–N5 4 P–K3 P–B4 5 P–QR3 B×N+
6 P×B   N–B3

Later it was found that 6 ... P–QN3! 7 B–Q3 B–N2 is much stronger, as White is forced to play the unfavourable 8 P–B3. Our note to White's 10th move will show how important this gain of a tempo is. Several games played subsequently have shown that 6 ... P–QN3! gives Black at least equality. The keen reader is advised to study the games Geller–Euwe (Candidates', 1953), Polugayevsky–Averbakh (23rd USSR Championship), Geller–

Smyslov (Candidates', 1956) and
Stoltz–Pachman (zonal, Marienbad
1951).

7	B–Q3	0–0
8	N–K2	P–QN3
9	P–K4	N–K1!

A very important part of Black's
plan, avoiding the powerful pin by
B–N5 and at the same time preparing to
answer a later P–KB4 with . . . P–B4.

10 B–K3?

From the point of view of basic
principles, this move is already a serious
mistake. In this position White must
seek compensation for his weak doubled
pawn in sharp piece play. For this
reason, quiet development, as
represented by the text move, is
completely out of place. It was essential
to prepare a K-side attack as speedily as
possible. In the game
Lilienthal–Najdorf (Saltsjobaden interzonal 1948) play went 10 0–0 P–Q3
11 P–K5! (in order to exploit the
unprotected black queen after *11 . . .
QP×P 12 P×KP N×P??* 13 B×P+ . Note
that this line would be impossible with
the black bishop already on QN2,
which is why *6 . . . P–QN3!* is the best
move.) 11 . . . QP×P 12 P×KP B–N2 13
B–B4 P–B4 14 P×Pep P–K4? (if *14 . . .
Q×P 15 Q–B2 P–N3 16 QR–K1* White
has the advantage, as in
Pachman–Jeney, Bucharest 1949, but
the text move loses quickly) 15
B×RP+ ! and White soon won. It
would have been better to set up an
attack on the QBP by 11 . . . N–R4
followed by . . . B–R3 but after 12 B–B4
B–R3 13 Q–B2, or an immediate 12
Q–B2 White has good attacking
chances. An even better continuation
was played in the game Averbakh–
Taimanov, 16th USSR Championship
1948: 10 P–K5! P–B4 11 KP×Pep Q×P
12 B–K3 P×P (or *12 . . . P–Q3 13 Q–B2
P–N3 14 P–KR4*) 13 P×P B–R3 14
Q–B2 with a clear advantage to White.

| 10 | . . . | P–Q3 |
| 11 | 0–0 | N–R4 (*132*) |

132
W

A typical position in which the
weakness of White's doubled pawn
counts for more than any counterplay
he may obtain on the K-side. White's
main trouble is that he cannot support
his attack with a pawn storm, as 12
P–B4 is immediately answered by 12
. . . P–B4! (but not *12 . . . B–R3 13
P–B5! B×P 14 P–B6! N×P 15 B–N5*
followed by *N–N3* with a mighty attack
for the two sacrificed pawns). Not only
does this effectively prevent the
advance of White's pawns, but the
mobility of his two bishops is severely
restricted.

| 12 | N–N3 | B–R3 |
| 13 | Q–K2 | Q–Q2! |

A very good move threatening to win
White's pawn on QB4 by . . . Q–R5. If
White now replies 14 P–QR4 then 14
. . . P×P 15 P×P P R–B1 still wins a pawn,
so 14 P–K5! is essential here, giving
White some tactical counter-chances
on the K-side.

14 P–B4? P–B4!

An excellent positional move,
blocking White's attack and at the same
time severely restricting the mobility of
his QB. His only chance is to force open
a line by P–Q5 or P–K5. After the
immediate 15 P–Q5 P–N3! 16 QP×P
Q×P 17 P×P P×P White has no time to
exploit Black's weakened K-side, as his
pawn on QB4 falls at once.

15 QR–K1

It was better to play the other rook to this square, followed by QR–Q1, when Black has to watch out for both P–Q5 and P–K5.

15 ...   P–N3!

16 R–Q1

It is now pointless to play 16 P–Q5 because of 16 ... N–N2, so White prepares for P–K5. Black still cannot play 16 ... Q–R5, as 17 P–Q5 B×P 18 QP×P B×P 19 P×P would give White a strong attack in which Black's decentralized queen would prove a serious disadvantage. However, the strength of Black's game resides in the fact that he does not have to hurry with the capture of the QBP.

16 ...   Q–KB2

17 P–K5   R–B1

18 KR–K1

After 18 KP×P N×P White's QBP falls at once. The text move involves a little trap, because 18 ... BP×P? fails to 19 B×QP! B×P? 20 P×P N×P 21 Q–K5 winning.

18 ...   QP×P!

Choosing the right moment, as White must now recapture with the QP (*19 BP×P? P×P* etc.). This means that Black has achieved a complete blockade of the centre, thus freeing his pieces for the final attack on White's weaknesses. The game is already decided from the strategic point of view.

19 QP×KP   N–KN2

20 N–B1   KR–Q1

21 B–KB2   N–R4!

22 B–N3

An awkward but essential move. His K3 square must remain available for the knight to defend the pawn on QB4, and 22 P–N3? would fatally weaken the long white diagonal (22 ... B–N2! followed by ... B–R1 and ... Q–QN2).

22 ...   Q–K1

23 N–K3   Q–R5

24 Q–R2   N×B

Black could win even more quickly with 24 ... P–KN4! but he probably did not want to give White some attacking chances after 25 P×P P–B5, even though he would have insufficient compensation for the piece.

25 P×N (*133*)

It is clear that Black has attained his strategic goal. He should now simply exchange queens and after 25 ... Q–N6 26 Q×Q N×Q 27 P–N4 P×P 28 N×P N–R4 29 N–K3 K–B2, followed by doubling rooks on the Q-file, he would win comfortably.

25 ...   P–R4?

In his haste to prevent P–N4 Black overlooks an interesting tactical point. White could now play 26 B–B2! when 26 ... B×P fails to 27 B×Q B×Q 28 B–Q7 R–N1 29 P–B4. Admittedly after 26 ... Q–B3 27 P–QR4 Black has still far the best of it, but White has at least countered the immediate threats to his Q-side.

26 B–K2?   K–B2

27 K–B2   Q–N6!

28 Q×Q   N×Q

29 B–Q3

Otherwise Black wins as follows: after ... N–R4 he plays ... K–K2, exchanges both pairs of rooks, plays his king to KR3 and then wins by ... P–KN4 and ... P–R5.

29 ...	K–K2(?)
30 K–K2	N–R4
31 R–Q2	R–B2(?)

A serious error, after which White obtains counterplay. The correct move was 31 ... K–B2! rectifying his mistaken 29th move. Both sides were now short of time.

32 P–N4!	R2–Q2

After 32 ... RP×P 33 R–KR1! White has strong counterplay down the KR-file.

33 P×BP	NP×P
34 R1–Q1??	

A blunder after which White has no reasonable moves left. 34 R2–Q1! followed by 35 R–KR1 was the correct plan, when it is by no means clear that Black could achieve the win.

34 ...	P–R5!
35 K–K1	N–N6
36 N–Q5+	P×N
37 B×P	N×R
38 R×N	P×P
39 B×R	R×B
40 R–KB2	K–K3
41 R–B3	R–Q6
42 K–K2	0–1

60 Geller–Lisitsin

22nd USSR Championship 1955, Nimzo-Indian Defence

1 P–Q4 N–KB3 2 P–QB4 P–K3 3 N–QB3 B–N5 4 P–K3 P–B4 5 B–Q3 N–B3 6 P–QR3 B×N+ 7 P×B P–Q3 8 N–K2 P–QN3

9 0–0	Q–Q2

In contrast to the previous game, Black now prepares to castle long. The immediate 9 ... B–R3 fails to 10 Q–R4.

10 P–K4	B–R3
11 B–N5	0–0–0 *(134)*

Once again Black intends to put pressure on White's doubled pawns by ... N–QR4 followed by ... Q–R5 if White defends by Q–K2 or Q–R2. So White must try his chances in an attack

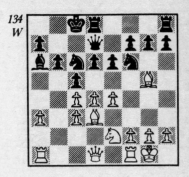

134
W

on the king instead of passively defending his pawn on QB4. In his game against Spassky, Geller played 12 N–N3 P–R3! 13 B×N P×B 14 N–R5 hoping to exploit Black's K-side weaknesses. However, the open KN-file gave Black a decisive initiative: 14 ... P×P 15 P×P N×P 16 N×P Q–K2 17 Q–R4? *(17 N–N4 is better)* 17 ... B–N2! 18 N–R5 KR–N1 19 Q–Q1 P–B4! 20 R–K1 Q–R5 and Black won on move 31. Geller's experience in this game convinced him that he had to find much more effective counterplay for his sacrificed pawn. The only possibility lies in an attack on the king. Although it seems incredible that White is in a position to build up an attack on the Q-side, Geller shows us it can be done. His first aim is to advance his QRP to R5, which is the point behind the following surprising move.

12 N–B1!	

An excellent positional sacrifice of a pawn. After 12 ... P×P 13 P×P N×QP 14 P–QR4 N–B3 15 N–N3 Black cannot prevent the opening of the Q-side by P–R5.

12 ...	N–QR4
13 N–N3!	Q–R5

Once again acceptance of the pawn would be to Black's disadvantage e.g. 13 ... N×BP 14 P–QR4 and 15 P–R5, or 13 ... B×P 14 N×N B×B 15 Q×B

P×N 16 QR–N1 etc. After 13 . . . N×N 14 Q×N Black cannot prevent P–QR4–5, so he decides to keep the Q-side blocked by recapturing on QR4 with his queen. However, this displacement of his queen allows White to begin operations in the centre.

14 N×N   Q×N

Black loses a pawn after 14 . . . Q×Q 15 QR×Q P×N 16 P–K5 QP×P 17 P×KP P–R3 18 B×N P×B 19 P×P.

15 Q–B2   P–R3
16 B–Q2!   P–Q4

This move is forced sooner or later. For, example, after 16 . . . K–N1 17 KR–N1! White would be threatening 18 R–N5! B×R 19 P×B trapping the black queen. After the text move, however, White eliminates his doubled pawn and comfortably exploits his central superiority in the further course of the game. Play continued: **17 BP×P P–B5 18 B–K2 P×P 19 P–K5 N–K5 20 B–K1 N–N4 21 P–QR4 B–N2 22 P–R4 N–K3 23 P–B4 B–B3 24 P–B5 N–B2 25 B–N3 B–Q2 26 Q–Q2 K–N2 27 P–R5 R–QB1 28 Q–B2 P–B3? 29 P–K6 B–B3 30 B–Q6 N–K1 31 B–K7 K–R1 32 KR–N1 R–QN1 33 B–B3 Q–R3 34 Q–B1 Q–N2 35 Q–R3 N–B2 36 B–Q6 KR–Q1 37 P–R5! P–QN4** if 37 . . . N–N4 38 R×N B×R 39 P×P Q×P 40 B–B5 winning **38 P–R6 Q–B1 39 B–B4 R–N3** if 39 . . . R–K1 40 Q–Q6 N×RP 41 B×QP R–N3 42 R×P! wins **40 Q–K7 N×RP 41 Q×NP B–N2 42 Q×BP P–N5 43 Q–K5 Q–B3 44 P×P N×P 45 P–K7 R–KN1 46 P–B6 Q–K1 47 R×N! R×R 48 Q–K6 Q–QB1 49 Q×Q+ R×Q 50 P–B7 1–0.**

PART TWO

The Centre

In an early chapter of this work (see volume 1 'The Development of Modern Chess') the reader was shown how the various schools of chess could be differentiated by their attitude to the struggle for the centre. It is vital for us to examine in more detail what is meant by the centre and wherein lies its importance.

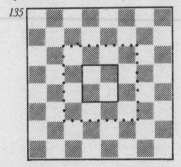

135

By the centre we usually mean the four squares in the middle of the board (see diagram 135) but sometimes the term 'large centre' is used, denoting the sixteen squares shown within the broken line in the diagram. Let us consider why the struggle for control of this central zone forms one of the most important aspects of chess strategy. We have already seen that the effectiveness of pieces and pawns depends upon the nature of the position. The more space they control, the more powerful they are, and pieces in the centre usually benefit in this way. We know, for example that a knight exerts its maximum power when posted in the

centre (see volume 1, 'The Minor Pieces'). The same applies to the other pieces, although it is rarely possible to post the major pieces in the centre until later in the game.

Control of the centre means then, above all, an improvement in the working power of our pieces. If our pawns control the centre, this restricts the space available to the enemy pieces. Moreover, the advance of a pawn may well force an enemy piece away from the central zone (for example, P–K5 can drive a knight from KB3 or a bishop from Q3). Thus our spatial superiority, directly resulting from control of the centre, not only allows us to manoeuvre our own pieces more effectively but also restricts the possibilities open to our opponent.

The best known and most common form of central control is brought about by a pawn centre, and indeed many players view the 'struggle for the centre' purely in terms of establishing a secure pawn structure on central squares. This was Tarrasch's incomplete concept of central control, hotly disputed by Nimzowitsch who demonstrated that the centre can be controlled by other means, such as centralization of pieces or pressure on the centre by pieces from the flanks (for example, White can control Q4 and K5 by playing his knight to KB3 and bishop to QN2). In other words the centre is a group of squares, not pawns, but as pawn control is more permanent than piece control, we shall first examine the various types of pawn centre.

8 The Classical Centre

Most openings used in the classical period of chess aimed at setting up pawns on Q4 and K4. For instance, in the Gioco Piano after 1 P–K4 P–K4 2 N–KB3 N–QB3 3 B–B4 B–B4 the continuation 4 P–B3 prepares P–Q4. However, this loss of time gives Black a chance to begin an effective counter-attack against the KP (4 . . . N–B3! 5 P–Q4 P×P 6 P×P B–N5+ 7 B–Q2 B×B+ 8 QN×B P–Q4!), so the Italian school attempted to improve White's plan by the Evans Gambit (4 P–QN4!? B×NP 5 P–B3) which gave him time to set up a pawn centre on Q4 and K4, at the price of a pawn. Another opening of the period, the King's Gambit, had a similar aim. After 1 P–K4 P–K4 2 P–KB4 P×P, White gambits a pawn in order to carry out the advance of his pawn to Q4 (apart from the strategic advantage he gains by the subsequent opening of the KB-file). The idea is clearly seen in the unsound Steinitz Gambit (1 P–K4 P–K4 2 N–QB3 N–QB3 3 P–B4 P×P 4 P–Q4?!) when, in order to achieve this central formation, White not only sacrifices a pawn but is also willing to gamble with the safety of his king (4 . . . Q–R5+ 5 K–K2).

This placing of pawns on Q4 and K4 was the only way then known of exploiting control of the centre, the idea being to use the dynamic power of the central pawns in order to drive back the enemy pieces and thus create opportunities for a successful attack by one's own pieces. A drastic example of this strategy can be seen in the following well-known variation of the Gioco Piano: **1 P–K4 P–K4 2 N–KB3 N–QB3 3 B–B4 B–B4 4 P–B3 N–B3 5 P–Q4 P×P 6 P×P B–N3?** (*136*)

136
W

| 7 P–Q5! | N–K2 |
| 8 P–K5 | N–K5 |

Or 8 . . . N–N5 9 P–Q6 P×P 10 P×P N–QB3 11 0–0 etc.

| 9 P–Q6 | P×P |
| 10 P×P | N×BP |

Or 10 . . . N–QB3 11 Q–Q5.

11 Q–N3	N×R
12 B×P+	K–B1
13 B–N5 winning	

The following games are more complex examples of the same theme.

61 Chigorin–Steinitz

World Championship 1892, Evans Gambit

1 P–K4 P–K4 2 N–KB3 N–QB3 3 B–B4

**B–B4 4 P–QN4 B×NP 5 P–B3 B–R4 6
0–0 P–Q3**

7 P–Q4   B–KN5

Lasker's 7 . . . B–N3 is the best defence
here, giving a pawn back after 8 P×P
P×P 9 Q×Q+ N×Q but eliminating
White's strong pawn centre and
obtaining good positional chances. The
text move on the other hand, like 7 . . .
P×P, allows White to achieve his goal of
setting up the classical pawn centre.

8 B–QN5

Another good continuation is 8
Q–N3 Q–Q2 9 P×P, or 8 Q–R4, but
the text move is the best way to force the
exchange of pawns in the centre.

8 . . .   P×P

Other moves are unsatisfactory e.g.

a. 8 . . . P–QR3 9 B×N+ P×B 10
Q–R4 etc.

b. 8 . . . B–Q2 9 B×N B×B 10 P×P
P×P 11 N×P Q×Q 12 R×Q B×KP
13 R–K1 B×N 14 N–B6+! (if *14
N–N6+ K–Q2 15 N×R B–B4*) 14 . . .
K–Q2 15 N×B B–B4 16 N×P N–B3
17 B–N5 with the better game for
White.

9 P×P   B–Q2 (*137*)

137
W

A typical Evans Gambit set-up.
White's strong centre gives him
compensation for the pawn, but he
must complete his development before
he can launch an attack by advancing
his centre pawns.

10 B–N2   N3–K2?

A faulty idea which leaves Black
seriously behind in development. In
later games of the match, Steinitz
played the correct 10 . . . N–B3, when
chances are about even.

11 B×B+   Q×B

12 N–R3!

The natural 12 N–B3 is much
weaker, as 12 . . . B×N would greatly
reduce White's attacking prospects.

12 . . .   N–R3

By no means an attractive square for
the knight, but on KB3 it would be
endangered by the advance of either
white pawn (P–K5, or P–Q5 followed
by B×N).

13 N–B4   B–N3

14 P–QR4   P–QB3

15 P–K5!?

After completing his development
White finally advances a pawn beyond
the fourth rank. A good alternative is 15
P–Q5 0–0 16 N×B P×N 17 Q–Q4 P–B3
18 Q×NP P×P 19 P×P, when White
not only regains his pawn (19 . . . N×P?
20 Q–N3) but has a definite positional
superiority thanks to his bishop on
QN2. Chigorin wants more, however,
so begins an attack on the K-side.

15 . . .   P–Q4

Steinitz prefers to strengthen his
centre rather than to castle. After 15 . . .
P×P 16 P×P Q×Q 17 KR×Q White
has strong threats (N–Q6+, or P–K6)
despite the exchange of queens.

16 N–Q6+   K–B1

17 B–R3   K–N1

18 R–N1!

White intends to play R–K1 followed
by P–K6 and N–N5, but first gains a
tempo (threat 19 P–R5) so that he can
later play his QR over to the K-side via
QN3, after the expected defensive move
18 . . . R–N1.

18 . . .   N3–B4(?)

(*138*)

Steinitz ignores the above threat in
his desire to exchange the strongly

posted knight. Apart from the above-mentioned 18 ... R–N1, he had the possibility of 18 ... N–B1, when Chigorin gives the following interesting variation: 19 P–R5 N×N 20 P×N B×RP 21 N–K5 Q–B1 22 Q–R5 P–B3 23 P–Q7 Q–Q1 24 R×P! P×N 25 P×P and the advance of White's pawns decides the game.

138
W

19 N×BP!?

A move which is typical of Chigorin's style of play, revealing his penchant for deep combinations and artistic moments in his games. However, most present-day masters would have settled for the following simpler line: 19 P–R5 B×RP 20 R×P Q–Q1 21 N–KN5 with a strong attack.

19 ...	K×N
20 P–K6+	K×P
21 N–K5!	

The point of the combination. Black's king is kept in the centre where it can be threatened by White's pieces.

| 21 ... | Q–B1 ? |

After this move White wins by force. Lasker later recommended the stronger defence: 21 ... Q–K1! 22 R–K1 K–B3 23 P–N4 P–KR4! 24 B×N+ Q×B and now:
a. 25 P×N QR–K1 26 N–N4+ P×N 27 R×Q R×R 28 Q×P R–R3 and Black can survive (Lasker).
b. 25 P–N5+! K×P 26 Q–Q2+ K–B3 27 P–R4 N×RP 28 Q–B4+ N–B4

29 N–N4+ P×N 30 R×Q K×R 31 Q–K5+! K–Q1 32 Q×N R–K1! 33 P–R5 B×RP 34 R×P B–B2 and Black has many defensive chances.

22 R–K1	K–B3
23 Q–R5	P–N3
24 B×N+	K×B

Or 24 ... N×B 25 Q–R4+ P–N4 26 N–N4+ K–B2 27 Q×NP winning.

25 N×NP+ +	K–B3
26 N×R	B×P

Or 26 ... Q×N 27 R–K5 Q–QB1 28 P–N4 winning.

27 R–N3!	Q–Q2
28 R–KB3	R×N
29 P–N4	R–KN1
30 Q–R6+	R–N3
31 R×N+	1–0

62 Keres–Fine

Ostend 1937, Queen's Gambit

1 N–KB3 P–Q4 2 P–Q4 N–KB3 3 P–B4 P–K3 4 N–B3 P–B4 5 BP×P N×P 6 P–K4 N×N 7 P×N P×P 8 P×P B–N5+ 9 B–Q2 B×B+ 10 Q×B 0–0

11 B–B4

This is the best square for the bishop, even though it appears to be 'biting on granite'. It is vital that this piece can successfully support the advance of the QP later in the game.

| 11 ... | N–Q2 |

For many years the move 11 ... N–B3 was considered best here, but about five years ago the following promising method of play was found against it: 12 0–0 P–QN3 13 QR–Q1 B–N2 14 KR–K1 R–B1 15 P–Q5! N–R4! (after *15 ... P×P 16 B×P N–R4 17 Q–B4!* White is clearly better, as was shown in the game Spassky–Petrosian from their 1969 match) 16 B–Q3 P×P 17 P–K5! The game Polugayevsky–Tal continued 17 ... N–B5 (both *17 ... R–K1 18 Q–B4 P–KR3 19 Q–B5 P–N3 20 Q–R3 K–N2*, and *17 ... Q–K2 18 N–Q4*

P–N3 seem better) 18 Q–B4 N–N7 (if *18 . . . R–B3 19 N–Q4*, or *18 . . . P–KR3 19 Q–B5 P–N3 20 Q–R3 K–N2 21 P–K6 P×P 22 N–Q4* etc.) 19 B×P+ ! K×B 20 N–N5+ K–N3 21 P–KR4! and White had a very strong attack, although the outcome was still unclear after 21 . . . R–B5! 22 P–R5+ K–R3! 23 N×P+ + K–R2 24 Q–B5+ K–N1 25 P–K6 Q–B3!

12 0–0	P–QN3
13 QR–Q1!	

At first sight 13 QR–B1 seems more natural, occupying the open file. However, it is essential to develop the pieces in support of the main strategic plan–the advance of the QP.

13 . . .	B–N2
14 KR–K1	R–B1
15 B–N3	N–B3

Black's best move here is clearly 15 . . . Q–B3! when, after 16 P–Q5, he can either capture or play . . . P–K4. The text move can be answered at once by 16 P–Q5! e.g. 16 . . . P×P 17 P×P R–B4 18 P–Q6 B–Q4 19 Q–B4 N–R4 20 Q–Q4 N–B3 21 R–K5! B×N 22 P×B and White's passed pawn is very strong. All this occurred in the game Olafsson–Unzicker, Lugano Olympiad 1968, but of course the theory of this opening variation was not so well known 31 years previously!

16 Q–B4	Q–B2
17 Q–KR4!	

Exchange of queens would obviously favour Black e.g. 17 Q×Q R×Q 18 P–Q5 P×P 19 P×P R–Q2 and the passed pawn is rendered harmless.

17 . . .	KR–Q1
18 R–K3(?)	

The following principle usually applies to the handling of pawns on Q4 and K4: never hurry to advance one of the pawns when your opponent can successfully blockade the remaining backward pawn. However, all rules have their exception, and in this

position White's actively placed pieces allow him to play 18 P–K5! with advantage e.g. 18 . . . N–Q4 (if *18 . . . B×N? 19 P×N* followed by *20 Q–N5* wins) 19 N–N5 P–KR3 20 N–K4 and this knight reaches the excellent strong-point on Q6; or 18 . . . N–K1 19 N–N5 P–KR3 20 N–K4 B–Q4 21 B×B R×B 22 R–Q3! with strong threats such as 23 N–B6+ P×N 24 Q×RP, or 23 R–KN3, or 23 N–B3 followed by 24 P–Q5.

18 . . .	P–QN4!
19 R1–K1	P–QR4

Black has used the slight breathing space to mobilize his Q-side majority, giving him an equal game.

20 P–QR4	P–N5 ? *(139)*

Black is understandably anxious to obtain a protected passed pawn whilst fixing White's QRP on the same colour as his bishop. However, it is vital to use the available tempo in order to prevent the attack down the centre and on the K-side. After 20 . . . P×P! 21 B×RP P–R3! the game would still be even.

139
W

21 P–Q5!

The beginning of a typical break-through combination. After 21 . . . P–K4 White would reply 22 Q–N5 R–K1 23 N–R4 P–R3 24 Q–N3 N–R4 25 Q–N4 N–B3 (*25 . . . N–B5 26 P–Q6!*) 26 Q–R3 threatening the powerful 27 N–B5.

21 . . .	P×P
22 P–K5!	N–Q2?

This leads to a forced loss, whereas 22 ... N–K5 still leaves the situation unclear. Keres intended 23 P–K6! P×P 24 R×N! P×R 25 N–N5 with strong attacking chances. Black is then forced to play 25 ... Q–B6! (if *25 ... Q–K4 26 Q×RP+ K–B1 27 N×P.K6+ K–K2 28 N×P*) when White has three possible continuations of the attack:

a. 26 Q×RP+ K–B1 27 N×P.K6+ K–K2 28 Q–R4+ Q–KB3 29 Q–N4 with attacking chances for the exchange.

b. 26 B×P+ K–B1 27 Q–B4+ K–K2 28 Q–KB7+ K–Q3 and White must take the perpetual check by 29 Q–B4+ K–K2 etc.

c. 26 B×P+ K–B1 27 R–KB1! with excellent attacking chances e.g. 27 ... R–B2 28 B–B5, or 27 ... B–R3 28 .Q–B4+ K–K2 29 Q–KB7+ K–Q3 30 N×KP+ etc.

23 N–N5   N–B1

Or 23 ... P–R3 24 P–K6! P×N 25 P×P+ K×P 26 R–K7+ when White wins after both 26 ... K–N3 27 Q–Q4 Q–B6 28 B–B2+! Q×B 29 R×P+ K–R4 30 P–R4, and 26 ... K–N1 27 Q×KNP Q–B6 28 B×P+ B×B 29 Q×B+ K–R2 30 Q–R5+ K–N1 31 Q–B7+ K–R2 32 R7–K3.

24 N×RP!   N×N

Or 24 ... N–N3 25 Q–R5 N–B5 26 N–B6+! wins.

25 R–R3   Q–B8
26 Q×N+   K–B1
27 R3–K3   P–Q5
28 Q–R8+   K–K2
29 Q×P   R–B1

After 29 ... B–Q4 30 Q–B6+ K–K1 31 P–K6! wins.

30 Q–B6+   K–K1
31 P–K6!   1–0

If 31 ... P×R 32 P×P+ R×P 33 B×R+ K–Q2 34 B–K6+ etc. forces the win.

63 Pachman–Vesely

Prague 1953, Queen's Gambit

1 P–Q4 P–Q4 2 P–QB4 P–QB3 3 N–QB3 N–B3 4 P–K3 P–K3 5 N–B3 QN–Q2 6 Q–B2 B–Q3 7 P–QN3 0–0 8 B–K2   Q–K2?

Better is 8 ... P×P 9 P×P P–K4 10 0–0 R–K1 11 B–N2 P×P 12 P×P N–B1. After the text move the exchange on ... Q5 will no longer be possible, as Black's queen will be driven away from the K-file with gain of tempo.

9 0–0   P×P
10 P×P   P–K4
11 R–K1!

As Black will be forced to play ... P–K5 and White will then wish to open up the centre by N–Q2 and P–B3, it would have been strategically better for the QR to go to K1. However, there is a slight tactical disadvantage to this plan: after 11 B–N2 R–K1 12 QR–K1 P–K5 13 N–Q2 N–B1 14 P–B3 P×P 15 B×P N–N5! Black equalizes, as White must play 16 B×N which gives his opponent compensation for the strong centre in the shape of the bishop pair.

11 ...   R–K1
12 B–N2   P–K5
13 N–Q2   N–B1 *(140)*

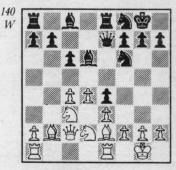

140
W

14 P–B3!

A frequently recurring method of eliminating the enemy KP and giving White a central pawn majority. When playing such a move, the possible weakness of the backward KP must always be taken into account. For instance, in the French Defence Black is often compelled to play . . . P-KB3 leaving him with pawns on Q4 and K3 which can become a serious weakness if White succeeds in blockading them. In the present case, however, White can easily force through P-K4, creating a strong pawn centre.

14 . . .	P×P
15 B×P	N-N5
16 N-B1	

Now we see the point of 11 R-K1. White retains his bishop pair for the moment and Black cannot prevent P-K4 (16 . . . P-KB4? 17 P-K4 P×P 18 R×P etc.).

| 16 . . . | Q-N4 |
| 17 P-K4 | B-B5 |

It is important to note that Black cannot attack White's centre with 17 . . . P-QB4 (hoping to blockade on K4 after *18 P-Q5?*), as White replies 18 P-K5 B-N1 (*18 . . . P×P? 19 N-K4 Q×P 20 N×B*) 19 N-K4 Q-N3 20 P-KR3 N-R3 21 P×P! B×KP 22 B×B R×B 23 Q-B3! P-B3 (*23 . . . R-K2? 24 N-B6+*) 24 N-Q6 with a winning position.

18 B×N!

Black was threatening 18 . . . N-K6, whereas now his KB is misplaced on the KR3-QB8 diagonal.

18 . . .   B×B?

It seems natural enough to develop a piece whilst recapturing, but this is a mistake. It was essential to take with the queen so as to allow the KB to retreat at once to KR3.

| 19 P-K5 | B-B4 |
| 20 Q-B2 | B-Q6 |

White was threatening 21 P-N3 which would now be answered by 21 . . . B×N 22 K×B B-Q7.

| 21 N-K4 | Q-R3 |
| 22 P-N3 | B.Q6×N |

23 K×B	Q-R6+
24 K-N1	B-R3
25 N-Q6	R-K2
26 P-Q5!	

This move is much better than 26 Q-B5 Q×Q 27 N×Q R-Q2. White has already attained his strategic goal of cramping the enemy position by the advance of his central pawns.

26 . . .	P×P
27 P×P	R-B2
28 QR-Q1	B-N4
29 R-K2	P-KR4
30 R-KB1!	

This attack on Black's KB2 leads to a quicker win than preparing to advance the passed pawns.

30 . . .	Q-Q2
31 P-KR4	B-R3
32 Q-B3	P-KN3
33 Q-N3!	N-R2

Black can no longer defend his KBP. After 33 . . . Q-Q1 White wins by either 34 N×NP or 34 N×BP R×N 35 P-Q6 Q-Q2 36 R2-KB2. Or if 33 . . . Q-N5 then simply 34 R2-KB2 wins.

| 34 N×BP | B-N2 |
| 35 P-Q6 | 1-0 |

In all these three games White reached a position with pawns on Q4 and K4. In the first case, Black had a pawn on Q3, in the second on K3, whereas in the third game Black had no QP or KP. Euwe termed this pawn configuration 'the absolute centre'. The QP and KP usually possess great mobility but can also become weak if subjected to pressure down the open files. So far the games in this chapter have shown us how White can advance the pawns after due preparation and use their mobility to achieve a breakthrough. Sometimes, however, such an advance is difficult to carry out. The importance of the pawn centre then lies in the fact that it restricts the activity of the enemy pieces which constantly have to guard against any possible break-through. The result is that the side with the strong pawn centre has a sound basis for operations of various kinds.

64 Kotov–Eliskases

Stokholm–Saltsjobaden interzonal 1952, Queen's Gambit

1 P–Q4 P–Q4 2 P–QB4 P–K3 3 N–QB3 N–KB3 4 B–N5 QN–Q2 5 P–K3 P–B3 6 Q–B2 Q–R4 7 P×P N×P 8 P–K4 N×N 9 B–Q2 P–K4 9 ... Q–R5! 10 P×N! P×P 11 P×P B–N5 12 R–N1! B×B+ 13 Q×B Q×Q+ 14 K×Q (*141*)

This game without queens reminds one of the game Alekhine–Treybal which was discussed in volume 1. In such positions it is much more difficult to use a central break-through as a basis for an attack on the wings. However, the pawn centre is an ideal protection for White's king which can become actively centralized, ready to penetrate quickly into the enemy position as soon as a break-through is achieved.

14 ...   N–N3
15 B–Q3

White cannot avoid further simplification. As Kotov gives, after 15 R–N4 B–K3 16 P–QR4 0–0–0 17 K–K3 P–KB4 18 P–B3 N–Q2 threatening 19 ... P–B4 or 19 ... N–B3 is good for Black.

15 ...   B–K3

16 P–QR4   0–0–0
17 N–K2

Not however 17 P–R5? N–B5+ 18 B×N R×P+! 19 B–Q3 B–B5 20 K–B3 B×B etc.

17 ...   N×P
18 R–R1   N–N7
19 R×P   K–N1
20 R1–R1   B–B5!

To give up the knight for the bishop would be a serious positional error, for White's knight would then be far stronger than Black's bishop, as it can effectively support the advance of the centre pawns.

21 B×B   N×B+
22 K–Q3   N–N3
23 P–N4!

White thus prevents the possible freeing move ... P–KB4 and at the same time prepares a pawn advance on the K-side.

23 ...   K–B2
24 P–B4   R–Q2

Black could exchange all four rooks here, but the unfavourable placing of his king and knight would lose him a pawn e.g. 24 ... R–R1? 25 R×R R×R 26 R×R N×R 27 N–N3 (threatening *N–R5*) 27 ... P–KN3 28 P–K5 K–Q2 29 N–K4 K–K2 30 N–B6 etc.

25 R7–R5   R1–Q1
26 R–KN5!

Along with the next move, this is a very good manoeuvre, preparing to advance the K-side pawns and then break through in the centre at an opportune moment. The immediate advance of these pawns (e.g. 26 P–B5 and 27 P–N5) would be pointless, as Black's pawns are not yet weakened. The aim of the rook move is to cause the necessary weakness.

26 ...   P–B3

After 26 ... P–N3 27 R5–QR5 White would be able to fix Black's K-side pawns by 28 P–N5 and then prepare P–R4–5 and P–B4–5.

27 R5–QR5

Threatening 28 P–B5 followed by K–K3 and N–B4–K6.

27 ...   N–B1!

28 P–B5(?)

This move complicates matters unnecessarily. More exact is 28 P–R4! N–Q3 29 N–B3 when White can continue P–B5, P–K5 or P–N5 depending upon the play.

28 ...   P–KN4!

29 P–R4   P–R3

30 P×P   RP×P

31 R–R1

Now White's sole winning plan is to post his pieces as favourably as possible and prepare P–K5.

31 ...   N–Q3

32 R–KR6   R–K2!

33 N–B3   R1–K1! *(142)*

Passive defence would give White an easy win by P–K5, so Black counter-attacks the KP and apparently prevents P–K5.

142
W

34 P–K5!   P×P

35 N–Q5+ !

The break-through is carried out by means of a little combination giving White the better rook ending.

35 ...   P×N

36 R–B5+   K–N1

Weaker is 36 ... K–Q2 37 R×P etc.

37 R×N   P×P

White would still have good chances after the better 37 ... P–K5+! 38

K–K3 R–KR1 39 R5×P R–R6+ 40 K–K2 R–R7+ 41 K–B1 P–K6 42 R–K6! R–QB2 43 R–B5, but it is doubtful whether he could force a win against best defence. Kotov now exploits his passed KBP in instructive fashion.

38 R5×P!   R–K6+

39 K–B4!   R–QB1+

40 K×P   R–KN6

41 P–B6   R×P+

42 K–K5   R–KB5

Or 42 ... R–K1+ 43 K–B5 R–KB5+ 44 K×P R1–K5 45 R–KB5 wins.

43 R–Q8!   R×R

44 R×R+   K–B2

45 R–KN8   K–Q2

46 R–N7+   K–K1

Or 46 ... K–B3 47 R×KNP R–B8 48 K–K6 R–K8+ 49 K–B7 P–N4 50 K–N7 wins.

47 R×QNP!

It is interesting to note that Black loses solely because his own KNP protects the white king from vertical checks by the rook!

47 ...   R–B7

48 K–K6   R–K7+

49 K–B5   P–N5

50 K–N6   R–KB7

51 P–B7+   K–B1

52 R–N8+   K–K2

53 R–K8+   1–0

The 'absolute centre' of pawns on Q4 and K4 is not in itself an advantage, as many other factors come into play. In many modern openings Black allows White to attain this set-up and then proceeds to weaken the pawn centre by attacks from the flanks. The relatively modern Grünfeld Defence is based on this idea. Here is an example.

65 Sliwa–Pachman

Moscow 1956, Grünfeld Defence

1 P–Q4 N–KB3 2 P–QB4 P–KN3 3

N–QB3 P–Q4 4 P×P N×P 5 P–K4
N×N 6 P×N B–N2 7 B–QB4 0–0
8 N–K2   N–B3

A very surprising move which
introduces a system devised by the
Soviet grandmaster Simagin. It is
surprising because it is well-known that
Black can attack the centre at once by 8
. . . P–QB4, so why should he now block
this pawn? After 8 . . . P–QB4 9 0–0
N–B3 10 B–K3 Black can adopt two
important systems about which theory
has not yet come to a definitive
conclusion:

a. 10 . . . P×P 11 P×P B–N5 12 P–B3
  N–R4. Now after 13 B–Q3 B–K3
  White has two sharp lines at his
  disposal, involving in turn the
  sacrifice of a pawn and the
  exchange: 14 R–B1 B×RP 15 Q–R4
  B–N6 16 Q–N4 followed by 17
  P–Q5, or 14 P–Q5!? B×R 15 Q×B
  P–B3! We advise the reader to study
  these variations thoroughly (they
  can be found in any book on the
  openings), for they reveal many
  interesting strategic points with
  regard to the problem of the centre.
  As, however, the correctness of both
  these sacrifices cannot be demonstrated (the pawn sacrifice can
  even be considered unsound!) we
  recommend instead the quiet
  continuation 13 R–B1! N×B 14
  R×N B–Q2 15 Q–N3 Q–R4! 16
  N–B3! when White's pawn centre is
  more than compensation for the two
  bishops.

b. 10. . . Q–B2 11 R–B1 R–Q1 12
  P–KB4. Once again, it is by no
  means clear whether White's
  aggressive pawn centre gives him a
  concrete advantage.

The text move 8 . . . N–B3 is part of a
plan to develop Black's Q-side first (. . .
P–N3 and . . . B–N2) and only then to
launch a direct attack against the
centre with . . . N–R4 and . . . P–QB4.

9 0–0   P–N3
10 R–N1 ?

The idea of this move is to make it
more difficult for Black to play . . .
P–QB4 e.g. if 10 . . . N–R4 11 B–Q3
P–QB4 12 P–Q5 P–K3 13 P–QB4! and
White's QR is not attacked. However,
the rook is better placed on QB1 after 10
B–K3 B–N2 (or *10 . . . N–R4 11 B–Q3
P–QB4 12 R–B1*) 11 R–B1!

10 . . .   B–N2 (*143*)

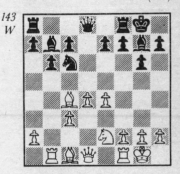

143
W

11 B–R3 ?

White wishes to prevent an attack on
his centre by guarding the QB5 square,
but in reality this only helps Black.
Once again 11 B–K3 was the correct
move and after 11 . . . Q–Q2 12 Q–Q2
KR–Q1 the game is approximately
even.

11 . . .   N–R4
12 B–Q3   Q–Q2
13 P–KB4(?)

Such an aggressive advance is only
effective when the central position is
strong enough. In the given
circumstances it constitutes a further
strategic error after which the imposing
looking White centre is speedily
shattered. White could not even
prevent . . . P–QB4 by repeating moves
with 13 B–N4 N–B3 14 B–R3. Black
would continue 14 . . . KR–Q1! 15
P–KB4 P–K3! 16 P–B5 KP×P 17 P×P
N–R4! 18 B–N4 P–B4! 19 B×N P×B 20
BP×P RP×P 21 B–B4 B–Q4 22 B×B

Q×B and Black's pressure against what is left of White's centre guarantees him the advantage.

13 ...	**P–QB4**
14 P×P	

After 14 P–Q5 Black would attack the centre from the other wing with 14 ... P–B4.

14 ...	**KR–Q1**
15 B–B2	**Q–B2**
16 Q–K1	

Black also has a decisive positional superiority after 16 Q–B1 N–B5.

16 ...	**N–B5**
17 P×P	**P×P**
18 B–B1	**N–R6!**

The QRP cannot run away, so Black has time to obtain the permanent positional advantage of the two bishops.

19 B×N	**R×B**
20 P–K5	

The attempt to protect his RP by 20 R–N2 fails to the tactical point 20 ... R×BP! 21 N×R B×N 22 Q–B1 B×R 23 Q×B R–Q7 24 R–B1 Q–B4+! followed by 25 ... B×P winning for Black. The text move attempts at least to block the long black diagonal.

20 ...	**R×RP**
21 B–N3	**R7–Q7**
22 R–B2	

Or 22 R–Q1 R×R 23 B×R P–K3 and 24 ... B–KB1.

22 ...	**P–K3**
23 R–Q1	**R×R**
24 B×R *(144)*	

All that is left of White's proud centre is his pawn on K5, shutting in Black's KB. But we soon see that even this last strong-point cannot be maintained.

24 ...	**P–KN4!**
25 P×P	

Or 25 P–N3 Q–B3 26 K–B1 Q–R8+ 27 N–N1 B–KB1 28 R–Q2 B–Q4 wins.

25 ...	**Q×KP**
26 P–R4	**Q–K6**
27 Q–B1	**R–Q7**

144
B

28 K–R1	**R×B**
0–1	

In this game Black liquidated his opponent's pawn centre by advancing his QBP. Another method is to apply pressure by pieces, when it is often possible to force a premature advance of the pawns, then to liquidate them by exchanging them for one's own pawns. Alekhine's Defence is a simple example of this method: 1 P–K4 N–KB3 2 P–K5 N–Q4 3 P–QB4 N–N3 4 P–Q4. If White's pawn were on K4 instead of K5, he would have a decisive advantage, whereas now Black can successfully break up the centre by 4 ... P–Q3 5 P–B4 P×P 6 BP×P N–B3 7 B–K3 B–B4 8 N–QB3 P–K3 9 B–K2, forcing the exchange of the QP (after 9 ... N–N5 10 R–B1 P–QB4) or the KP (after 9 ... B–K2 and 10 ... P–KB3).

Here is a clear-cut example of the same method used in the Grünfeld Defence.

66 Euwe–Reshevsky

A.V.R.O. tournament 1938, Grünfeld Defence

1 P–Q4 N–KB3 2 P–QB4 P–KN3 3 P–B3 P–Q4 4 P×P N×P 5 P–K4 N–N3 6 N–B3 B–N2

7 B–K3	**0–0** *(145)*

This is more exact than 7 ... N–B3 8 B–QN5 when White can maintain his strong pawn centre longer.

145
W

8 P–B4!?

The sharpest continuation by which White strengthens his centre (. . . P–K4 is prevented) and vacates KB3 for his knight. After 8 Q–Q2 N–B3 9 0–0–0 Black equalizes by 9 . . . P–K4 10 P–Q5 N–Q5.

8 . . .   N–B3!

The only correct way to liquidate White's centre. After 8 . . . P–QB3 (preventing P–Q5 and preparing to exert lasting pressure on the QP) White obtains active play on the K-side by 9 N–B3 B–K3 10 Q–Q2 N–B5 11 B×N B×B 12 P–B5! etc.

9 P–Q5

Or 9 N–B3 B–N5! 10 P–Q5 N–N1 and once again Black can successfully attack the centre e.g. 11 B–K2 P–QB3 12 Q–N3 P×P 13 P×P N1–Q2 14 0–0 P–K3.

9 . . .   N–N1

Less clear is 9 . . . N–R4!? 10 B×N RP×B 11 R–B1 threatening 12 P–QN4.

10 N–B3?

White must play energetically if he is to maintain equality e.g.

a. 10 B–Q4 B×B 11 Q×B P–QB3=
b. 10 P–QR4 P–QB3 11 P–R5 N3–Q2 12 P–K5 P×P 13 Q×P N–QB3= Or here 10 . . . P–K4!? 11 P–R5 N3–Q2 12 N–B3 P×P 13 B×BP R–K1 with an equal game.

10 . . .   P–QB3

11 Q–N3

After 11 P×P N×P followed by 12

. . . B–N5 Black has good play down the long Black diagonal.

11 . . .   P×P
12 N×P   N×N
13 P×N   N–Q2
14 B–K2   Q–R4+ !

All that remains of White's centre is his pawn on Q5 whose weakness Black now exploits to gain a decisive advantage.

15 B–Q2

Other possibilities are:

a. 15 N–Q2 N–B3 16 B–B3 R–Q1 winning the QP.
b. 15 K–B2 N–B3 threatening both . . . N–N5+ and . . . N×P.

15 . . .   Q–N3!
16 B–B3

After 16 Q×Q N×Q White loses either his QP or QNP, and Black answers 16 0–0–0 with 16 . . . Q×Q 17 P×Q N–B4! 18 B–B4 P–QN4! B×P N×P+ 20 K–B2 R–N1 etc.

16 . . .   B×B+
17 P×B

Or 17 Q×B N–B3 18 R–Q1 R–Q1 19 B–B4 B–N5 with a clear advantage to Black.

17 . . .   Q–K6

This wins a pawn, as 18 P–N3 loses to 18 . . . N–B4 19 Q–B2 N–K5 etc. The game concluded: **18 P–B4 Q×P 19 0–0 Q–B2 20 K–R1 N–B3 21 Q–K3 B–N5 22 Q–R6 B×N 23 R×B P–QN4! 24 P×P Q–K4 25 R–K1 N×P 26 R–KR3 Q–N2 27 Q–Q2 P–K3 28 R–Q3 QR–N1 29 P–QR4 N–N3 30 Q–N4 R–N1–B1 31 P–R5 N–Q4 32 Q–N3 R–B4 33 B–B3** if 33 P–N6 R×P 34 P–N7 R–N1 35 Q–B4 Q–B1, or here 35 R–QB1 R–R8 **33 . . . R–N1 34 B×N R4×P!** not 34 . . . R1×P? 35 B–B4! R×Q 36 R–Q8+ etc. **35 Q–R2 P×B 36 R×P Q–B6 37 R–KB1 R–N7 38 Q–R4 R–N8 39 R5–Q1 R×R 40 R×R P–QR3 41 P–R3 R–N4 42 R–R1 K–N2 43 Q–R2 Q–N7 44 Q–R4 R–N4 45 R–R2 Q–B6 46 R–R1 P–R4 47**

**Q–R2 R–KB4 48 K–R2 P–N4 49
Q–R4 R–B5 50 Q–R2 P–N5 51 P×P
Q–K4 52 P–N3 R–K5 53 Q–N1
R–K7+ 54 K–R3 P×P+ 55 K–R4
R–R7+ 56 K×P Q–K7+ 0–1.**

We can now attempt to draw up some basic principles governing positions with the 'classical centre':

For the side with the pawn centre

1. Post the pieces in such a way that they guard the centre pawns and at the same time are ready to support their advance.
2. Force the enemy pieces onto unfavourable squares.
3. Advance the pawns at an opportune moment, creating tactical threats on either wing in conjunction with a central break-through.

For the side fighting against the pawn centre

1. Place the pieces so as to restrain the enemy pawns.
2. By pressure against the pawns, force the enemy pieces to defend passively.
3. Weaken the enemy centre by forcing one of the pawns to advance, then blockading the other.
4. Eliminate one or both centre pawns by advancing the QBP or KBP.

Summing up, the classical pawn centre is strong only when it is adequately defended by pieces and has sufficient mobility. It is weak when it can be restrained or, even better, blockaded.

9 The 'Little Centre'

By this expression we mean that one side has a pawn on K4 or Q4, whilst the other side has a pawn on the third rank on the adjacent central file. Diagram 146 shows this clearly.

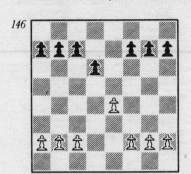

146

White has more space in the centre. If Black's QP were on Q4 and White's KP on K3, then Black would be in possession of the 'little centre'. In volume 1 we have already discussed this pawn formation (see the chapter 'The Rooks'), showing that the most important strategic idea for White is to occupy the 'outpost' on the open file (Q5 in the diagram), whereas Black aims to utilize his K4 square. Here is where the importance of the 'little centre' comes in. As White's Q5 square is in his opponent's half of the board, a piece posted on it, especially a knight, will exert much greater pressure on the enemy position than a corresponding black piece posted on K4. In other

words, the side who possesses the 'little centre' has a space advantage which he can use to manoeuvre his pieces more freely.

Here are two games which illustrate how such a space advantage can be used to carry out an attack on the enemy position.

67 Tarrasch–Schlechter

Leipzig 1894, Ruy Lopez

1 P–K4 P–K4 2 N–KB3 N–QB3 3 B–N5 P–Q3 4 P–Q4 B–Q2 5 N–B3 N–B3 6 0–0 B–K2

    7 R–K1   N×QP

After 7 ... P×P 8 N×P 0–0 9 B×N P×B we have a different type of pawn formation which was thoroughly examined in our chapter on 'The Doubled Pawn'.

    8 N×N   P×N
    9 B×B+   Q×B
    10 Q×P   0–0 (*147*)

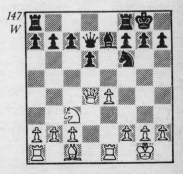

147
W

11 P–QN3!

White's bishop will be placed to maximum advantage on QN2 and will prevent in particular the regrouping of Black's pieces by ... R–K1, ... B–B1, ... R–K3, ... P–KN3 and ... B–N2, converting his passive KB into an active one.

11 ...	KR–K1
12 B–N2	B–B1
13 QR–Q1	

Threatening P–K5. As can be seen, the 'little centre' contains a certain dynamism, even though its mobility is naturally by no means as great as that of the 'classical centre'.

13 ...	Q–B3
14 R–Q3	R–K3
15 R3–K3	R1–K1
16 P–KR3	Q–N3

It is doubtful whether Black can improve the co-ordination of his pieces by 16 ... P–KN3, as White would then be able to make effective use of his Q5 square e.g. 17 N–Q5! B–N2 18 P–QB4 N–R4 19 Q–Q2 with a clear advantage in view of the weakness of Black's KB3 square.

17 Q–Q3   **P–B3**

This move is essential, as White is threatening 18 P–KN4 followed by P–N5 and N–Q5, but this weakening of the QP is already a strategic success for the first player.

18 N–R4!   **Q–B2**
19 P–QB4

An important manoeuvre, preventing ... P–Q4 and freeing his knight for work on the K-side, a strange result of 18 N–R4!

19 ...   **N–Q2?**

This was Black's first and last chance to play ... P–KN3. Admittedly his bishop would then have to give up the defence of his QP, but this would be compensated by its activity along the KR1–QR8 diagonal. Black chooses a passive defence instead, allowing White

to exploit his space advantage in a K-side attack.

20 K–R1

Not only placing the king on a safer square but freeing KN1 for a rook which will support an attack down the KN-file nine moves later.

20 ...	P–B3
21 Q–B2	N–K4
22 N–B3	

Threatening N–K2–N3.

22 ...	N–B2
23 P–KN4!	

Not however 23 N–K2? P–KB4! giving Black immediate equality by liquidating White's 'little centre'.

23 ...	Q–R4
24 R–Q1	Q–N3
25 P–KR4!	

It was still too early to play 25 N–K2, as 25 ... N–N4 would immediately force the knight back to QB3.

25 ...	N–K4
26 R–N3	N–B2
27 P–B3	N–R1 *(148)*

Black has no chances of counterplay, so must simply await events.

148
W

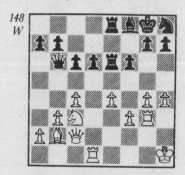

28 N–K2	Q–B2
29 R1–KN1!	

White's plan is simple. He intends to open the KN-file by P–N5, then transfer his knight to KB5, thus attacking KN7 four times, Black is helpless.

29 ...	Q–B2
30 N–Q4	R3–K2
31 P–N5	P×P
32 R×P	P–KN3
33 N–B5	R–K4

Or 33 ... R–Q2 34 Q–B3 etc.

34 P–B4!	R×N
35 P×R	B–N2
36 P×P	1–0

68 Lasker–Capablanca

Moscow 1935, French Defence

1 P–K4 P–K3 2 P–Q4 P–Q3 3 N–QB3 B–N5 4 KN–K2 P×P 5 P–QR3 B–K2 6 N×P N–KB3 7 N2–B3? N2–N3! 7 ... QN–Q2? 7 ... N–B3! 8 B–KB4 N×N 9 N×N N–B3 10 B–Q3 0–0 11 N×N+ B×N 12 P–QB3 *(149)*

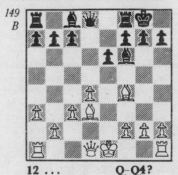

149
B

12 ...   Q–Q4?

When fighting against the 'little centre', the simplest method is to liquidate the central pawns by exchanges. It is therefore understandable that Black wishes to force through ... P–QB4 or ... P–K4 in the present situation, and that this queen move is the best means available, as it not only attacks the KNP but also contains a subtle trap. However, Lasker has a very neat refutation at hand. Nor was 12 ... P–B4 possible, as after 13 P×P Q–Q4 14 Q–B2! White retains his extra pawn. All this means that Black cannot liquidate White's QP, so he should

settle for 12 ... P–B3, giving him a passive but solid position.

13 Q–K2

Capablanca had planned for the variation 13 Q–B2 Q×NP 14 B×RP+ K–R1 15 B–K4 Q–N5! 16 B×BP P–K4! when 17 P×P R–K1 18 P–B3 B–R5+ gives him a strong attack. After the text move, however, 13 ... Q×NP fails to 14 B–K4 Q–R6 15 B×BP followed by 16 0–0–0, and if 13 ... P–B4 14 B–K4 wins a pawn for White.

13 ...   P–B3
14 0–0

A typical Lasker move. Most players would prefer to castle long in order to support the K-side attack by advancing the pawns on that wing. However, Lasker does not wish to give his opponent the slightest counter-chance, calculating that piece play along with a definite space advantage ('little centre'!) should be sufficient to win the game.

14 ...   R–K1
15 QR–Q1   B–Q2
16 KR–K1(?)

One important aspect of this position is that all the knights have disappeared, thus reducing the value of the strong-points (White's on K5 and Black's on Q4). Nevertheless, White can exploit his K5 square, as pointed out by Rabinovich, with 16 B–K5! B–K2 (Black loses a pawn after *16 ... B×B 17 B×P+ K×B 18 P×B*) 17 Q–B2 P–KR3 18 P–QN4! when Black must retreat his QB in order to avoid the loss of his queen.

16 ...   Q–QR4
17 Q–B2   P–KN3

This weakening move is forced, as 17 ... Q–R4 fails to 18 B–K5! threatening 19 R–K3.

18 B–K5!   B–N2(?) *(150)*

It was clearly better to play 18 ... Q–Q1 when White would have to prepare his next move.

19 P–KR4!

The following attack clearly emphasizes White's advantage in space. Black's pieces can neither counter-attack nor effectively defend the K-side.

19 ...	Q–Q1
20 P–R5	Q–N4
21 B×B	K×B
22 R–K5	Q–K2

After 22 ... P–KB4 White would win by directing his pieces at the weak KP (R1–K1, B–B4, Q–N3). However, 22 ... Q–R3 gives an interesting situation, as it would clearly be pointless for White to continue with his K-side attack, because Black is already threatening ... P–B3 followed by ... Q×P. Instead White could exploit the fact that Black's queen is out of play and continue 23 B–K2 followed by Q–N3–N4–Q6 with a strong Q-side attack. This switching from one wing to another is once again typical of positions where one side has a space advantage.

23 R1–K1	R–KN1
24 Q–B1!	

Preventing the escape of Black's king, as 24 ... K–B1 now fails to 25 Q–R6+ .

24 ...	QR–Q1
25 R1–K3	B–B1

The white rook on K5 exerts uncomfortable pressure, as 25 ... P–B3 allows 26 R–R5 P–QR3 27 P×P P×P 28 R–N3 B–K1 29 R–R3 winning. This

is a good example of a strong-point occupied by a rook.

26 R–R3	K–B1

Black finally decides to retreat his king. If 26 ... P–B3 27 P×P P×P 28 Q–R6+ K–B2 29 R–N3! wins, and after 26 ... R–KR1 then 27 Q–B4 is strong, planning 28 R–KN5 followed by P×P and Q–K5+ .

27 Q–R6+	R–N2
28 P×P	RP×P
29 B×P!	Q–B3

Of course 29 ... P×B loses to 30 Q–R8+ and 31 R–B3+ .

30 R–KN5!

Black's only method now of prolonging the agony is to give up his queen for rook and bishop.

30 ...	K–K2
31 R–B3	Q×R.B6
32 P×Q	R1–N1
33 K–B1	

There is a quicker win by 33 Q–R4. In the remaining part of the game Lasker does not find the most exact winning plan but calmly manoeuvres until the adjournment is reached, when Capablanca must finally capitulate: 33 ... R×B 34 R×R R×R 35 Q–R2 K–Q2 36 Q–B4 P–B3 37 P–B4 P–R3 38 Q–R4 R–N4 39 Q–R7+ K–Q1 40 Q–R8+ K–B2 41 Q×P K–KB4 42 Q–N7+ B–Q2 43 K–K2 K–B1 44 Q–R8+ K–B2 45 Q–R2+ K–B1 46 Q–Q6 R–KR4 47 K–K3 R–KB4 48 K–K4 R–KR4 49 Q–B8+ K–B2 50 Q–B4+ K–B1 51 Q–Q6 R–KB4 52 K–K3 R–KR4 53 K–Q3 R–KB4 54 K–K2 R–KR4 55 K–Q2 R–KB4 56 K–K3 R–KR4 57 Q–B8+ K–B2 58 Q–B4+ K–B1 59 Q–Q6 R–KB4 60 Q–N3 R–KR4 61 Q–N4 R–KB4 62 Q–N8+ K–B2 63 Q–N3+ K–B1 64 Q–N6 K–B2 1–0.

In both the above games White's space advantage allowed him to carry out a K-side attack. It is important to note the vital part played by the white centre pawn, well guarded by the BP in both cases, supporting the knight on KB5 in game 67 and the bishop, then rook, on K5 in game 68. With this pawn set-up of QB3, Q4 or KB3, K4 the central pawn is not particularly mobile, but it allows the pieces to manoeuvre freely, as they are not tied down to its defence. If the BP goes to the fourth rank, then the central pawn immediately gains in mobility but at the same time loses its natural defence and can become in certain circumstances an object of attack.

Pressure against the centre pawn is thus one method of combating the 'little centre', but the most usual method is to liquidate the pawns by advancing one's own. Opening theory provides us with numerous examples of this strategem. For example, in the Rubinstein variation of the French Defence, after 1 P–K4 P–K3 2 P–Q4 P–Q4 3 N–QB3 P×P 4 N×P, Black's aim is to attack White's centre by a subsequent ... P–QB4. We also meet the advance ... P–K4 in similar situations (e.g. 1 P–K4 P–K3 2 P–Q4 P–Q4 3 N–QB3 B–N5 4 KN–K2 P×P 5 P–QR3 B–K2 6 N×P N–KB3 7 N2–N3 0–0 8 B–K2 N–B3 9 N×N+ B×N 10 P–QB3 P–K4! etc.) In the same way, the KP is often liquidated by a timely ... P–Q4 (e.g. 1 P–K4 P–K4 2 P–Q4 P×P 3 Q×P N–QB3 4 Q–K3 N–B3 5 N–QB3 B–K2! 6 B–Q2 P–Q4!)

The 'little centre' is therefore an unstable structure which can only be maintained for a short time. When the centre pawns are liquidated the resulting open file can often be occupied with advantage by the defending pieces. In our next game, White tries to use his 'little centre' as a basis for a K-side attack, but Black obtains strong counterplay by seizing the open file after liquidating White's QP.

69 Smyslov–Pachman

Moscow 1947, French Defence

1 P–K4 P–K3 2 P–Q4 P–Q4 3 N–QB3 N–KB3 4 B–KN5 P×P 5 N×P B–K2 6 B×N B×B 7 N–KB3 N–Q2 8 P–B3 Q–K2 9 B–Q3 P–QN3
   10 N×B+

White can obtain a slight but lasting positional advantage by 10 B–N5! B–N2 11 N×B+ P×N 12 Q–K2. Sooner or later Black is forced to play ... P–QB4 and after P×P White has a mobile Q-side pawn majority whereas Black's weakened K-side pawns have limited mobility. Smyslov plans to attack on the K-side, so wishes to use the K5 square for his knight.

   10 ...   **N×N**
   11 N–K5!   **0–0**

Forced because of the threatened B–N5+

   12 Q–B3   **B–Q2**

White's last two moves have compelled Black to develop his bishop on this unfavourable square rather than on QN2.

   13 Q–R3

This momentarily prevents 13 ... P–B4 when 14 P×P Q×P? 15 N×B wins for White. However, Black's counterplay is delayed for only one move, so perhaps the simple 13 0–0 is better, followed by QR–Q1, KR–K1 etc., as White's queen is now decentralized. If then 13 ... P–B4 White could exchange and try to exploit his Q-side pawn majority.

   13 ...   **KR–Q1**
   14 0–0

Q-side castling would fit in better with White's plan of attacking on the K-side, but a two-edged position would then arise, with chances to both sides. Black could play either 14 ... P–B4 15 P×P P×P (*15 ... Q×P? 16 N×B R×N 17 B×P+*) with an attack down the QN-file, or even better 14 ... B–R5 15

R–Q2 (*15 P–QN3? Q–R6+ 16 K–N1 B×P*) 15 . . . P–B4, or here 15 B–B2 B×B 16 K×B R–Q3, ensuring Black an equal game.

14 . . .   **P–B4** (*151*)

151
W

15 Q–R4   **P–KR3**

The threat was 16 B×P+ In order to maintain his pawn on Q4, White must allow it to become isolated, but it would then constitute a serious weakness, hardly compensated by any attacking chances he might have. For example, after 16 QR–Q1 P×P 17 P×P QR–B1 18 KR–K1 B–B3 Black stands better (19 R–K3 N–Q4).

16 P×P   **Q×P**
17 QR–K1

All that remains of White's 'little centre' is his control of K5 which he now aims to consolidate whilst building up an attack by R–K3, R1–K1, R–N3 etc. Black must rapidly set up counterplay down the Q-file.

17 . . .   **B–B3**

The bishop finally reaches the correct diagonal and after 18 N×B R×B! 19 N–Q4 Q–Q4 Black would already stand better.

18 R–K3   **B–N2**
19 R1–K1   **R–Q4**
20 P–QN4

If White wishes to pursue his attack, he must first drive away the black queen from its strong position.

However, in doing so he seriously weakens his Q-side pawns, clearly banking everything on the coming attack.

20 . . .   **Q–Q3**
21 Q–R3

In the tournament book Botvinnik recommended 21 B–B2 after which I intended 21 . . . R–Q7! 22 R–N3 (if *22 N–B4 Q–Q4 23 R–N3 N–R4*) 22 . . . K–B1! with a very promising game (*23 B–N3 N–K5!*). Six moves later the thought of this king move was to linger fatefully in my memory.

21 . . .   **R–Q1**
22 B–B2!

White cannot begin an immediate attack on the KP by 22 B–B4 because of 22 . . . R–Q8! when 23 N×P fails 23 . . . K×N 24 R×P R×R+ 25 R×R+ K–B1 winning. Now, however, White is threatening 23 B–N3 followed by 24 N×P.

22 . . .   **Q–B2**
23 B–N3   **R4–Q3**
24 Q–R4 (*152*)

Now that Black has defended against the sacrificial threats, White is in a quandary about how to continue his attack.

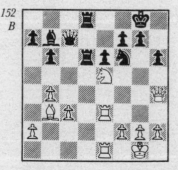

152
B

I could already obtain a clear advantage by 24 . . . B–Q4 25 P–QB4 B–N2 26 R–N3 K–B1 followed by 27 . . . R–Q5. Or here 25 B–B2 B×RP 26 R–N3 K–B1 27 P–R3 R–Q7. Or finally

25 P–KR3 B×B 26 P×B R–Q8 etc. The move I play is a little risky, but correct nevertheless.

24 ... R–Q7!?
25 P–KR3!

Black wins after 25 N×P K×N 26 R×P B–Q4! 27 R×N+ P×R 28 Q×RP K–N1! 29 Q×R B×B. Or if 25 R–N3 Q×N wins.

25 ... B–Q4!

With the same ideas as given in our note to move 24, where we pointed out that after 26 P–QB4 B–N2 Black's Q5 is made available for his rook.

26 R–N3 K–B1 ??

In all previously mentioned variations this was the right square for the king, so I played it here too quickly without realizing that in this position it constitutes a gross blunder. After the correct 26 ... K–R2! White must play very sharply to avoid serious positional disadvantage. Smyslov had then intended 27 R1–K3 B×B 28 R×P+ but after 28 ... K×R 29 R–N3+ K–R2 30 Q×N R–Q8+ 31 K–R2 R–KN1 he would have insufficient compensation for the exchange. The same applies to the variation 28 P×B R–Q8+ 29 K–R2 R–QB8 30 R×P+ K×R 31 R–N3+ K–R2 32 Q×N R–KN1 33 N×P R×R 34 Q×RP+ K–N1 35 P×R R×P 36 Q–N6+ K–B1 etc.

27 Q–KB4!

This double threat against the rook and the queen (N–N6+) settles matters. The game ended: **27 ... Q–K2 28 Q×R B×B 29 Q–K2 B–Q4 30 P–QB4 B–N2 31 R–Q3 R×R 32 Q×R Q–B2 33 Q–Q4 1–0.**

10 Other Types of Pawn Centre

There are obviously many possible kinds of pawn structure in the centre. In the above two chapters we only mentioned those in which one side has a central superiority. From a strategic viewpoint we hardly need to consider symmetrical formations such as the one arising after 1 P–K4 P–K3 2 P–Q4 P–Q4 3 P×P P×P. In such positions the fight for the centre is carried out by the pieces which strive to control or occupy central points. As for positions with the pawns locked in the centre (e.g. white pawns on Q4, K5 and black pawns on Q4, K3), the reader will see a full treatment of them in the chapter 'The Blocked Pawn Chain' (volume 3). In the same volume we shall again discuss the problem of the pawn centre in relation to 'The Pawn Majority on the Wing', examining amongst other formations the one with white pawns on QR2, QN2, K4, KB2, KN2, KR2, and black pawns on QR2, QN2, QB2, KB2, KN2, KR2.

In game 67 which we used to explain the 'little centre', by move 19 White had pawns on QB4 and K4 and Black's pawns were on QB3 and Q3. White's QBP lent splendid support to the KP by controlling Q5 and thus preventing . . . P–Q4. In various modern openings we arrive at the pawn structure shown in diagram 153.

Black has retained both his centre pawns whereas White's QP has been exchanged for Black's QBP. Neverthe-

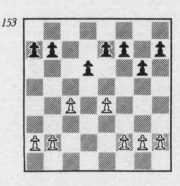

153

less it is White who has the central superiority because his pawns restrict the mobility of the black pawns. Black's QP is completely fixed by White's QBP and KP, and . . . P–K3 or . . . P–K4 would weaken it considerably. Such a pawn structure provides much more space advantage than was the case with the 'little centre', so it is strategically vital for the defence to liquidate either the QBP or KP. Opening theory shows us how this is done in practice. For example, after 1 P–K4 P–QB4 2 N–KB3 N–QB3 3 P–Q4 P×P 4 N×P P–KN3(?) 5 P–QB4! B–N2 6 N–B2(?) P–Q3 7 B–K2 Black usually continues 7 . . . N–R3! 8 0–0 P–B4! with a satisfactory game. Equally, with the situation reversed after 1 P–QB4 P–QB4 2 N–QB3 N–KB3 3 P–KN3 P–Q4(?) 4 P×P N×P 5 B–N2 N–B2 6 P–Q3 P–K4, White has the promising 7 P–B4! or sometimes even prevents 6 . . . P–K4 by playing 6 P–B4!? instead of 6

P-Q3. The game Botvinnik–Fine, Nottingham 1936, began with the moves 1 N-KB3 P-Q4 2 P-B4 P×P 3 N-R3 P-QB4 4 N×P N-QB3 5 P-QN3 P-K4 6 B-N2 P-B3 7 P-N3 KN-K2 8 B-N2 N-Q4 9 0-0 B-K2 10 N-KR4! 0-0 11 Q-N1 R-B2 12 N-B5 B-K3 13 P-B4! P×P 14 P×P when White already stood a little better.

Let us now examine a few games which illustrate the most important strategic problems arising from such a pawn structure.

70 Lisitsin–Botvinnik

Leningrad 1932, English Opening

1 N-KB3 P-QB4 2 P-B4 N-KB3 3 P-KN3 P-Q4 4 P×P N×P 5 B-N2 N-QB3 6 0-0 P-K4 7 P-Q3 B-K2 8 QN-Q2? 0-0 9 N-B4 P-B3 10 B-K3 B-K3

11 P-QR4

White adopts a faulty strategic plan. This move admittedly secures his knight on QB4 but it weakens his Q-side and above all permanently cuts out the possibility of liquidating Black's QBP by P-QN4.

11 ... Q-Q2
12 Q-Q2 P-QN3! *(154)*

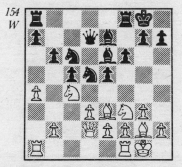

154
W

Black's QBP and KP are towers of strength, giving him such a space advantage that he can calmly prepare his attack against the white position.

13 KR-B1	QR-B1
14 Q-Q1	K-R1
15 B-Q2	KR-Q1
16 Q-N3	N-B2
17 B-B3	R-QN1
18 Q-B2	N-Q4
19 N3-Q2	R.N1-B1
20 N-B1	N-Q5!

A move which is typical of such positions. However, it is important to play it only when its capture is unfavourable for the defence. In this case Black can recapture with his KP and put pressure down the open K-file.

| 21 Q-Q1 | B-N5! |

Forcing White to exchange on Q4, albeit unwillingly.

22 B×N	KP×B
23 Q-Q2	B-B1
24 R-K1	R-K1
25 P-R4	

Intending to play his knight to KR2. He could not try 25 P-K4 in view of 25 ... P×Pep 26 P×P N-N5 etc.

| 25 ... | B-R6 |

Black plans to attack the enemy king, so it is logical to try to remove White's most important defensive piece, the fianchettod bishop.

26 B-B3	R-K2
27 N-R2	R1-K1
28 K-R1	B-K3!
29 P-N3	N-N5!

Still aiming to exchange bishops by ... B-Q4. Note that 29 ... N-B6? fails to 30 P-K4!

30 B-N2	B-Q4
31 N-B3	R-B2

Played in order to bring his KB back into play.

32 K-R2	B-Q3
33 B-R3	Q-Q1
34 QR-N1	R2-K2
35 N-N1	B-QB2
36 N-R3	B-N2!

Finally exchanging the white-squared bishop because of the threatened 37 ... Q-Q4.

37 B–N2	B×B
38 K×B	N–Q4
39 N–B2	Q–Q3! *(155)*

155
W

The time is ripe for the final attack. White has no defence to the entry of Black's knight at ... K6.

40 N–QR3	N–K6+ !
41 K–R1	N–N5
42 Q–B4	

Or 42 K–N2 N×P 43 K×N Q×P+ 44 K–B1 R–K6 45 N–B3 Q–R6+ 46 K–N1 B–R7+ winning.

42 ...	Q×Q
43 P×Q	N×P+
44 K–N2	N×P
0–1	

71 Pachman–Kuzelka

Prague 1943, Sicilian Defence

1 P–K4 P–QB4 2 N–KB3 N–QB3 3 P–Q4 P×P 4 N×P P–Q3(?) 5 P–QB4 P–KN3 6 B–K2 B–N2 7 N–B2 7 B–K3! 7...N–B3? 7...N–R3! 8 N–B3 0–0 9 0–0 B–Q2

| 10 B–K3 | Q–B1 |

Like White in the previous game, my opponent fails to prepare a counter-attack against my centre and is content to carry out piece manoeuvres. The threat is 10 ... N–KN5.

| 11 P–B3 | N–K4 |
| 12 P–QN3 | B–B3 *(156)* |

A position has arisen which is very similar to the one in diagram 154. In

156
W

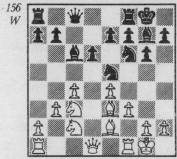

particular, it is worth noting that the QBP and KP are supported in the same way by pawns on QN3 and KB3.

| 13 Q–Q2 | R–Q1 |

By guarding his QP Black reveals his intention of trying for ... P–Q4 after a preparatory ... P–K3.

| 14 N–Q5 | B×N |
| 15 BP×B! | |

In most cases the correct plan is to recapture with the KP, as in the previous game, but after 15 KP×B P–QN4!? (16 P×P N×QP) Black obtains counterplay. After the text move White's chances of exploiting the QB-file are increased by the awkward placing of the black queen.

| 15 ... | N4–Q2? |

This is already the decisive mistake. It was essential to play 15 ... Q–Q2 and after 16 P–KR3 (threatening 17 P–B4) then 16 ... Q–K1, although White would still have a significant positional plus.

| 16 N–Q4 | Q–N1 |
| 17 QR–B1 | P–QR3 |

After 17 ... R–QB1 18 N–N5 P–QR3 19 R×R+ Q×R 20 R–B1 Q–Q1 21 N–R7 Black is completely hemmed in, as 21 ... N–N3 fails to 22 Q–R5 N.B3–Q2 23 N–B6! P×N 24 P×P N–B4 25 P–QN4 N4–R5 26 P–B7 etc.

18 R–QB2	R–QB1
19 R1–B1	R×R
20 Q×R	N–K1 *(157)*

157
W

White's space advantage has now given him the only open file, the two bishops and an advanced pawn on Q5 which restricts the movement of Black's pieces. It is not difficult for him to increase his Q-side pressure.

21 P–QN4!

Vacating QN3 so that the knight can reach QR5 and completely tie Black down. There are two possible defences:
1. 21 . . . B×N which would sooner or later give Black a hopeless position.
2. 21 . . . Q–Q1 with the idea of playing . . . N–N3 followed by . . . R–B1. However, this allows a decisive break-through combination, as the game continuation shows.

21 . . .	**Q–Q1**
22 N–B6!	**P×N**
23 P×P	

This passed pawn is already as strong as a piece. The main variation runs 23 . . . R–B1 24 B×P R–B2 25 P×N! R×Q 26 P×N= Q+ Q×Q 27 R×R Q–Q2! (*27 . . . Q–R5 28 R–B8+ B–B1 29 B–R6 Q–Q8+ 30 B–KB1 wins*) 28 R–B8+ B–B1 29 P–N5! winning. After 23 . . . N–K4 24 P–B4 wins.

23 . . .	**N–B1**
24 P–B7	**N×P**

Or 24 . . . Q–B1 25 Q–B6 when the threat of 26 Q×R forces transposition to the game line.

25 Q×N	**Q–K1**
26 Q–B6	**Q–N1**

As the ending would be hopeless, Black sets a little trap.

27 B×P	**B–N7!**
28 R–N1!	

But not 28 R–B2? Q×P 29 Q×R Q–K8+ 30 B–KB1 Q×B.K6+ followed by . . . B–Q5.

28 . . .	**B–B3**
29 P–QR4	

Preparing the subsequent queen sacrifice which is the quickest way to settle matters (see move 31).

29 . . .	**N–K3**
30 B–N7	**N–Q5**
31 B×R!	**N×Q**
32 B×N	

The Q-side pawns cannot now be stopped.

32 . . .	**B–B6!**
33 P–N5	

Not, however, 33 P–R5? Q–B2 34 B–Q5 B×P 35 R×B Q–B6.

33 . . .	**P–K3**
34 P–N6	**P–Q4**
35 P–N7	**K–N2**

After 35 . . . B–K4 (*35 . . . P–Q5? 36 B–B4*) there is the pretty finish 36 P–B4! B–B2 37 B–Q4! B×P 38 P–K5.

36 K–B1	**P×P**

Or 36 . . . B–K4 37 P–B4 B×P 38 B–Q4+ P–K4 39 B–R7 etc.

37 B–R7	**Q×RP**
38 P–N8= Q	**B–K4**
39 B–N1	**Q–B5**
40 B–Q4	**1–0**

72 Bielicki–Evans

Havana 1964, English Opening

1 P–QB4 N–KB3 2 N–QB3 P–Q4 3 P×P N×P 4 P–KN3 P–QB4 5 B–N2 N–B2 6 N–B3 N–B3

7 0–0

If White intends to fianchetto his QB it is better to do so at once. The game Taimanov–Bivshev, USSR 1951, went 7 P–N3 P–K4 8 B–N2 B–K2 9 R–QB1 P–B3 10 N–QR4 P–QN3? (*10 . . .*

N–R3! is essential) 11 N–R4! N–Q4 12 P–QR3 B–K3 13 P–QN4! and Black's position was shattered after 13 ... P–KN4!? 14 N–KB3 N–Q5 15 N×N! BP×N 16 P–K3! 0–0 17 P×P P×P 18 0–0 B–B2 19 R–K1 Q–Q2 20 B×P etc.

7 ...   P–K4

8 P–N3

Now it is best to proceed 8 P–Q3 B–K2 9 N–Q2! followed by N–B4 and P–B4.

8 ...   B–K2

9 B–N2   0–0(?)

An inexactitude. After 9 ... P–B3! 10 R–B1 P–QN3! Black consolidates his centre and has a good game.

10 R–B1   P–B3

11 N–K1   B–Q2

12 N–R4 (*158*)

158
B

White is launching an attack on Black's KP and QBP, first putting pressure on the latter then planning P–B4. How should Black now defend his QBP?

12 ...   N–R3(?)

The first error. It is worth sacrificing the exchange in order to maintain the pawn centre, so 12 ... P–QN3! is called for. After 13 P–QN4!? N×P! 14 B×R Q×B Black has positional compensation for the loss of the exchange.

13 N–Q3   Q–R4?

And this second error already gives Black the worst of it. Admittedly he now maintains material equality but

his knight on QR3 and queen on QR4 have deserted the K-side. This allows White to attack energetically on this side of the board by eliminating the enemy KP.

14 P–B4!   P×P

15 N×KBP   B–Q3

16 P–K3!

Despite White's modest looking central position he is already threatening a mating combination with 17 B–Q5+ K–R1 18 N–KN6+! P×N 19 R–QB4! etc.

16 ...   B×N

17 R×B   QR–Q1

18 B–Q5+!

This plan needed precise calculation, as otherwise the bishop would prove vulnerable here and Black would obtain pressure down the Q-file.

18 ...   K–R1

19 R–R4!

Threatening the well-known tactic 20 R×RP+! K×R 21 Q–R5 mate.

19 ...   P–KR3

20 R1–B4! (*159*)

159
B

White has achieved his strategic aim. Black's forces are tied down to the defence of his QBP and his king's position is unprotected. The sacrifice R×RP+ is already in the air.

20 ...   B–B4

Black accepts a doubled QBP so that he can use his bishop in defence of his king. Other possibilities are:

a. 20 . . . P–QN4? 21 R×RP+ ! P×R
22 Q–R5 K–N2 23 R–R4 wins.

b. 20 . . . B–N5 21 Q×B R×B 22 Q–N6
R–N4 23 R×RP+ ! P×R 24
Q×RP+ K–N1 25 B×P R×B 26
Q×R.B6 maintaining an attack
with three pawns for a piece.

c. 20 . . . B–K1 21 Q–B3! (threatening
22 R×RP+ P×R 23 B×P+) 21 . . .
R–Q3 22 B–B3 Q–Q1 23 B–K4
B–B2 24 Q–B5 B–N1 25 Q–N6!
Q–K2 26 R×RP+ ! P×R 27
Q×RP+ B–R2 28 B×B Q–N2 29
Q–R3! etc.

21 B×N	**P×B**
22 B–B3!	

Winning at least a pawn (after 22 . . .
Q–Q1!) but obtaining a combinative
finish if Black elects to hang on to his
QBP.

22 . . .	**Q–N4?**
23 R×RP+ !	**P×R**
24 Q–R5	**N–B2?**

Hastening his defeat but after 24 . . .
R–Q3 25 Q×B Q–N2 26 N×P N×N 27
R×N White would have two pawns for
the exchange and his bishop would be
worth at least a rook!

25 Q×P+ !	**K–N1**
26 B×P	**N–K3**

Or 26 . . . R×B 27 Q×R R–KB1 28
Q–N5+ K–R1 29 R–R4+ B–R2 30
Q–K5+ etc.

27 R–KN4+ !	**K–B2**

Or 27 . . . B×R 28 Q–N6+ mates.

28 R–N7+ !	**1–0**

160

The final sacrifice leads to an
unusually pretty finish after 28 . . .
N×R 29 Q×N+ K–K3 30 Q–K7+
K–Q4 31 N–B3 mate!

Now let us examine another type of
pawn centre, as shown in diagram 160.

Once again White has central
superiority because his QP is mobile
whereas Black's . . . P–Q4 is made more
difficult because of the white QBP.
Such a pawn structure is usually of a
temporary nature, as White often plays
P–Q5 to obtain a space advantage and
vacate Q4 for his knight or bishop, or
Black plays . . . P–Q4, when White can
gain space on the Q-side by P–B5.
Sooner or later . . . P–Q4 is essential, or
else White can exploit his strong centre
to build up promising piece play, as in
the following game.

73 Boleslavsky–Bondarevsky

Leningrad 1948, Alekhine's Defence

**1 P–K4 N–KB3 2 P–K5 N–Q4 3 P–Q4
P–Q3 4 P–QB4 N–N3 5 P×P KP×P
6 B–Q3   P–KN3**

This move was recommended by
Mikenas in place of the earlier . . .
B–K2. The fianchettod bishop will
obtain good play on the long diagonal,
should White play P–Q5, or else it will
attack the QP which Black can fix by
. . . P–Q4.

7 N–K2	**B–N2**
8 0–0	**0–0**
9 QN–B3	**N–B3**
10 B–K3 (*161*)	
10 . . .	**N–N5**

Black goes for the pair of bishops but
neglects the centre. He should play 10
. . . P–Q4! 11 P–B5 N–Q2! (not *11 . . .
N–B5 12 B×N P×B 13 Q–R4*) followed
by . . . N–B3, . . . N–K2 and . . . B–B4
with equality.

11 P–QN3	**N×B**

Now 11 . . . P–Q4 is not so effective
because after 12 P–B5 N–Q2 13 B–N1

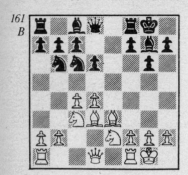

followed by 14 P–QR3 and 15 P–QN4
White can build up a Q-side attack
with gain of time.

12 Q×N   R–K1

And now 12 . . . P–Q4 is dubious on
account of 13 P–B5 N–Q2 14 N×P
P–QB3 15 N5–B4 P–KN4 (the only
way to recover the pawn) 16 N–R5
N×P 17 Q–B2 etc., when Black's K-
side is seriously weakened.

13 QR–Q1   N–Q2
14 Q–Q2   P–QB3

Black rejects 14 . . . N–B1 because
after 15 B–N5 he must either block the
diagonal of his KB by 15 . . . P–KB3 or
else exchange bishops by 15 . . . B–B3.
However, in both cases he would have
better prospects than after the text
move which admittedly gives his queen
more scope but at the same time
seriously weakens his QP.

15 KR–K1   Q–R4

It was still preferable to play 15 . . .
N–B1. After 15 . . . N–B3 White has 16
B–N5 Q–B2 17 N–N3 B–Q2 18
N.N3–K4.

16 B–B4   B–B1
17 N–N3   R×R+
18 R×R *(162)*

By simple means White has obtained
a winning position. Against the threat
of 19 R–K8 Black can play neither 18
. . . N–B3? 19 N–Q5! Q–Q1 20 N×N+
Q×N 21 B–N5 Q–N2 22 R–K8, nor 18
. . . Q–Q1 19 N.N3–K4 N–N3 20 B–N5
B–K2 21 B×B Q×B 22 Q–B4 etc.

18 . . .   P–QN4

So that his QB can go to N2 in
answer to 19 R–K8.

19 N.N3–K4   P×P

Or 19 . . . P–N5 20 N–N1 P–Q4 21
N–Q6 B–QR3 22 P–B5 with a decisive
positional plus to White.

20 B×P   B–QR3

Or 20 . . . P×P 21 B×B N×B 22
N–B6+   K–R1 (if *22 . . . K–N2 23
N–K8+* and *24 Q–R6*) 23 R–K8 K–N2
24 R–K5! followed by 25 N–K8+
winning.

21 P–QN4   Q–KB4
22 B×B   R×B
23 P–Q5!   N–K4

Or 23 . . . P×P 24 N×P K–N2 25
N–K7 Q–K3 26 N–QB5 wins.

24 P×P   P–B3

Black loses a piece after 24 . . . N×P
25 P–N5 B×P 26 N–Q6.

25 P–N5   B–B1
26 Q–Q4   P–QR3
27 N–Q5   K–N2
28 N4×P   1–0

28 . . . R×N 29 N×R K×N 30 P–B4.

11 Tension in the Centre

Many pawn structures which we have examined arose as a result of pawn exchanges, after which one side obtained a space or a pawn advantage in the centre. For example White obtains 'the little centre' against the French Defence after the moves 1 P–K4 P–K3 2 P–Q4 P–Q4 3 N–QB3 P×P 4 N×P. Let us now consider the position after the first two moves, before the exchange of pawns. Such a situation illustrates what we mean by tension in the centre and is usually of a transient nature. Sooner or later one side must release this tension. If White plays 3 P×P then 3 ... P×P produces a symmetrical structure and the release of tension has given Black full equality. Equally 3 P–K5 removes the tension, giving a blocked pawn chain which we shall discuss later. To maintain the tension White can guard his KP by, say, 3 N–QB3, when it is Black who must make a decision. He can continue the struggle for the centre with 3 ... N–KB3 or 3 ... B–N5, or can immediately release the tension by 3 ... P×P.

After 3 ... P×P Black has exchanged his only centrally posted pawn. Tarrasch termed such an exchange as 'giving up the centre', considering it a mistake in practically all cases. Nimzowitsch disputed this opinion, pointing out that such an exchange does not necessarily relinquish central control and that the struggle for the centre can be maintained by pressure against White's Q4 and K4. We have already shown how the 'little centre' can be countered by piece play or by an advance of either BP. Both Tarrasch and Nimzowitsch went to opposite extremes in their concept of the centre. The former over-estimated the importance of a pawn centre whereas the latter placed insufficient value on the 'little centre'. We now realize that 3 ... P×P in the French Defence gives White a definite space advantage, which is why the move is not very popular. In order to evaluate the pros and cons of the above type of pawn exchange we must always examine the specific characteristics of a given position.

Tension in the centre leads to very complex strategic and tactical problems, as both sides must often assess well in advance the positions that can arise after various alterations in the central pawn structure. As we have already stated, tension in the centre is usually of a transient nature, and this is especially the case when both sides have pawns on Q4 and K4. For example, after the moves 1 P–K4 P–K4 2 N–KB3 N–QB3 3 B–N5 P–QR3 4 B–R4 N–B3 5 0–0 B–K2 6 R–K1 P–QN4 7 B–N3 P–Q3 0–0 9 P–KR3 N–QR4 10 B–B2 P–B4 11 P–Q4 Q–B2 12 QN–Q2 B–N2 13 N–B1 BP×P 14 P×P QR–B1 15 B–N1 P–Q4! (163)

We have reached the well-known

variation of Panov's counter-attack which results in the liquidation of all four central pawns. Play might go 16 KP×P P×P 17 B-N5 QR-Q1! 18 Q-Q3 P-N3 19 Q×QP N×P, or 16 QP×P N×P 17 N-N3 P-B4! 18 P×Pep B×P 19 B×N P×B 20 N×P etc. It is interesting to note that with temporary pawn structures like this it is often preferable to force our opponent to exchange rather than release the tension ourselves. The reason for this is that our opponent has usually calculated the consequences of an immediate liquidation in the centre but may fail to take into account the results of our maintaining the tension for a little longer. The following game emphasizes this point.

74 Foltys–Zita

Ostrava 1946, French Defence

1 P-K4 P-K3 2 P-Q4 P-Q4 3 N-Q2 N-QB3 4 KN-B3 P-K4!? (*164*)

Zita had played his last move after carefully working out that immediate pawn exchanges in the centre would give White nothing. e.g. 5 QP×P P×P 6 N×P Q×Q+ 7 K×Q B-KN5 8 B-KB4 0-0-0+ followed by 9 . . . KN-K2 with very good play for Black. Or 5 KP×P N×P! 6 N×N (*6 N×P Q×P*) 6 . . . P×N 7 B-N5+ B-Q2 8 Q-K2+ Q-K2 with equality. However, White chooses a far more

powerful move which compels Black to exchange in the centre, highlighting his lack of development.

| 5 B-N5! | KP×P |
| 6 0-0! | |

The real point of his previous move. Black could equalize after 6 N×P B-Q2 7 N×N P×N 8 B-Q3 B-QB4, whereas now the central tension reacts against him, as total liquidation is impossible e.g. 6 . . . P×P 7 N×KP B-Q2 8 R-K1 B-K2 9 B-N5 P-B3 10 B-KB4 etc., or 6 . . . B-QB4 7 P×P Q×P 8 R-K1+ when 8 . . . K-B1 is forced, as 8 . . . N-K2 or 8 . . . B-K3 lose a piece to 9 R-K5.

6 . . .	B-Q2
7 P×P	N-N5
8 Q-K2+	B-K2

He loses after 8 . . . Q-K2? 9 B×B+ K×B 10 Q-N5+ etc.

| 9 P-Q6! | P×P |
| 10 N×P | P-QR3? |

This hastens defeat, but Black would still be in difficulties after the correct 10 . . . N-QB3, in view of his weak QP and lack of development.

11 B×B+	Q×B
12 N-B4	N-Q4
13 N-B5!	K-B1

Forced, as 13 . . . 0-0-0 loses to 14 N5-K3! KN-B3 15 N×N N×N 16 Q-B3 Q-B3 17 Q×N!, whilst 13 . . . Q×N? allows 14 N×P+ winning the queen.

| 14 Q-B3 | R-B1 |

If 14 . . . KN–B3 then 15 B–N5 wins, so Black decides to give up a rook and two minor pieces for the queen. The game finished as follows: **15 Q×N R–B4 16 N×B R×Q 17 N×R P–QN4 18 N4–N6 Q–B3 19 B–B4 N–K2 20 N×N K×N 21 KR–K1+ K–B3 22 QR–Q1 R–K1 23 R×R Q×R 24 R×P+ K–B4 25 B–K3 P–B3 26 P–KR3 Q–K2 27 R–Q4 K–N3 28 P–QR4 Q–QB2 29 P×P P×P 30 P–QB4 P×P 31 R×P Q–K4 32 P–QN4 K–B2 33 R–B5 Q–R8+ 34 K–R2 P–N4 35 P–N5 P–R4 36 N–B4 Q–QN8 37 P–N6 K–K3 38 R–B6+ K–Q4 39 N–B5+ K–K3 40 N–R3 Q–N5 41 N–N5 1–0.**

This example demonstrates that a central liquidation of pawns favours the better developed side. In our next game it is White who opens up the centre rather than obtaining less promising play against the isolated QP.

75 Negyesy–Szabo

Hungarian Championship 1951, Queen's Gambit

1 P–Q4 P–Q4 2 P–QB4 P–K3 3 N–QB3 P–QB3 4 N–B3 N–B3 5 P–K3 QN–Q2 6 B–Q3 B–N5 7 P–QR3 B–R4 8 0–0 0–0 9 Q–B2 B–B2 10 B–Q2 P–QR3 11 QR–Q1 P–K4 12 BP×P BP×P (*165*)

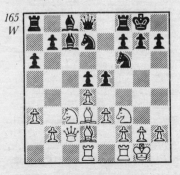

The natural continuation now seems to be 13 P×P N×P 14 N×N B×N, but Black would then have very good attacking chances on the K-side in compensation for his isolated QP. If White then decided to open up the game by 15 P–K4 Black could equalize by 15 . . . Q–B2 16 N×P B×RP+ 17 K–R1 N×N 18 P×N Q×Q 19 B×Q B–Q3. However, White shows that he can effectively open up the position at once.

13 P–K4!   **KP×P**

This loses a pawn without compensation, but even after 13 . . . QP×P 14 N.QB3×P P×P 15 N×N+ N×N 16 B–N4 R–K1 17 N×P Black's position is equally unsatisfactory, as his queen can find no protection from White's pressure down the open lines.

14 N.QB3×P   **N×N**
15 P×N   **N–K4**

Other moves are even worse e.g. 15 . . . N–B3 16 B–KN5, or 15 . . . P–R3 16 B–N4 R–K1 17 KR–K1, or 15 . . . P–KN3 16 B–KN5 P–B3 17 N×P etc. After the text move White comfortably exploited his extra pawn as follows: **16 N×N B×N 17 P–B4 B–B3 18 B×KRP+ K–R1 19 B–K4 B–N5 20 R.Q1–K1 B–R5 21 P–KN3 P–B4 22 B–N2 B–K2 23 Q–Q3 B–B4 24 P–N4 B–R2 25 R–K5 Q–Q2 26 P–R3 B–R4 27 P–N4 B–KN3 28 R–K6 R–B3 29 R–K5 P×P 30 P–B5 B–N1 31 R–K6 B–R4 32 P×P B×P 33 Q–K4 R×R 34 BP×R Q–Q3 35 B–B4 1–0.**

Now let us examine central pawn structures in which the tension can be maintained for long periods, in particular those positions with pawns on Q4 and K4 facing pawns on Q3 and K4. In the next game Black tries to maintain the centre, but this entails limited space in which to manoeuvre his pieces. As a result White opens up the centre at the right time, exploiting Black's unfavourably posted pieces and obtaining a strong attack.

76 Smyslov–Lublinsky

17th USSR Championship, 1949, Ruy Lopez

1 P–K4 P–K4 2 N–KB3 N–QB3 3 B–N5 P–QR3 4 B–R4 P–Q3 5 P–B3 B–Q2 6 P–Q4 N–B3 7 QN–Q2 B–K2 8 0–0 0–0 9 R–K1 *(166)*

166
B

In this position Black's usual plan is to fight against the classical centre after 9 ... P×P 10 P×P N–QN5 11 B×B Q×B 12 N–B1 P–QB4! etc.

9 ...   B–K1

With this continuation (the so-called Kecskemet variation) Black intends to maintain the centre by playing ... N–Q2 and ... P–KB3.

10 B–N3!

A dual purpose move. On the one hand White prevents the central action that could arise after 10 N–B1 P×P 11 P×P P–Q4 12 P–K5 N–K5, and on the other hand, he makes it more difficult for Black to play ... P–KB3 which would be possible, for example, after 10 P–KR3 N–Q2 11 N–B1 P–B3 etc.

10 ...   N–Q2
11 N–B1   B–B3?

Black mixes his systems. The logical continuation is 11 ... K–R1 and 12 ... P–B3 when Black has at least a solid centre in compensation for his passively placed pieces.

12 N–K3   N–K2

He cannot play 12 ... P–KN3 13 N–Q5 B–N2 because of 14 B–N5.

13 N–N4   N–KN3
14 P–N3   B–K2
15 P–KR4!

Beginning his K-side attack by creating a post for his knight on KN5.

15 ...   N–B3
16 N–N5   P–R3
17 N×N+   B×N
18 Q–R5!   N–R1 *(167)*

167
W

19 P×P!

Perfectly timed! Black must accept the opening of the Q-file, as 19 ... B×P 20 P–KB4 B–B3 21 N–B3 gives White mobile pawns in the centre (P–K5) and on the K-side (P–N4–5).

19 ...   P×P
20 B–K3!   Q–K2

If Black accepts the knight sacrifice, then after 20 ... P×N 21 P×P P–KN3 22 Q–R4 B–N2 White obtains a decisive attack down the KR-file: 23 K–N2 B–QB3 24 R–R1 R–K1 25 Q–R7+ K–B1 26 B–B5+ R–K2 27 Q×N+! winning.

21 B–Q5!   P–B3

The lesser evil would be 21 ... B–B3 22 B×B P×B but Black's pawn would then be very weak and he would have the 'bad' bishop. After the text move White's attack breaks through.

22 B–N3   B–Q2

White's previous move prevented the active posting of this piece on QB3, and this gives him time to double rooks on the Q-file.

23	QR–Q1	QR–Q1
24	R–Q2	B–B1
25	R1–Q1	R×R
26	R×R	Q–B2

White still has a clear advantage after 26 ... P×N 27 P×P P–KN3 28 P×B Q×P 29 Q–R6 Q–N2 30 Q–R4. With the text move Black hopes to force the knight away but allows a pretty combination which wins for White.

27 B–B5!   R–Q1

If 27 ... P×N 28 B×R, or 27 ... B–K2 28 B×B Q×B 29 N–B3 R–K1 30 Q×KP! Q×Q 31 N×Q R×N 32 R–Q8+ wins a pawn.

28	R×R+	B×R
29	N×P!	N×N
30	B–N6!	Q–Q2

After 30 ... Q×B 31 Q×N+ K–R2 32 P–R5 it is mate next move.

31	B×B	K–R2
32	B×N	Q×B.Q1
33	B–N6+	1–0

As can be seen from this game, White's active placing of pawns on Q4 and K4 gave him a positive advantage in space. For this reason it is never good policy for the defending side to maintain the central tension for too long. Our next two games illustrate two of the most important methods of defence against such a centre:

1. to exchange pawns at the appropriate moment, then liquidate the enemy pawn centre.
2. to force the attacking side to release the tension, by exerting pressure on his centre pawns.

77 Tarrasch–Alekhine

Baden-Baden 1925, Giuoco Piano

1 P–K4 P–K4 2 N–KB3 N–QB3 3 B–B4 B–B4 4 P–B3 B–N3 5 P–Q4 Q–K2 6 0–0 N–B3 7 R–K1 P–Q3 8 P–QR4 P–QR3
9 P–R3
White has certain problems in trying

to maintain the centre in this line. He must prevent ... B–N5 in order to keep control of his Q4 square.

9 ...	0–0

10 B–KN5

There are stronger alternatives in 10 P–QN4 in order to develop the bishop on QR3, or 10 N–R3 in order to strengthen the centre after N–B2.

10 ...	P–R3

11 B–K3 (*168*)

After 11 B–R4 P–KN4? 12 N×NP P×N 13 B×NP White has a decisive attack, but Black can simply prepare ... P–KN4 by first playing ... K–R1 and ... R–KN1.

168 B

White's QB is awkwardly placed, as it hinders the protection of his KP. However, it is by no means easy for Black to exploit this circumstance. The immediate 11 ... N×KP? fails to 12 P–Q5 N–R4 13 B×B P×B 14 B–R2 P–KB4 15 P–QN4 winning a piece. Alekhine manages to find an extremely subtle way of eliminating his opponent's central advantage.

11 ...   Q–Q1!

A splendid positional move! Black threatens 12 ... P×P 13 P×P P–Q4, and if White does not wish to exchange queens by 12 P×P, he must withdraw his KB from its active post to maintain his centre.

12 B–Q3

He cannot play 12 B–R2 because of 12 . . . R–K1! 13 QN–Q2 P×P when White is forced to recapture with the bishop.

| 12 . . . | R–K1 |
| 13 QN–Q2 | B–R2! |

An excellent waiting move, anticipating a possible N–QB4.

14 Q–B2(?) (*169*)

White wishes to transfer his knight on Q2 to KN3, but this placing of the queen is tactically unfavourable and gives Black the opportunity of liquidating the enemy pawn centre. Better was the eccentric-looking 14 Q–N1! so that after 14 . . . P×P 15 P×P! N–QN5 the KB can retreat to KB1 (16 . . . N×P? 17 N×N B–KB4 18 B–Q2!).

169 B

| 14 . . . | P×P |
| 15 N×P | |

After 15 P×P Black obtains the advantage by the interesting variation 15 . . . N–QN5 16 Q–B3 N×B 17 Q×N N×P! 18 N×N B–KB4 19 B–B4! Q–K2! (*19 . . . P–Q4 20 B×BP!*) 20 N–B5 Q–B3 21 N–K4 Q–N3. After the text move Black succeeds in completely liquidating White's pawn centre.

15 . . .	N–K4
16 B–B1	P–Q4!
17 QR–Q1	

After 17 P–KB4 N–N3 18 P–K5 N–R4 Black wins a pawn.

17 . . .	P–B4!
18 N4–N3	Q–B2
19 B–KB4	

White should be satisfied with the modest 19 P×P N×P with a slight advantage to Black.

19 . . .	N–B6+ !
20 N×N	Q×B
21 P×P?	

Black's advantage now leads to a rapid victory. Alekhine recommends as best 21 P–K5 B–B4 22 Q–Q2 Q×Q 23 R×Q N–K5 24 R2–Q1 (if *24 R×P? B–K3*) 24 . . . QR–Q1 when Black's bishop pair gives him a lasting initiative.

| 21 . . . | B–B4 |
| 22 B–Q3 | |

Or 22 Q–Q2 Q×P 23 N–B1 B–B7 24 R×R+ R×R 25 R–K1 N–K5 26 Q–B4 P–B5 27 N–Q4 B×N 28 P×B Q–N5! (Alekhine). White now hopes for 22 . . . B×B? 23 Q×B P–B5 24 Q–Q2!

22 . . .	B×P!
23 P×B	Q×N
24 R×R+	R×R
25 B–B1	R–K4
26 P–B4	R–N4+
27 K–R2	N–N5+
28 P×N	R×NP
0–1	

78 Pachman–Minev

Zonal tournament 1954, Tartakower's Opening

1 P–K4 P–K4 2 N–KB3 N–QB3 3 B–K2 N–B3

| 4 P–Q3 | P–Q4 |

This is a natural reply to White's seemingly tame opening, and yet it contains the seeds of Black's later difficulties. We have reached a Philidor's Defence with colours reversed, giving White an important tempo and thus allowing Black none of the tactical possibilities which are the sole means of taking advantage of this positionally sound defence.

| 5 QN–Q2 | B–K2 |

If Black follows the normal

development of pieces against the Philidor by 5 ... B–QB4, then the threat against White's KB2 no longer has any relevance, and the bishop would only help a subsequent attack by White on the Q-side (P–QN4 would gain a tempo).

6 0–0	0–0
7 P–B3	P–QR4
8 Q–B2	B–KN5
9 R–K1	

It was more exact to play 9 P–QN3 at once, as Black could now play 9 ... P–R5 forcing White to prepare further by 10 R–QN1.

9 ...	P–R3(?)
10 P–QN3	R–K1
11 B–N2	B–KB1
12 P–QR3! (170)	

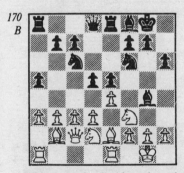

170
B

White's passive-looking pieces have in reality great latent power. He is already threatening P–N4–5 and there is always a possibility in the air of playing P×P followed by P–B4 with pressure on the KP. To prevent this Black must exchange pawns himself within the next two or three moves, but prefers to do so at once, in order to regroup his pieces for White's coming action on the Q-side. It is interesting to note how Black is immediately forced onto the defensive, as soon as he has released the tension in the centre.

12 ...	P×P
13 P×P	N–Q2

14 QR–Q1	N–N3
15 P–N4	Q–B3
16 N–N3	B–K3
17 N.B3–Q2	R.K1–Q1
18 B–N5	

It was also possible to play the immediate 18 P–N5 and 19 P–QB4 but I was intending to adopt this plan with the gain of a tempo, after the best defence 18 ... N–R2 19 B–KB1 N–B3. Black's next move only increases the effectiveness of White's Q-side play, as the weakness of the QRP will soon be felt.

18 ...	P–R5
19 N–QB1	

Not however, 19 N–B5 B×N 20 P×B N–Q2 21 B×P N×P 22 B×N P×B and Black's pieces have suddenly become very active.

19 ...	N–K2
20 B–B1	P–B4

This prevents White's threat of P–QB4–5 followed by N–B4, but at the same time gives him an operation base on Q5.

21 N–Q3	N–Q2
22 P–QB4	

Threatening the powerful 23 P–B4!

22 ...	P–KN4
23 P–N5	N–KN3
24 N–B1	

Beginning the trek to Q5.

24 ...	N–N3
25 N–R2	N–B5
26 N–QB3	R×N?

A faulty combination, as Black fails to see the idea behind White's 29th move. However, after other moves White obtains a decisive advantage by 27 N–Q5 B×N 28 KP×B, not so much because of the protected passed pawn but because of the pressure down the QR1–KR8 diagonal.

27 R×R	B×P
28 B×B	N×B
29 N–Q5!	

In this way White retains his

important bishop and can now exploit his advantage without great difficulty. The game ended: **29 . . . N×N 30 Q×N N–B5 31 R–Q7** threatening 32 B×P **31 . . . B–N2 32 R1–Q1 P–N5 33 B–B1 P–R4 34 B×N P×B 35 P–K5! Q–B4 36 Q×QBP P–R5 37 Q–K7 P–R6 38 P–K6! Q×KP 39 Q×Q P×Q 40 R–Q8+ R×R 41 R×R+ K–B2 42 R–Q7+ K–B3 43 R×P B–B1 44 R–QR7 B×P 45 R×P B–Q3 46 P–N6 P–N6 47 RP×P BP×P 48 NP×P 1–0.**

When a player has pawns on Q4 and K4, his opponent tries to force him to release the tension in the centre, and this struggle often begins in the opening stages. For example, in the well-known closed variation of the Ruy Lopez after the moves 1 P–K4 P–K4 2 N–KB3 N–QB3 3 B–N5 P–QR3 4 B–R4 N–B3 5 0–0 B–K2 6 R–K1 P–QN4 7 B–N3 0–0 8 P–B3 P–Q3 it is no longer considered best to play the immediate 9 P–Q4. Black can then play 9 . . . B–N5 forcing 10 P–Q5. If instead 10 B–K3 then Black can liquidate in the centre by 10 . . . P×P 11 P×P N–QR4 12 B–B2 N–B5 13 B–B1 P–B4. This is why White usually plays 9 P–KR3, when Black must use sharper means to release the central tension e.g. the Chigorin manoeuvre 9 . . . N–QR4 10 B–B2 P–B4 11 P–Q4 Q–B2 12 QN–Q2 N–B3 forcing either 13 P–Q5 or 13 P×BP.

In positions with pawns on Q4 and K4 facing pawns on Q3 and K4, the active side will therefore, as a rule strive to maintain the central tension (unless, of course, the release of tension ensures him an advantage), whilst the defending side will aim to reduce this tension, providing that he at the same time eliminates his opponent's central superiority.

So far we have dealt with positions in which both sides had a KP and QP. However, situations often arise when one side has a single pawn in the centre,

supported by the pieces. Diagram 171 shows us a typical pawn structure.

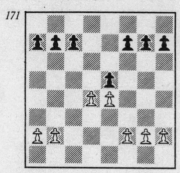

171

The difference here is that an exchange of pawns does not bring about central equilibrium. We shall discuss this pawn structure more fully in the chapter 'Pawn Majority on the Wings'. At first sight it does not seem to matter which side exchanges pawns in the centre, but in practice there is often a significant tactical difference. This is because the exchange allows our opponent to centralize his pieces advantageously (a white piece on Q4 or a black piece on K4). Let us consider the position after the moves 1 P–Q4 P–Q4 2 P–QB4 P–K3 3 N–QB3 P–QB3 4 N–B3 N–B3 5 P–K3 QN–Q2 6 B–Q3 B–Q3 7 0–0 0–0 8 P–K4 P×BP 9 B×P P–K4. It is clear that 10 P×P N2×P 11 N×N B×N allows Black to develop his forces effectively, so White usually plays 10 B–KN5 when 10 . . . P×P 11 Q×P threatening 12 P–K5 is good for him! (11 . . . Q–K2 12 B×N Q×B 13 Q×Q P×Q 14 QR–Q1). After 10 . . . Q–K2! 11 R–K1! Black still cannot exchange because of 11 . . . P×P 12 P–K5 N×P 13 N–K4 with a sharp attack for White.

As we can see from this simple example, it is once again vital to maintain the central tension, even if this can only be done for a short time. In this particular case (see diagram 171) the move P–Q5 would be even worse than normal, as it consolidates Black's KP and at the same time provides an excellent blockading square for a black piece on Q3.

79 Keres–Lipnitsky

19th USSR Championship, 1951, Nimzo-Indian Defence

1 P–Q4 N–KB3 2 P–QB4 P–K3 3 N–QB3 B–N5 4 P–K3 0–0 5 B–Q3 P–Q4 6 N–B3 N–B3
7 0–0   P–KR3

The immediate 7 ... P×P 8 B×BP B–Q3 offers more prospects, as 9 P–K4(?) is answered by 9 ... P–K4 when Black has a good game after both 10 P–Q5 N–K2 followed by ... N–N3, and 10 B–K3 B–KN5! 11 P–Q5 N–Q5! etc. After 9 B–QN5! Black can continue in gambit style with 9 ... P–K4! 10 B×N P×P 11 B×P B×B 12 N×P Q–Q2 with excellent chances for Black, so White plays here 11 P×P P×B 12 B–N5 with a good game. It is this last possibility that Black wishes to eliminate by the preparatory 7 .... P–KR3, wrongly assuming that White has no way of utilizing the extra tempo e.g. 8 P–QR3 P×P! 9 B×P B–Q3 etc.

8 P–KR3!

This is much more than a copy of Black's move, as it anticipates the coming central structure, when it will be essential to maintain the tension in the centre by preventing both ... B–KN5 and ... N–KN5 (see White's 11th move).

8 ...   P×P

There are two other interesting waiting moves in 8 ... P–R3 and 9 ... Q–K2.

9 B×P   B–Q3
10 P–K4!   P–K4
11 B–K3! *(172)*

We can now appreciate the point of 8 P–KR3. As it would be clearly unfavourable for Black to liquidate by

11 ... P×P 12 N×P N×N 13 B×N R–K1 14 R–K1 B–K4 15 B×B R×B 16 P–B4 and 17 P–K5, he has the difficult task of trying to force White to release the central tension.

11 ...   P–R3
12 R–K1   B–Q2(?)

This bishop should be used to apply more pressure against the enemy centre by 12 ... P–QN4 13 B–KB1! B–N2 (not *13 ... P–N5 14 N–QR4 N×KP 15 Q–B2*) threatening to win the KP by ... P–N5. After 14 P–R3 R–K1! 15 P–Q5 N–K2 Black has chances of equality despite his Q-side weaknesses. After the text move White obtains a positional advantage.

13 Q–B2   R–K1 ?

But it is only now that the game clearly swings White's way. Black had to play 13 ... P–QN4! 14 B–KB1 N×QP 15 N×N P×N 16 B×QP P–B4 17 B×N Q×B 18 N–Q5 Q–N3 19 Q–Q2 B–B3 20 P–K5 B×N 21 Q×B B–K2 when the opposite-coloured bishops offer him drawing chances.

14 P–R3

Preventing the threatened 14 ... P–QN4 when 15 B–K2 N×QP 16 N×N P×N 17 B×QP P–B4 18 B–K3 P–N5 19 N–Q5 N×P 20 B×KRP! is good for him. However, 14 QR–Q1 is even more effective.

14 ...   P×P
15 N×P   N–K4
16 B–KB1 *(173)*

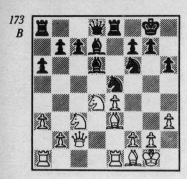

173
B

We can now see the result of the exchange which Black has been forced to make. White's KP is very strong and he already threatens to win a piece by 17 P-B4 and 18 P-K5.

16 ...	N-N3
17 QR-Q1	Q-K2
18 P-KN3!	

Threatening 19 B-N2 and 20 P-B4, so Black is driven into the following complications.

18 ...	N×P!
19 B-B1	P-KB4
20 B-N2	

But not 20 P-B3 B×NP 21 P×N B×R 22 R×B Q-K4 when Black stands better.

20 ...	N-K4
21 N×P	B×N
22 N×N	

Threatening 23 Q-N3+ and 24 Q×P

22 ...	N-B2!
23 Q-N3	QR-N1
24 B-Q2	

White aims for the advantage of the two bishops which is sufficient to bring about a decision in such an open position. After 24 ... B-K4 then 25 B-N4 is very strong, and after the relatively best 24 ... B-K3 he can play either 25 Q-B2 B-KB4 26 Q-B1 or 25 Q-KB3 B-Q4 26 B-B3.

24 ...	Q-K3
25 Q×Q	R×Q
26 N×B	P×N

If 26 ... R×N 27 B-B4. Or 26 ... R×R+ 27 R×R N×N 28 R-K7 etc.

27 B-Q5!	R×R+
28 R×R	K-B1
29 R-QB1	N-Q1
30 R-B7	B-K3

Black cannot shake off the domination of White's rook on the seventh rank, as 30 ... R-B1 fails to 31 B-R5! N-B3 32 R-B7+ K-K1 33 B-QB3 etc.

The game ended: **31 B×B N×B 32 R-Q7 N-N4** if 32 ... N-B4 33 R×QP N-K5 34 B-N4! **33 B×N P×B 34 R×QP R-B1 35 K-N2 R-B4 36 R-QN6 R-B2 37 K-B3 R-B2+ 38 K-N4 R×P 39 R×NP R-R7 40 P-QR4 P-R4 41 R-N5 1-0.**

12 Centralization of Pieces

We mentioned earlier that a strong pawn centre is not the sole means of controlling the centre. Let us now examine how the centralisation of pieces represents an important method of fighting for central superiority. Here is an opening variation: 1 P–Q4 P–K3 2 N–KB3 P–QB4 3 N–B3 P–Q4 4 P–K4 QP×P 5 N×P P×P 6 Q×P Q×Q 7 N×Q (*174*)

174
B

The only central pawn belongs to Black and yet it would be wrong to assume from this that he has a central advantage. In actual fact, White's two knights dominate the centre and immediate attempts to drive them away fail e.g. 7 ... P–K4 8 N–QN5, or 7 ... P–B4 8 N–KN5. If instead Black plays the preparatory move 7 ... P–QR3 then White can obtain at least the bishop pair by 8 B–KB4 and 9 N–Q6+ .

However, such a piece centre is rare, and in most cases there is only one centralised minor piece which is nevertheless sufficient to make its influence felt over the whole board. In volume 1, the game Ahues–Alekhine was an excellent example of the power of a centralised knight. This short-stepping piece needs centralisation more than any other piece, but all pieces do in fact benefit from being posted in the middle of the board. Our next game illustrates the effectiveness of a centralised bishop.

80 Botvinnik–Kan

Leningrad 1939, Nimzo-Indian Defence

1 P–Q4 N–KB3 2 P–QB4 P–K3 3 N–QB3 B–N5 4 N–B3 P–B4 5 P–QR3 B×N+ 6 P×B Q–R4? (Both 6 ... P–Q3 and 6 ... P–QN3 are better. **7 B–Q2 N–K5 8 Q–B2 N×B 9 N×N P–Q3**

10 P–K3

Not, however, 10 P–K4? P×P 11 P×P N–B3 12 Q–Q3 P–K4! and Black can fix White's pawns on the same colour as the white bishop.

10 ...   P–K4?

Whereas now this move is a serious strategic error, as it allows the white bishop to reach Q5 via K4.

11 P×KP!

This seemingly weakens his central position and lays bare his doubled QBP, but in reality it is the first step towards domination of the centre.

11 ...	P×P
12 B–Q3	P–KR3
13 0–0	0–0 (*175*)

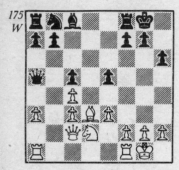

It is clear that White is striving to occupy Q5 and at first sight a knight seems best suited for this rôle. However, this does not work, as after 14 P–K4? N–B3 15 KR–Q1 B–K3 16 N–B1 QR–Q1 17 N–K3 N–K2 18 N–Q5 B×N! 19 BP×B N–B1 and 20 ... N–Q3 Black's blockading set-up gives him the better of it.

14 P–B4!

A vital part of the plan! This pawn will go to KB5 to prevent ... B–K3 and thus increase White's control of Q5. In view of White's advantage in development 14 ... P×P 15 P×P would be in his favour.

14 ...	N–Q2
15 P–B5	N–B3(?)

This only helps White to clarify matters in the centre. Black should reserve this knight for a later exchange of White's bishop when it reaches Q5, and play at once 15 ... P–B3 to eliminate any tactical possibilities arising from the advance of White's KBP to B6. However, after 16 B–K4 and 17 B–Q5+, White would still have the advantage.

16 N–K4!	Q–Q1
17 N×N+	Q×N
18 B–K4	R–N1
19 QR–Q1	P–QN3

Black is clearly hoping to solve his problems by ... B–N2 exchanging bishops. However, he cannot carry out this manoeuvre because of the danger of White seizing the Q-file. Another disadvantage is that Black's queen is tied down to KB3 in order to prevent P–B6 smashing up his K-side.

20 P–KR3

Giving his king a loop-hole in anticipation of 20 ... B–N2 21 B×B R×B 22 Q–K4! when he can double the rooks on the Q file after both 22 ... R2–N1 23 R–Q7 or 22 ... R–K2 23 R–Q5. So Black decides to complicate matters by preparing ... P–QN4.

20 ...	B–R3
21 B–Q5	P–QN4
22 P×P	R×P(?)

According to Botvinnik, Black should play 22 ... B×P 23 P–B4 B–B3 24 Q–K4 B×B 25 R×B when he loses a pawn but has drawing chances with the major pieces only on the board.

23 P–B4	R–N3 (*176*)

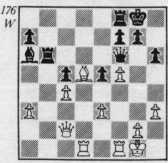

White's strongly posted bishop gives him a clear advantage. Note that it is Black who would stand better if White's bishop were on Q3 and his pawn on K4. White's bishop would then be 'bad' compared with the black bishop. However, in the present situation, despite the fact that most of White's pawns are on the same colour as his bishop, the latter is obviously far stronger than Black's piece on QR3 which must wander about aimlessly within its own lines. Black now threatens to exchange bishops by . . . B-N2, so White immediately prevents this.

24 R-N1!   **R-Q1**

After 24 . . . R1-N1 25 R×R R×R *(25 . . . Q×R? 26 P-B6! threatening 27 Q-N6!)* 26 Q-R4 Q-K2 27 P-B6! P×P 28 Q-B2 K-N2 29 R-B3 White has a strong attack. Also possible here is the simple 26 R-N1.

25 R×R	**P×R**
26 P-K4	**B-B1**
27 Q-R4	**B-Q2**
28 Q-R7	**B-K1**
29 R-N1	**R-Q3**
30 P-QR4	

Black cannot now prevent P-R5 winning a pawn. The game ended as follows: **30 . . . K-R2 31 P-R5 P×P 32 Q×RP R-R3 33 Q×P R-R7 34 Q-K3 Q-R3 35 R-N8 Q-R5 36 K-R2 R-R6 37 Q-B5 R-R7 38 R-R8 Q×R 39 B×Q R×B 40 Q×P B-B3 41 Q-B7 1-0.**

In our note to move 20 of the above game, we saw how White could win by posting his rook on Q5 and centralising his queen on K4. We do not meet this type of centralisation as much as the one involving minor pieces, but in certain circumstances it can be just as effective. Usually it is combined with pressure against the KP, as the following typical example illustrates.

81 Botvinnik-Chekhover

Leningrad 1938, Nimzo-Indian Defence

1 P-Q4 N-KB3 2 P-QB4 P-K3 3 N-QB3 B-N5 4 N-B3 0-0 5 B-N5 P-Q3 6 P-K3 Q-K2 7 B-K2 P-K4 8 Q-B2 R-K1 9 0-0 B×N 10 P×B P-KR3 11 B-R4 P-B4 12 QR-K1 B-N5

13 B×N!

Beginning the fight for the occupation of Q5, as in this connection Black's knight is more important than White's QB.

13 . . .   **Q×B**
14 Q-K4   **B×N(?)**

This gives White immediate control of the vital Q5 square. Botvinnik recommends 14 . . . B-B4! 15 Q×NP N-Q2 when Black has good piece play for the pawn.

15 B×B	**N-B3**
16 P×BP!	**P×P**
17 R-Q1	**QR-Q1**
18 R-Q5	**P-QN3**

There is nothing to be gained from 18 . . . R×R 19 P×R N-K2 20 P-Q6! Q×P 21 Q×NP Q-QN3 22 R-N1, but somewhat better is 18 . . . Q-K2 19 R1-Q1 P-KN3 when White would have to play 20 P-N4! in order to maintain his queen on K4.

19 R1-Q1	**N-R4**
20 P-KR3	**R×R**
21 R×R *(177)*	

A characteristic position has arisen in which the pressure against Black's KP stops him exchanging the heavy pieces e.g. 21 . . . R-Q1 22 R×KP N×P? fails to 23 R-K8+ R×R 24 Q×R+ K-R2 25 Q-K4+ . It is interesting to note that Black's pawn structure is far superior to White's, as the doubled QBP would be a serious weakness in the ending.

However, he cannot co-ordinate his forces because of White's beautifully centralized pieces.

| 21 ... | Q–K2 |
| 22 B–N4 | Q–N2 |

Preventing 23 R–Q7.

23 B–B5! (*178*)

White has achieved maximum effectiveness for his centralised pieces. His bishop now guards the queen, so that R–Q7 can no longer be prevented, and after 23 ... P–N3 24 B×P P×B 25 Q×NP+ K–B1 26 R–Q6 wins.

23 ...	Q–N1
24 R–Q7	R–Q1
25 Q×P	N×P
26 Q×Q	R×Q
27 B–K4!	

And now the bishop heads for Q5! This factor, in conjunction with the rook on the seventh rank, is enough to guarantee a comfortable win. The game ended: **27 ... N–R6 28 B–Q5 R–KB1 29 P–K4 P–QR4 30 P–QB4 P–QN4 31 P×P N×P 32 P–K5 P–R5 33 P–B4 N–Q5 34 K–B2 P–N4 35 P–N3 P×P 36 P×P N–K3 37 K–K3** finally the king is centralized, a typical occurrence in the endgame **37 ... P–B5 38 P–B5 N–B4 39 R–B7 N–Q6 40 P–K6 1–0.**

In both the above games White's centralized pieces were beautifully co-ordinated. The placing of a piece on a central square does not in itself

guarantee an advantage unless it is co-ordinated with the other pieces. Our next game contrasts the effectiveness of centralized pieces in the light of this statement.

82 Teichmann–Chigorin

Cambridge Springs 1904, Queen's Gambit

1 P–Q4 P–Q4 2 P–QB4 N–QB3 3 N–KB3 B–N5 4 P×P B×N 5 P×N B×BP 6 N–B3 P–K3 7 B–B4 N–B3 8 P–K3 B–N5 9 Q–N3 N–Q4 10 B–N3 0–0 11 B–Q3 Q–N4!

12 Q–B2

Not 12 0–0? B×N 13 P×B N×KP!

12 ...   P–B4!

Securing Q4 for his knight. At the same time this move gives White's bishop a square at K5, but as we shall see this centralized piece has little influence on the remainder of the game.

13 B–K5	R–B2
14 0–0–0	B×N
15 P×B	(*179*)

At first sight White's position does not look too bad. He has the two bishops, a central pawn majority and a centralized bishop on K5 which seemingly gives him the possibility of a later K-side attack. Nevertheless, within the space of a few moves Black manages to shatter the somewhat weakened enemy king's position. What is the explanation for such a rapid collapse of White's game? The answer lies in the excellent co-ordination of the black pieces. The centralized knight is well supported by the bishop, and the queen can quickly be transferred to the Q-side. White's bishop on K5 proves in reality to be practically useless, as White has no time to open up the KN-file in order to put pressure on the KNP (Black will of course refrain from capturing the white KNP!). Nor can the bishop be used for defence, as it is completely cut off from the Q-side by its own QP.

15 ...	P-N4!
16 KR-N1	Q-K2
17 QR-B1	

White also loses quickly after 17 K-N2 R-N1 18 P-N4 P-N5 19 P-QB4 N-B6 20 QR-KB1 N-R5+ 21 K-R1 P-N6 etc.

17 ...	Q-R6+
18 K-Q2	P-N5
19 P-QB4	B-R5!
20 Q-N1	N-B6

White's position is now in ruins and Black has various ways of building up his attack. The game ended as follows: **21 Q-R1 R-Q1 22 P-N3 N-K5+ 23 K-K2 N-B4 24 Q-N1 N×B 25 Q×N Q×P+ 26 K-B3 B-B7! 0-1.**

Our next game is instructive because Black achieves complete centralization of his pieces, whereas the White pieces, which are partially decentralized, do not exert the same influence on the game.

83 Novotelnov-Averbakh

19th USSR Championship 1951, Catalan System

1 P-Q4 N-KB3 2 P-QB4 P-K3 3 N-KB3 P-Q4 4 P-KN3 B-K2 5 B-N2 0-0 6 0-0 QN-Q2 7 Q-B2 P-B3 8 B-B4(?) P-QN3 9 N3-Q2 B-N2 10 P-K4 R-B1!

11 N-QB3	P-B4!

Black chooses the right moment to liquidate pawns in the centre whilst increasing the activity of his pieces.

12 BP×P	KP×P

Also good is 12 ... BP×P 13 P-Q6 P×N 14 P×B Q×P 15 P×P P-K4 followed by 16 ... N-B4, but Black plans to clear the centre of pawns and post his pieces there.

13 N×P	N×N
14 P×N	P×P
15 Q-R4	N-B4!
16 Q×QP	N-K3
17 Q-K4	R-B4!
18 B-K3	B×P
19 Q-N1	

The point of Black's whole manoeuvre beginning at move 12 is that White's queen has to be content with retreating to QN1, limiting its own activity and that of the QR. Other queen moves would have cost at least a pawn e.g. 19 Q-Q3 B×B 20 Q×Q R×Q 21 K×B R-B7. Or 19 Q-KN4 B×B 20 K×B R-B7 21 KR-Q1 R×P 22 N-B4 Q-R1+. Or finally 19 Q-QR4 R-R4 20 Q-B2 B×B 21 K×B R×P! 22 R×R Q-Q4+ etc.

19 ...	B×B
20 K×B	R-Q4
21 R-Q1	

Or 21 N-B3 B-B3 and White can find no squares for his pieces.

21 ...	B-B3
22 K-N1	

He cannot play either 22 N-B4 P-QN4 or 22 N-K4 B×P!

22 ...	R-K1
23 P-QR4	(*180*)

To prepare 24 N-B4.

Black's superiority is self-evident but there still remains the problem of exploiting it. After 23 ... N-B4 (threatening ... *N-Q6*) 24 B×N R×N 25 B-R3 R1-K7 White can defend by 26 R×R Q×R 27 Q-KB1 when both 27 ... B×P 28 R-Q1 and 27 ... B-Q5 28 R-Q1 B×BP+ 29 K-R1 are

180
B

insufficient. So Black must first prevent back-rank mates.

23 ...   **P–KR4!**

In order to answer 24 P–R4 with 24 ... N–B4 or the equally strong line given by Euwe: 24 ... N–Q5 25 B×N R×B 26 N–B4 B×P! 27 P×B R–KN5+ 28 K–B1 Q–R1! etc. So White must allow the advance of Black's KRP which soon creates serious mating threats.

24 N–B4   **P–R5**
25 Q–B2   **P–R6**
26 Q–K2

Also insufficient is 26 P–B3 N–Q5 27 B×N R×B threatening 28 ... Q–Q4.

26 ...   **N–Q5**
27 Q–B1

Or 27 Q–N4 R–K5! 28 Q×R N–K7+ 29 K–B1 R×R+ 30 K×N R×R. After the text move Black could win at once by 27 ... N–B6+ 28 K–R1 R×R 29 R×R Q–R1, but in the rest of the game both sides commit errors.

27 ...   **Q–B1 ?**
28 B×N   **B×B**
29 R–Q2   **Q–N5**
30 R1–Q1 ?

White could still hold the position with 30 R–B1!

30 ...   **B×BP+ !**
31 Q×B   **Q×R+**
0–1

The next game is interesting because, although both sides have pieces in the centre, Black outnumbers White in

pieces which control the central squares.

84 Chekhover–Pirc

Moscow 1935, Queen's Gambit

1 P–Q4 P–Q4 2 P–QB4 P–QB3 3 N–KB3 N–KB3 4 P–K3 P–K3 5 B–Q3 P×P 6 B×BP QN–Q2 7 N–B3 P–QN4 8 B–Q3 P–QR3 9 P–K4 P–N5 10 N–K2 10 N–QR4! **10 ... P–B4 11 P–K5 N–Q4 12 0–0 B–N2 13 N–N3 P×P 14 N–K4 P–R3! 15 B–Q2 P–N4? 16 N×QP?**

Much stronger is 16 Q–R4! but White is counting on the fact that he can afford to give up his KP in order to obtain an attack against the enemy king in the centre. As it turns out, however, it is not so much the pawn that matters as the control that Black now obtains over his K4 square.

16 ...   **N×P**
17 B–B2   **Q–N3!**
18 B–R4+   **K–K2**
19 R–K1   **B–N2!** *(181)*

181
W

A fascinating position has arisen in which all four knights are in the centre! However, whereas the black knights are well supported by the bishops, and Black's queen is also directly aimed at the centre (the immediate threat is 20 ... Q×N 21 B×KNP† P×B 22 Q×Q N–KB6+ etc.), there is only the white KR at the moment which is supporting the central pieces.

20 N-B2

To safeguard his threatened piece White has to withdraw the knight from the centre, but this allows a decisive invasion by the black pieces.

20 ... N-Q6!

In order to obtain an irresistible attack after 21 B×KNP+ P×B 22 Q×N B-K4 etc.

21 B-K3 N×B
22 Q×N N-Q4
23 N-K3 KR-Q1
24 N-KB5+

An attempt to conjure up complications. Black could now play 24 ... P×N 25 N-B5+ K-B3 (or *25 ... K-B1 26 R-K8+ R×R 27 N-Q7+ K-N1 28 N×Q N×N 29 B×R R×B*) 26 N-Q7+ R×N 27 B×R N-K2, but instead Pirc chooses a more cautious defence in which he gradually eliminates the enemy threats. The game ended: **24 ... K-B1 25 N×B K×N 26 Q-KN3 N-B5 27 B-B2** 27 P-R4 R-Q6 **27 ... B×N 28 B×B QR-B1 29 P-KR4 Q-N4 30 P×P P×P** not 30 ... N-K7+? 31 R×N Q×R 32 Q-K5+! K-B1 33 P×P **31 Q-K3 R-B5 32 P-KN3 N-R6+ 33 K-N2 P-N5 34 B-Q3 Q-Q4+ 35 B-K4 Q-Q7 36 Q-K2 P-B4 37 B-N7 R-B7 38 K-B1 Q-Q6! 0-1.**

We have already seen in diagram 173 and game No. 82 that centralized pieces can be more important than a central pawn majority. A typical illustration of this point is given by the Sicilian Defence. After 1 P-K4 P-QB4 2 N-KB3 N-QB3 (or 2 ... P-Q3) 3 P-Q4 P×P 4 N×P, Black has obtained two pawns against one in the centre by exchanging his QBP for White's QP. However, White's pieces control Q4, a factor which can also prove important if Black manages to play ... P-Q4, as shown in our next game.

85 Maroczy-Euwe

Scheveningen 1923, Sicilian Defence

1 P-K4 P-QB4 2 N-KB3 N-QB3 3 P-Q4 P×P 4 N×P N-B3 5 N-QB3 P-Q3 6 B-K2 P-K3 7 0-0 B-K2 8 K-R1 The more exact modern method of development, suggested by Boleslavsky, is 8 B-K3 0-0 9 P-B4 P-QR3 10 Q-K1 Q-B2 11 R-Q1 followed by 12 Q-N3, achieving maximum centralization of the pieces. **8 ... 0-0 9 P-B4 Q-B2 10 N-N3 P-QR3 11 P-QR4 P-QN3**

12 B-B3 B-N2

With this move and his next, Black aims for ... P-Q4, but it is better to build up Q-side counterplay by 12 ... R-Q1 13 B-K3 N-QR4!

13 B-K3 N-QN5
14 Q-K2 P-Q4
15 P-K5 N-K5

Or 15 ... N-Q2 16 Q-B2 B-B4 17 N-Q4 N-QB3 18 N3-K2 followed by 19 P-B3 when White's solid central position gives him the basis of a K-side attack which he can build up in comfort.

16 B×N P×B
17 Q-B2 P-QN4

Even worse is 17 ... B-Q1 18 N-Q4. Black does not lose his QNP after the text move, but by attacking it White gains time to centralize his knight on N3.

182
W

18 P×P   **P×P**
19 N–Q4   **B–QB3** (*182*)

Black defends his QNP by his indirect threat against White's QBP (20 N×NP? B×N 21 N×B Q×BP), but his position remains difficult. White's knight on Q4 is directed against both wings, allowing White to build up a dangerous K-side attack.

20 Q–N3!

Preparing P–B5.

20 . . .   **R×R**
21 R×R   **R–N1?**

This passive defence of the QNP gives White a vital attacking tempo, as at the critical moment his bishop will be threatening the rook. Euwe should have tried 21 . . . R–B1 or 21 . . . R–R1 22 R×R+ B×R 23 N3×NP Q–B5 with counterplay for the pawn.

22 P–B5   **P×P**
23 N×BP   **B–B1**
24 B–B4!   **R–R1**
25 R–QB1!

Very accurate play! Weaker are both 25 R×R B×R 26 P–K6 Q–R2 threatening 27 . . . Q–R8+ , and 25 R–KB1 N–Q4 26 N×N B×N 27 P–K6 Q–B5.

25 . . .   **P–N3**
26 P–K6   **Q–N2**
27 P–K7!   **B–N2**

Or 27 . . . B×P 28 N×B+ Q×N 29 B–Q6 winning.

28 N×B   **K×N**
29 Q–R4   **P–B3**
30 Q–R6+   **K–N1**
31 B–Q6   **1–0**

13 Control of the Central Squares

In several games from the previous section it was clear that the struggle for the centre was carried out not only by those pieces which were posted on the central squares but by other pieces which controlled these squares from a distance. In game 82 the black bishop on QB3 controlled Q4 and K5. In game 83 Black's knight on K3, bishop on KB3, rook on K1 and queen on Q1 were all directed at the centre. A similar function was performed by the bishops and queen in game 84.

For this reason it is important to distinguish between 'control' and 'occupation' of the centre. As soon as a piece occupies a central square it loses the control it exerted over this square. For example, after the moves 1 P-Q4 N-KB3 2 N-KB3 N-K5, leaving aside the fact that Black's last move is an important loss of time, we can see that by occupying K5 with his knight Black has given up his control of this square.

This means that the centralization of pieces cannot be carried out effectively until a side has achieved adequate control of the central squares. For example, it would be pointless to proceed 1 N-KB3 P-Q4 2 N-K5? as Black can immediately drive away this centralized piece by 2 . . . P-KB3.

Let us see how Black can increase his control of K5 after 1 P-Q4 N-KB3 2 N-KB3. There are basically two methods:

1. 2 . . . P-Q4, posting a pawn in the centre.
2. 2 . . . P-QN3 and 3 . . . B-N2 putting piece pressure on Q4 and K5.

We have already explained in sufficient detail the importance of a pawn centre. Nimzowitsch and Reti, creators of the 'Hypermodern School', demonstrated that, whilst a pawn centre guarantees a stable control of some central squares, it also has the disadvantage of restricting the action of one's own pieces. For instance, after the above moves 1 P-Q4 N-KB3 2 N-KB3 P-Q4, Black's QP would block the diagonal of his fianchettod QB (e.g. in the Tartakower system of the Queen's Gambit). In the French Defence, after 1 P-K4 P-K3 2 P-Q4 P-Q4 3 N-QB3, Nimzowitsch recommended 3 . . . P×P precisely because it offers Black better prospects of directing his pieces at the central squares (the major pieces down the Q-file and the QB on the QR1-KR8 diagonal). In fact, the opening systems advocated by the Hypermoderns can be characterized by the basic strategic idea of exerting pressure on the centre by means of pieces and pawns rather than occupying the centre immediately with pawns.

We have already dealt with the use of either BP to exert pressure on the enemy centre. Piece pressure on the centre is usually brought about by a fianchettod bishop. Examples are the Queen's Indian Defence (1 P–Q4 N–KB3 2 P–QB4 P–K3 3 N–KB3 P–QN3), the Nimzowitsch system (1 N–KB3 P–Q4 2 P–QN3) and the Reti system (1 N–KB3 P–Q4 2 P–QB4 P–K3 3 P–KN3, or here 2 ... P–QB3 3 P–QN3). A vital strategic element is also the exchange of enemy pieces controlling the central squares. For instance, in the Nimzo-Indian Defence, after 1 P–Q4 N–KB3 2 P–QB4 P–K3 3 N–QB3, the move 3 ... B–N5 pins and later intends to exchange White's QN which is controlling Q5 and K4.

It is of course true that there is nothing new about using pieces and pawns to exert pressure on the centre. The basic theme of the Ruy Lopez (1 P–K4 P–K4 2 N–KB3 N–QB3 3 B–N5) is to increase White's pressure on Q4 and K5. In the Scotch Game, after 1 P–K4 P–K4 2 N–KB3 N–QB3 3 P–Q4 P×P 4 N×P Black defends by applying pressure either on Q5 (4 ... B–B4 5 B–K3 Q–B3) or on K5 (4 ... N–B3 5 N–QB3 B–N5). The use of pawns for the same purpose is the strategic idea behind not only the Queen's Gambit (1 P–Q4 P–Q4 2 P–QB4) but also one of the oldest openings the King's Gambit (1 P–K4 P–K4 2 P–KB4).

However, such a use of pieces and pawns in the struggle for central control was viewed solely as a means of occupying the centre, until the Hypoderns demonstrated that control of the centre is possible without the direct occupation of it by pawns or pieces. Let us consider a few examples to illustrate these points.

86 Nimzowitsch–Wolf

Karlsbad 1923, Nimzowitsch–Larsen Opening

1 N–KB3 P–Q4 2 P–QN3 N–KB3 3 B–N2 P–B4

4 P–K3   N–B3

The first inaccuracy, allowing White to exchange his KB for Black's QN which is much more important as regards the struggle for central control.

5 B–N5!   B–Q2
6 0–0   P–K3
7 P–Q3   B–K2

From a strategic point of view 7 ... B–Q3 would be better, protecting the vital K4 square, but White could then play 8 P–K4 (threatening *9 P–K5*) as 8 ... P×P 9 P×P N×P fails to 10 R–K1.

8 QN–Q2   0–0
9 B×N!   B×B *(183)*

183
W

This position clearly illustrates our theme. Although none of White's pawns has passed the third rank, he has a definite central superiority.

10 N–K5   N–Q2

Black must immediately take up the struggle for the central squares. After 10 ... R–B1 or 10 ... B–K1 White would gain a vital tempo to secure control of K5 and obtain a clear advantage e.g. 10 ... R–B1 11 P–KB4 N–Q2 12 Q–N4 N×N 13 B×N B–B3 14 R–B3 (Nimzowitsch-Spielmann, New York 1924), or 10 ... B–K1 11 P–KB4 N–Q2 12 N×N Q×N 13 P–K4 P–B3 14 Q–B3 (Nimzowitsch-Rubinstein, Semmering 1926). After the text move both 11 N×B P×N 12 P–K4 B–B3 13 B×B Q×B and 11 N×N B×N 12 P–KB4 B–KB3 give Black equality.

11 N2–B3   **R–B1**

An illogical move. 11 ... B–B3! would give Black chances of complete equality.

12 Q–K2   **N×N(?)**

It was still vital to play 12 ... B–B3! instead of giving White full control of K5.

13 N×N   **B–K1**

White could now answer 13 ... B–B3 with 14 P–KB4 as 14 ... B×N 15 P×B gives him a strong K-side attack. On the other hand, after 13 ... P–B3 14 N×B R×N 15 P–QB4, Black remains with the 'bad' bishop.

14 Q–N4   **P–B4**

The disadvantage of this move is that it increases the scope of White's bishop. Black could prevent the threatened N–B6 or N–Q7 by 14 ... B–KB3 although 15 P–KB4 still gives White the better game.

15 Q–K2   **B–KB3**
16 P–QB4!   **Q–K2**
17 P–B4! (*184*)

White's last two moves have increased his control of the centre which in conjunction with his powerful bishop gives him attacking prospects on the K-side. Nevertheless, it is still doubtful whether White can win against accurate and active defensive play.

184 B

17 ...   **B–B2**

To connect his rooks. After 17 ... P–QN4 18 QR–B1 NP×P 19 QP×P

followed by 20 KR–Q1 White would have strong pressure against the QBP and QP.

18 P–KR3   **KR–Q1**
19 K–R2   **R–B2**
20 R–B2   **B–K1**
21 R–KN1   **P×P**
22 NP×P   **B×N?**

The decisive error, increasing White's attacking chances. It was essential to play 22 ... P–QN4 and 23 ... R–N2.

23 B×B   **R2–Q2**
24 P–N4!   **P×P**
25 Q×P   **B–N3**
26 P–Q4   **P×P**
27 P×P   **B–B4**
28 Q–R5   **B–N3**
29 Q–K2   **R–KB1**
30 R–N5   **R–B4**
31 R2–N2   **R×R**
32 R×R   **Q–B1**
33 Q–N4   **B–B4**
34 Q–N2

White intends to increase his pressure on the KNP by creating a passed QP. The contrasting activity of the bishops already spells defeat for Black.

34 ...   **P–KR3**
35 R–N3   **K–R2**
36 P–Q5!   **R–KB2**

Or 36 ... P×P 37 P×P P–QN4 38 P–Q6 followed by 39 Q–Q5. After the text move Black is soon in zugzwang, as his bishop cannot stop the passed pawn.

37 P–Q6   **P–KN3**
38 P–B5   **Q–B1**

White's quickest winning method is now 39 P–B6 Q×P 40 Q×Q P×Q 41 R–N3 etc., but Nimzowitsch's continuation also leads to a clear win. The game ended: **39 R–QB3 Q–B3 40 Q×Q P×Q 41 P–KR4 K–N1 42 R–QN3 R–Q2 43 R–N8+ K–B2 44 R–QB8 B–K5 45 K–N3 P–KR4 46 K–B2 B–Q4 47 K–K3 B–N7 48 K–Q4 B–B6 49 B–R8! P–K4+** or 49 ... B–N7 **50 K–K5 B–B6 51 B–B6 B–Q4 52 B–N5**

B–N7 53 R–B7 wins **50 K×P B–Q4 51
B–B6 B–B6 52 B–N5 K–N2 53 P–B5!
B–N5 54 P–B6+ K–R2 55 R×P 1–0.**

Our next game contains an extremely interesting transition from one kind of centre to another. First of all Black exerts pressure against White's pawn centre, then he occupies the centre himself with pieces and finally he establishes a firm pawn centre himself.

87 Feigin–Flohr

Kemeri 1937, Grünfeld Defence

**1 P–Q4 N–KB3 2 P–QB4 P–KN3 3
N–QB3 P–Q4 4 Q–N3 P×P 5 Q×BP
B–K3 6 Q–N5+? 6 Q–Q3! 6 . . . N–B3
7 N–B3 N–Q4 8 N×N** 8 P–K4!?
N4–N5 9 Q–R4 B–Q2 10 Q–Q1 P–K4!
produces complications **8 . . . B×N 9
P–K3 P–K3 10 B–Q2 P–QR3
11 Q–R4   B–Q3!**

White's misguided 6th move, at the time considered best, has given his opponent a lead in development which Black has used to obtain a clear advantage in the centre by controlling his Q4 and K5 squares. Black's bishop stands better on Q3 than on KN2, as it makes its influence felt on both sides of the board, being in particular directed against the K-side.

**12 B–K2   0–0
13 Q–B2   N–N5**

Not a particularly good move, as the knight is momentarily taken away from the centre. The immediate 13 . . . P–B4 is better.

**14 Q–N1   P–KB4
15 0–0   N–B3!**

Otherwise White could advantageously simplify by 16 B×N B×B 17 N–K5. Admitting his mistake, Flohr plans an effective knight tour to KB3.

**16 B–B3   Q–K2
17 R–Q1   N–N1!
18 N–Q2**

After 18 N–K5 B×N 19 P×B Q–N4

20 B–B1 N–Q2 Black obtains a clear advantage thanks to his actively posted pieces and his Q-side pawn majority.

**18 . . .   N–Q2
19 B–B3   N–B3** (*185*)

185
W

Black's timely knight manoeuvre has given him complete control over his K5 square, as 20 P–K4? fails to 20 . . . P×P 21 N×P N×N 22 B×N Q–R5 etc., a variation which points to the usefulness of the black bishop on Q3.

20 Q–Q3   N–K5!

Finally Black can occupy his strong-point at K5. White cannot win a pawn, as 21 N×N P×N 22 B×P allows 22 . . . B×KRP+ etc.

21 Q–K2   N–N4!

The knight temporarily leaves his central post in order to force the exchange of white-squared bishops by the threat of . . . Q–N2–R3. White prefers to exchange himself in the mistaken belief that Black will go for the two bishops by . . . N×B+?, but the text move makes Black's task easier.

22 B×B(?)   P×B

Black now has a decisive positional advantage in view of his central control, the K-file with its outpost on K5, and his 'good' bishop.

**23 N–B3   N–K5
24 QR–B1   P–B3
25 B–K1   QR–K1
26 P–KN3   Q–Q2
27 Q–B1   P–KN4**

White has no counterplay what-soever and is helpless against the coming attack. Flohr concluded the game as follows: **28 R–Q3 P–B5 29 KP×P P×P 30 N–R4 K–R1 31 Q–N2 P×P 32 RP×P N–N4 33 P–B3 N–R6+ 34 K–R1** if 34 K–R2 N–B5 **34 ... B–K2 35 B–Q2 B×N 36 P×B Q–B4 37 R–N3 R–KN1 38 Q–R2 R–K3 39 R–B1? N–B7+ 0–1.**

We have already seen how a flank attack can demolish an enemy pawn centre. Here is an illustration of the same strategy, with the slight difference that the QP is used for the final blow. Such use of a pawn which has lain dormant for a long time often occurs in variations of the Reti opening.

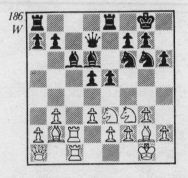

186
W

This position (*186*) arose in the game Reti–Yates, New York 1924. White now smashed the enemy centre as follows: **17 P–Q4 P–K5 18 N–K5 B×N 19 P×B N–R2 20 P–B4 P×Pep 21 P×P N–N4 22 P–B4 N–R6+ 23 K–R1 P–Q5 24 B×P QR–Q1 25 R×B P×R 26 B×BP N–B7+ 27 K–N2 Q×B.Q5 28 Q×Q R×Q 29 B×R N–K5 30 P–K6 R–Q7+ 31 K–B3 1–0.**

It is clear that the initial advance of White's QP was made possible because of the piece pressure against the centre. Here are three games to illustrate this point.

88 Kavalek–Pomar

Skopje Olympiad 1972, English Opening

1 P–QB4 N–KB3 2 N–KB3 P–K3 3 P–KN3 P–Q4 4 B–N2 B–K2 5 0–0 0–0 6 P–N3

At one time 6 P–Q4 was common here, strengthening White's central position and intending (after, say, ... QN–Q2) 7 Q–B2 followed by P–N3, B–N2, QN–Q2 (or B3). An interesting variation after 6 P–Q4 goes 6 ... P×P 7 Q–B2 (*7 N–K5 is stronger according to present theory*) 7 ... P–QR3! 8 Q×BP P–QN4 9 Q–B2 B–N2, and Black is content to control the central squares and to attack the centre later with ... P–QB4. However, the text move contains a completely different strategic idea. White holds his centre pawns back for the moment while he increases his pressure against the central squares. Only later will he use his QP and KP as attacking weapons.

6 ...   P–B4

7 P–K3

He can also play 7 B–N2 at once, as 7 ... P–Q5 has its darker side after 8 P–K3 N–B3 9 P×P P×P 10 R–K1! followed by N–R3–B2 or 8 P–QN4 with an attack on the QP.

7 ...   N–B3

8 B–N2   P–QN3

9 Q–K2

Perhaps a little more accurate than 9 N–B3 when Black has amongst other things 9 ... P×P(!) 10 P×P (*10 N–K5? N×N 11 B×R B–R3*) 10 ... B–N2 when White cannot become active in the centre on account of his weak QBP e.g. 11 P–Q4? P×P 12 P×P N–QR4 etc. So for the time being Kavalek leaves his knight on QN1, as it may later be required on Q2.

A typical example of play in this variation was seen in the game Botvinnik–Larsen (Palma de Mallorca,

1967): 9 N–B3 B–N2 10 P–Q3 R–B1 11 R–B1 R–B2 12 Q–K2 R–Q2 13 KR–Q1 R–K1 14 P×P N×P 15 N×N R×N 16 P–Q4! Q–R1? (*16 ... R–Q2!* was better) 17 P×P R×R+ 18 R×R B×P 19 N–N5! P–KR3 20 N–K4 B–KB1 and now White could have won immediately with 21 N–B6+! P×N 22 Q–N4+ K–R2 23 B–K4+ P–B4 24 R–Q7! N–Q1 25 R×P+! N×R 26 B×P+! P×B 27 Q×P+ K–N1 28 Q–N6+ followed by mate; or here 24 ... N–K2 25 R×N! R×R 26 B×P+! P×B 27 Q×P+ K–N1 28 Q–B6 K–R2 29 P–KN4! and again Black will be mated.

9 ...   B–N2
10 P–Q3

The immediate 10 R–Q1 is also possible.

10 ...   R–K1

The alternative 10 ... Q–B2 11 N–B3 QR–Q1 seems better.

11 R–Q1   B–Q3

As we saw in the above-quoted game Botvinnik–Larsen, White's usual plan in these positions is to play P×P followed by P–Q4. For this reason Pomar places his pieces so that P×P can be answered by ... P×P! when his rook on K1 'X-rays' the white queen.

12 N–B3   P–QR3 (*187*)

187
W

13 P–Q4!

A typical Reti move. The centre

pawn is not advanced until development is complete. As the black queen is now in the line of White's rook, the opening of the centre will favour White.

13 ...   BP×P
14 N.KB3

Not of course 14 KP×P which would close the diagonal of his QB and allow Black to equalize completely by ... N–K2 followed by ... Q–B2 and ... QR–Q1.

14 ...   N×N
15 R×N   B–K4
16 R–Q3!

The correct retreat. White intends to double rooks on the Q-file, but 16 R–Q2 allows 16 ... R–QB1 when 17 P×P fails to 17 ... B×N.

16 ...   P–QR4!

In order to win the exchange after 17 P×P B–R3

17 R1–Q1!   B–R3?

As his own QP is pinned this pin does not help much, whereas 17 ... Q–N1! would have freed his QP from both pins, threatening 18 ... P×P. White could then obtain two pawns for the exchange by 18 P×P B–R3 19 P×P R–R2! 20 P×P+ R×P 21 N–Q5 B×R 22 R×B B×B 23 Q×B with advantage, but the win would be by no means clear. White could also try 18 N–R4 B×B 19 Q×B with good pressure on the Q-side.

18 P–K4!   Q–N1

This is now too late, but after 18 ... B×N 19 R×B! P–Q5 20 P–K5! Kavalek had planned to give up two rooks for the queen, as 20 ... P×R 21 R×Q QR×Q 22 B×P N–Q2 23 B–B6 is in his favour.

19 KP×P   B×N
20 R×B   N×P

Or 20 ... P×P 21 R–K3! R×R 22 Q×R and the pin of the QP ensures White material advantage.

21 R3–Q3!

Threatening 22 P×N, so Black's

answer is forced because other retreats of the knight would lose the exchange. However, the knight is soon trapped.

21 ...	N–N5
22 R–Q7!	R–R2
23 R×R	Q×R
24 P–QR3	N–R7

Or 24 ... N–Q4 25 B×N and now it is the KP which is pinned!

| 25 B–QR1 | 1–0 |

89 Pachman–Donner

Rotterdam 1955, English Opening

1 P–QB4 P–KN3 2 N–QB3 B–N2 3 P–KN3 N–KB3 4 B–N2 0–0 5 P–K4 P–K4 5 ... P–B4! 6 KN–K2 P–Q3 7 0–0 N3–Q2 8 P–Q3 P–KB4 9 P×P   P×P

Although Black now has a central pawn majority, this position is in White's favour. My plan is simple: P–B4 will add to the pressure on the enemy centre which can then be smashed later with P–Q4. White's control of the central squares, in particular Q5 and K4, play a vital part in all this.

10 B–K3

Even the immediate 10 P–B4 is possible, but it is usually best not to reveal one's strategic plan too early in the game. It is logical to complete the development of the pieces first.

| 10 ... | N–KB3 |
| 11 Q–Q2 | P–B3 |

If 11 ... N–N5 then 12 B–N5

12 P–KR3   N–R4? (*188*)

After 12 ... P–Q4 13 P×P P×P 14 P–Q4 P–K5 15 N–B4 followed by 16 KR–B1 White stands better, but the text move creates much more difficult problems for Black. Instead of preventing White's next move, he makes it more effective by decentralizing his knight and beginning an unjustified action on the wing.

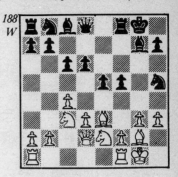

13 P–B4!

We have already pointed out the strategic significance of this move. Its tactical justification lies in the variation 13 ... P×P 14 N×P! N×P? 15 R–B3 Q–R5 (*15 ... Q–N4 16 N–K6*) 16 B–B2 etc.

13 ...	Q–K1
14 K–R2	Q–N3
15 Q–K1!	

The NP must be protected so that after ... P×P White can recapture with the knight.

15 ...   N–Q2

This blocks the line of his QB, so 15 ... N–R3 would have been better.

| 16 R–Q1 | K–R1 |
| 17 P–Q4 | |

The fight for the centre has reached its climax. If now 17 ... P–K5 then 18 P–KN4! P×P 19 N×P P×P 20 B–B3 and White's beautifully centralized position in conjunction with the open file gives him a decisive K-side attack. This variation shows how a pawn which is two files away from the centre can still take part in the struggle for the central squares!

17 ...	R–KN1
18 Q–B2	B–B3
19 QP×P	P×P
20 R–Q6!	

The logical culmination of White's play in the centre. Black now decides that the time is ripe to open up the position on the K-side, but he fails to take into account a little combination.

20 ...   P×P
21 N×P!

An unpleasant surprise for Black! Once again White's KNP cannot be taken, as after 21 ... Q×P+ 22 Q×Q N×Q 23 R1–Q1! Black is helpless e.g. 23 ... R–N2 24 R×B! N×R 25 R–Q8+ R–KN1 26 B–Q4! R×R 27 B×N+ winning.

21 ...   N×N
22 B×N   Q–B2
23 R–K1!

Reinforcing the central pressure and preventing ... N–K4! (centralization!) If now 23 ... Q×P White wins by 24 R×B! N×R 25 B–K5 Q–B2 26 N–K4! or here 25 ... R–KB1 26 N–K4! P×N 27 R×P! Q–B2 28 R–KB4 winning.

23 ...   B–N2
24 R6–K6   N–B1

Similar play arises after 24 ... N–B3

25 R–K7   Q×P? *(189)*

Black could put up a longer but still hopeless resistance with 25 ... Q–B3 26 R×B! R×R 27 B–K5 Q–B2 28 N–K4! etc.

189 W

The following exchange sacrifice is now almost thematic and requires little calculation. Black's KB is his only active piece (aiming at the centre!) and its elimination leaves the white pieces in full control of the board.

26 R×B!   R×R

Or 26 ... K×R 27 B–K5+ K–B2 28 N–K4!, a recurring centralization of the knight which decides the issue.

27 R–K8

This is the real idea behind the sacrifice, tying down the black pieces. It would be pointless merely to regain the exchange by B–K5?

27 ...   K–N1

After 27 ... Q–B2 or 27 ... R–KB2 White first plays 28 Q–K3! when Black cannot defend against the many threats.

28 B–Q6   R–KB2
29 Q–K3   P–B5

Otherwise 30 Q–N5+ follows.

30 Q–K5   R–B4
31 R×N+ !   R×R
32 Q–KN5+   1–0

White wins easily after 32 ... K–B2 33 Q–K7+ K–N3 34 Q×R followed by 35 B–K4+ . In the closing stages of this game White's pieces completely dominated the centre.

The final game of this section is a very interesting and complex illustration of pieces fighting for control of the central squares.

90 Tarrasch–Lasker

World Championship 1908, Ruy Lopez

1 P–K4 P–K4 2 N–KB3 N–QB3 3 B–N5 N–B3 4 0–0 P–Q3 5 P–Q4 B–Q2 6 N–B3 B–K2 7 R–K1 P×P 8 N×P N×N 9 Q×N B×B 10 N×B 0–0 11 B–N5 P–KR3 12 B–R4 R–K1 13 QR–Q1 N–Q2
    14 B×B(?)

White has better prospects with 14 B–N3 P–R3 (if *14 ... B–B3? 15 Q–B4 P–R3 16 N×BP R–QB1 17 B×P B–K4 18 Q–Q3*) 15 N–B3 B–B3 16 Q–Q2.

14 ...   R×B
15 Q–B3 *(190)*

Intending to gain a tempo to centralize the knight on Q4

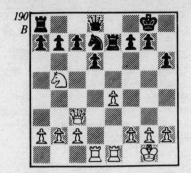

190 B

Lasker's next manoeuvre will be incomprehensible without a closer examination of the position. We already know about this central pawn structure which we have called the 'little centre' and which gives White some spatial advantage. His main advantage lies in the increased mobility of his major pieces, with both rooks able to occupy the central files and to be transferred via the third rank to either side of the board. Black on the other hand has only the K-file at his disposal, with the only safe square on the file being K1. On K4 the rook can be threatened by P–KB4 and on K3 or K2 it can be attacked by the knight on Q4 or KB5. For this reason Lasker has the original idea of transferring one rook to QB4 or QB5 so that he can play his other rook to K1 and maintain control of the central squares.

15 ...	R–K4!
16 N–Q4	

Not of course 16 N×BP? R–QB4 etc.

16 ...	R–QB4
17 Q–QN3	N–N3

This is played not only to protect the QNP but to provide for a later ... R–QB5.

18 P–KB4

Cutting off Black's rook from K4 and planning to harass if not trap it by a Q-side pawn advance. However, the text move has the disadvantage of

weakening the KP, thus giving Black chances of counterplay.

18 ...	Q–B3
19 Q–KB3	R–K1
20 P–B3	

After 20 P–QN3 intending P–B4, Black has 20 ... N–Q4! 21 P–N3 (*21 P×N R×R+ 22 R×R Q×N+*) 21 ... R–B6.

20 ...	P–QR4
21 P–QN3	

White cannot win a pawn by 21 N–N3 R–QN4 22 Q–Q3 P–B3 23 Q×P Q×Q 24 R×Q, as 24 ... P–R5 regains the pawn with advantage.

21 ...	P–R5
22 P–QN4(?)	

A serious positional error. After the correct 22 P–B4 White could restrict the central activity of the black rook on QB4, but 22 ... P×P 23 P×P R–QR4 followed by 24 ... R1–R1 would give Black play down the QR-file.

22 ...	R–B5
23 P–N3	R–Q1!

Preparing the decisive central attack by ... P–B4. As White cannot prevent this, he tries to exploit tactically the coming weakness of the QP but misses a subtle counter-combination.

24 R–K3 (*191*)

It is important for White's 'combination' that this rook should be guarded in this way.

191 B

24 ...	P–B4!

25 N–N5

There is no salvation either in 25 N–B5 P×P 26 Q–N4 (threatening 27 P–K5) 26 . . . P–R4! 27 Q×RP P×P e.g. 28 P–K5 P×P 29 R×KP R×R+ 30 Q×R P–B7! 31 R–K8+ K–R2 32 Q–R5+ Q–R3 etc.

25 . . .	P×P
26 R×P!?	R×R
27 P–K5	R×KBP!

Refuting White's play and justifying the placing of this rook on QB5. Black now maintains his material advantage and wins comfortably. The game ended: **28 NP×R Q–N3+ 29 K–R1 Q–QN8+ 30 K–N2 R–Q7+ 31 R–K2 Q×P 32 R×R Q×R+ 33 K–N3 P–R6 34 P–K6 Q–K8+ 35 K–N4 Q×KP+ 36 P–B5 Q–B5+ 37 N–Q4 P–R7 38 Q–Q1 N–Q4 39 Q–R4 N×P 40 Q–K8+ K–R2 41 K–R5 P–R8=Q 0–1.**

14 The Partially Blocked Centre

In this final section we shall consider positions with a partially blocked centre i.e. pawns on Q4 and K3, or K4 and Q3, on either side. From such a pawn structure, it is possible to obtain a central advantage in two main ways.

1. by exchanging the advanced enemy pawn whilst retaining one's own e.g. playing P-QB4 when the enemy pawn is on Q4
2. by advancing the back pawn i.e. P-Q4 or P-K4.

This second method can result in various central formations, either a pawn or a piece centre, which is why we have left to the end our treatment of this theme.

The exchange of a centre pawn for a wing pawn often occurs in variations of the Queen's Gambit. If Black plays inexactly after . . . QP×BP, White can obtain a decisive advantage in the centre, as we saw in the Alekhine-Treybal game (volume 1). For this reason, it is the second method which we shall be examining in this section, using three games as examples.

91 Opocensky-Ivkov·

Rogaska Slatina 1948, Queen's Gambit

1 P-Q4 P-Q4 2 N-KB3 N-KB3 3 P-B4 P-B3 4 P×P P×P 5 N-B3 N-B3 6 B-B4 B-B4 7 P-K3 P-K3

8 B-QN5

The move 8 Q-N3 has been robbed of its sting by the answer 8 . . . B-QN5,

so the text move is the strongest here. The threat of 9 N-K5 forces Black to move his KN away from the control of his K5 square.

8 . . .	N-Q2
9 0-0	B-K2
10 Q-K2	B-KN5?

If it were not for this de-centralization, White would hardly be able to play P-K4 in view of his weak QP. Correct was 10 . . . 0-0, as 11 P-K4 gives Black the better game after both 11 . . . B-KN5 12 B×N P×B and 11 . . . P×P 12 B×N P×B 13 N×P Q-N3.

11 P-KR3	B×N
12 Q×B	0-0
13 QR-B1	R-B1
14 KR-Q1	Q-N3
15 Q-K2	P-QR3
16 B-Q3	KR-Q1
17 B-N1	N-B3 (192)

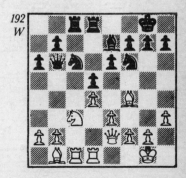

192
W

White's sole advantage lies in his two bishops, so he must strive to open up the position in order to increase their effectiveness.

18 P-KN4!   N-QR4?

The point of White's last move was to drive Black's KN from the centre, but Black wrongly assumes that it is the prelude to a K-side attack, so immediately begins a counter-attack down the QB-file. However, this further decentralization allows White to break through powerfully in the centre.

19 P-N5   N-K1

Or 19 ... N-Q2 20 P-K4 P×P 21 P-Q5! as in the game, when 21 ... P-K4 fails to 22 Q×KP threatening mate.

20 P-K4!   P×P
21 P-Q5!

In this way White at least liquidates the centre after 21 ... P×P 22 N×QP Q-K3 23 R×R R×R 24 Q×KP Q×Q 25 B×Q with a clear advantage in view of the powerful bishops and his centralized pieces.

21 ...   P-B4
22 NP×Pep   N×P
23 B-K3!   Q-Q3
24 N×P   N×N
25 R×R   R×R
26 B×N   P-K4

Black loses a pawn after 26 ... P×P 27 B×QP+ K-R1 28 B×P Q-KN3+ 29 B-N2.

27 P-N3   P-QN4
28 Q-N4   R-Q1
29 R-QB1

White's central break-through has given him a decisive positional advantage. His centralized bishops dominate the game, and there is already a threat of 30 B-QB5 Q-KB3 31 P-Q6! B×P 32 B-QN6, or here 30 ... Q-B2 31 Q-K6+ K-B1 32 Q-B5+ etc. There is no defence e.g. if 29 ... N-N2 30 R-B6, or if 29 ... Q-KB3 30 Q-K6+ Q×Q 31 P×Q etc.

29 ...   Q-Q2?

30 B-QN6   Q×Q+
31 P×Q   N-N2
32 R-B7   1-0

92 Stahlberg-Ojanen

Trencianske Teplice 1949, Queen's Indian Defence

1 P-QB4 P-K3 2 N-KB3 N-KB3 3 P-KN3 P-QN3 4 B-N2 B-N2 5 P-Q4 B-K2 6 0-0 0-0 7 Q-B2 P-Q4 8 P×P P×P 9 N-B3 P-B3 10 B-B4 R-K1 11 QR-Q1!

This is much stronger than 11 KR-Q1 KN-Q2 12 QR-B1 N-B1 13 B-R3 N-N3 14 B-N5 P-KR3 15 B-K3 B-Q3 with a good game for Black. (Zamikhovsky-Botvinnik, Moscow 1931). By placing his KR on K1 in conjunction with the text move, Stahlberg aims to play P-K4, as this is the only way of seizing the initiative.

11 ...   QN-Q2
12 KR-K1   N-B1
13 B-QB1

The final preparation for P-K4, in order that Black cannot gain a tempo by a later ... N-Q4.

13 ...   Q-B1(?)

The idea of this move is sound enough, as Black intends to answer 14 P-K4 with 14 ... P-B4 15 P-K5 N-K5 with counterplay. However, as we shall see, this proves a bad square for the queen, so Black's best defensive chance is 13 ... N-N3 14 P-K4 P×P 15 N×P N-Q4 16 N-K5 Q-B2, although White has a central advantage.

14 N-KN5!   N-N3? *(193)*

The second mistake which makes White's last move even stronger. Black had to play 14 ... P-KR3 15 B-R3 Q-Q1 16 N-B3 when White stands better e.g. 16 ... N-N3 17 N-K5! N×N 18 P×N N-Q2 19 P-K6 with attacking chances.

193
W

| 15 | P–K4! | P–KR3 |

Black can no longer achieve equality by 15 ... P×P 16 N5×KP N–Q4, as after 17 N×N P×N 18 Q×Q QR×Q 19 N–B3 Black has difficulty defending his weak QP, despite the reduction in material (if 19 ... R.B1–Q1 20 N–N5 etc.). Now, however, White smashes open Black's position with a splendid knight sacrifice.

16	B–R3	Q–Q1
17	N×BP!!	K×N
18	P–K5	N–K5

Clearly forced, as any other move of the knight allows 19 P–K6+ winning.

| 19 | B–B5! | N–R1 |

The threat was 20 B×N.N6+ K×B 21 P–B3, and if 19 ... N–B1? White wins at once with 20 R×N! P×R 21 Q–N3+ etc.

| 20 | N×N | P×N |
| 21 | B×KP | |

Threatening both 22 Q–N3+ followed by 23 R–Q3, and also the simple 22 B×BP after which the advance of the QP decides matters. Black now overlooks another move, but even after his best defence 21 ... Q–B1 22 R–Q3! K–N1 White wins by 23 R–QB3 e.g. 23 ... P–B4 24 P–Q5 etc.

| 21 | ... | Q–Q2? |
| 22 | B–N6+! | K–B1 |

The queen is lost after 22 ... N×B 23 P–K6+

| 23 | P–K6 | Q–Q1 |
| 24 | B×R | Q×B |

25	Q–R7	N–N3
26	R–Q3	B–B3
27	B×P!	P–B4

Or 27 ... P×B 28 R–KB3 winning.

28	P–Q5	N–K4
29	R×N!	B×R
30	B×P+!	1–0

A neat finish, as 30 ... B×B loses to 31 R–KB3+ K–K2 32 Q×B+ etc.

It is interesting to note that White played P–K4 without a preliminary P–KB3, with the result that ... P×P gave him an isolated QP. However, he had no need to fear this, in view of his well-placed pieces and Black's weak QBP. In many cases, however, such an isolated pawn can be a disadvantage, despite the temporary gain of space. In our final game. White managed to play P–K4 after a preliminary P–KB3, thus obtaining a strong 'classical centre'.

93 Botvinnik–Keres

20th USSR Championship 1952, Queen's Gambit

1 P–Q4 N–KB3 2 P–QB4 P–K3 3 N–QB3 P–Q4 4 P×P P×P 5 B–N5 B–K2 6 P–K3 0–0 7 B–Q3 QN–Q2 8 Q–B2 R–K1 We have already seen that White has various possibilities in this position, one of which is to prepare P–K4 by playing P–B3, as Botvinnik decides to do here. **9 KN–K2 N–B1 10 0–0 P–B3 11 QR–N1**

The immediate 11 P–B3 would allow 11 ... P–KR3 12 B–R4 N–K3 13 B–B2 P–B4! when Black's isolated QP would be no weaker than White's KP. So Botvinnik first goes in for the well-known Q-side 'minority attack' (see volume 3), whilst preserving the option of switching to the alternative plan if need be.

11 ... B–Q3(?)

This move is the cause of Black's later difficulties. We shall deal in volume 3 with the correct methods of defending against the 'minority attack' of P–QN4 etc. White easily parries the threat of . . . B×P+ after the text move.

12 K–R1!   N–N3
13 P–B3!

After 13 P–QN4 Black had planned 13 . . . P–KR3 14 B.N5×N Q×B with a K-side counter-attack, whereas now White obtains a clear advantage after 13 . . . P–KR3 14 B.N5×N Q×B 15 P–K4. This is a good example of the flexibility involved in logical strategic planning

13 . . .   B–K2 *(194)*

This prevents 14 P–K4 in view of 14 . . . P×P 15 P×P N–N5! 16 B×B Q×B threatening both . . . N–K6 and . . . Q–R5.

194
W

14 R.N1–K1!   N–Q2

Black cannot prevent P–K4 by 14 . . . N–R4, as White continues 15 B×B Q×B 16 P–KN4! N–B3 17 N–N3 etc.

His best chance lies in 14 . . . B–K3 15 N–N3 (if *15 P–K4 P×P 16 P×P N–N5 17 B–B1 B–N4!*) 15 . . . Q–N3 16 N–B5 B×N 17 B×B QR–Q1 when Black has given up one of his bishops but has made it difficult for White to play P–K4.

15 B×B   R×B
16 N–N3   N–B3
17 Q–B2   B–K3
18 N–B5

Again 18 P–K4 is premature because

of 18 . . . P×P 19 P×P N–N5. The following exchange is useful for White because the black KBP now loses a defender.

18 . . .   B×N
19 B×B   Q–N3
20 P–K4   P×P
21 P×P   R–Q1
22 P–K5!   N–Q4

No better is 22 . . . N–K1 23 B×N RP×B 24 R–K4 when White threatens to attack on the KR-file. After the text move White's knight obtains a powerful post on Q6, justifying the P–K5 advance which allowed Black to blockade White's backward QP.

23 N–K4   N–B1
24 N–Q6   Q–B2

The threat was 25 N–B8, and if 24 . . . N–K3? then 25 N×BP and 26 B×N wins, a variation which is also possible after 24 . . . R–B2 e.g. 25 N×BP! K×N (if *25 . . . R×N 26 B–K6*) 26 B–K6+ K×B 27 Q–B5+ K–K2 28 Q–B7 mate.

25 B–K4   N–K3

Or 25 . . . N–QN3 26 Q–N3! N–K3 (if *26 . . . P–N3 27 N–B5 R2–Q2 28 Q–N5*) 27 R–K3 threatening 28 B×RP+ ! followed by 29 Q–R4+ and 30 R–KR3.

26 Q–R4!   P–KN3
27 B×N   P×B
28 R–B1   Q–Q2
29 R–QB3   R–KB1

Otherwise 30 R–KR3 wins, a move which Black can now parry with 30 . . . P–B4. However, the placing of Black's king allows a rapid finish.

30 N–B5!   R1–K1

After 30 . . . P×N 31 R–KN3+ followed by 32 Q–B6, White mates in three moves. White now prefers to continue with his attack, rather than win the exchange.

31 N–R6+   K–B1

Or 31 . . . K–R1 32 Q–B6+ N–N2 33 N×P+ etc.

32 Q–B6   N–N2

33 R3–B3	R–B1

Mate in three was threatened.

34 N×P	R–K3
35 Q–N5	N–B4
36 N–R6	Q–N2
37 P–KN4	1–0

The move P–K4 is often a strategic necessity when Black has played ... P–QB5, attacking on the Q-side. It is obvious that similar situations arise with the Q3, K4 pawn structure. White has to decide whether to play P–Q4 directly or after P–QB3. Opening theory provides us with many examples of both methods, especially in various systems of the open game.

This concludes for the moment our treatment of the important struggle for the centre. However, in the next volume and in particular in the section 'Superiority on The Wings', we shall return to this vital question.

Index of Games

Index of Positions

Index of Openings